Washington
In Spring

Also by Robert K. Musil

Rachel Carson and Her Sisters:
Extraordinary Women Who Have Shaped America's Environment

Hope for a Heated Planet:
How Americans Are Fighting Global Warming and Building a Better Future

Washington In Spring:

A Nature Journal for a Changing Capital

Robert K. Musil
Author of *Rachel Carson and Her Sisters*

A
RACHEL
CARSON
COUNCIL
BOOK

Bartleby Press
Washington • Baltimore

A
RACHEL
CARSON
COUNCIL
BOOK

For more information on Rachel Carson Council
8600 Irvington Avenue
Bethesda, MD 20817
(301) 214-2400
rachelcarsoncouncil.org

ISBN 978-0935437-46-1

Library of Congress Control Number: 2016937042

Published by:

Bartleby Press

P.O Box 858
Savage, MD 20763
800.953.9929
BartlebythePublisher.com

Manufactured in the United States of America

For my daughters, Rebecca and Emily,
who share my passion to build a better future.
And for my grandchildren,
Catherine, Alex, Nora, and the newest, Desmond,
who bring forth a sense of wonder and delight in life.

Contents

Preface

I never intended to write a nature journal, nor, at first, to have it published for you to hold and dip gently inside the rhythms of my life. *Washington in Spring* grew unexpectedly, like a tiny tulip poplar seedling amongst my flowers, as I searched for rest, relief, renewal after decades of advocacy for the environment and for peace. I had spoken, organized, raised funds, and lobbied for the environment—to save it and us from toxic chemicals, air pollution, global climate change. I had loved the outdoors and nature in my childhood on Long Island before it was mostly paved. As a young man, I was an active, avid birder. The birds led me not only outside, but to places I never would have ventured—swamps, lagoons, winter beaches, rocky promontories, sea-swept islands, prairies, glacier-laden mountains, distant lakes and streams. Through birding, I came to understand and finally to appreciate the necessity and the beauty of the ecosystems on which we all depend. I became an environmentalist. But I also lived and worked and wrote mostly indoors or caught some hurried exercise or glimpse of nature on a schedule after I left a day of meetings or of moving swiftly through the marbled halls of Washington.

I had begun to lose touch with the very nature, the environment, I so desperately was working to protect. It was rare for me to ramble through the woods, follow a spring migration, or wander lazily, like a butterfly or bee, from flower to flower in the spring. I stepped down from many years of running Physicians for Social

Responsibility to write my first book on global warming, to teach, and to find time to restore my somewhat weary activist soul. I began to ride my bike along the C&O Canal, to go on long walks, and to take snapshots of landscapes in spring and fall. I could feel youthfulness, openness, fresh thoughts returning. But I was not yet ready to stop, linger, observe, or feel real kinship with the nature all around me. It was the women naturalists, scientists, birders, and advocates about whom I wrote in *Rachel Carson and Her Sisters: Extraordinary Women Who Have Shaped America's Environment* (Rutgers University Press 2014) who slowly drew me into a renewed, deepened connection with and love for nature. But, as importantly, they inspired me to share with others what I was observing, learning, feeling as I walked and rode and rambled. These women were trained in science and in letters. But they shared equally a love and concern for their fellow humans, as well as a belief that unless we humans developed a sense of wonder, awe, imagination, and actual *feeling* for our fellow creatures, for all of nature, we would become a dangerous species that might ultimately destroy the planet and ourselves. And so they revelled in nature and wrote about it in hopes their readers would step outside to see and smell and touch and feel the glories of the springtime.

Moved by their words and their example, I stepped outside again. Began to see and feel more deeply. In the course of writing about Rachel Carson, I came upon the Rachel Carson Council which now I head. Rachel Carson is best known for her book, *Silent Spring*, and her courageous stand in exposing, and then opposing, the chemical companies and their reactionary allies who soon attacked her. She had dared to reveal that their miracle pesticides like DDT were actually harming birds and fish and animals and *people*. But Rachel cared so deeply, acted so bravely, because she was raised by her learned, Presbyterian mother to wander freely around the farm and fields and woods of western

Pennsylvania where she grew up. She was taught to observe and study and love all of God's creation.

As I labored over *Rachel Carson and Her Sisters*, I was slowly drawn back to my own youth, to birding and to nature. I walked. I rode my bike. I rambled around greater Washington, often in the footsteps of Rachel Carson and her friends, noted nature writers and environmental advocates like Louis Halle and Roger Tory Peterson, or Shirley Briggs, Rachel's close friend and colleague, who carried on her work and her love of nature through the Rachel Carson Council.

Washington in Spring, then, is written by a somewhat rusty naturalist and birder, an amateur, who, you will discover, must identify and learn the wildflowers, the birds, and the budding trees anew or, in many cases, for the first time ever. My ramblings and observations of the natural beauty that still suffuses much of Washington have been and remain a joy, as I hope your own will be for you, your family, and your friends. The old nature writers, like Florence Merriam Bailey, were part of a broad nature-study movement at the end of the nineteenth century and the dawn of the twentieth. They believed that we learn best when we are not forced to memorize and absorb Latin names of genus and species, but rather when we open ourselves to the experience of nature. Only when we know and love and feel for the creation around us will we be moved to protect and save it. I have come to believe that, too.

But you will find, as you read, that though I returned to nature and the glories of Washington in spring, I could not always ignore or escape the signs of slowly, steadily changing flora and fauna in our capital. The nature writers of two and three generations ago who inspired me did not fully face, as we do, the threat to nature and to humanity from rampant development, depletion of natural resources, the continued use and spread of toxic chemicals, or of global climate change. I have worked and written on these subjects as an academic and as an environmental and public health advocate. I have appealed to the facts of policy and of science. But I have come to believe that you and I must listen, not just to the facts, but to our senses and to our hearts. For that, we must find ourselves in nature and the discovery of self and spirit that it brings.

This book, then, is meant as an act of faith, that even in the sprawling metropolis that is our nation's capital and beyond, there are readers like you who want to literally step outside the dulling routine of our hectic, increasingly virtual lives. Smell the roses. Breathe in the erotic scents of iris, lilac or viburnum. Listen to the haunting hoot of an owl in moonlight. Stand silent in awe as an elegant Wood Duck leads her ducklings with gentle clucks along a shaded stream. That is what I hope to share.

I am indebted for my own renewal and writing to many people, in addition to the women naturalists both before and after Rachel Carson. The Rachel Carson Council (RCC) allowed me to complete *Washington in Spring: A Nature Journal for a Changing Capital* and to publish it as a "Rachel Carson Council Book" with Bartleby Press. It is the first book from the Rachel Carson Council since Shirley Briggs' 1992 classic *Basic Guide to Pesticides*. The RCC is blessed to have on board a talented book and graphic designer in Ross Feldner of New Age Graphics. His labor of love has made this publication possible at reasonable cost to the RCC and to you the reader. Chad B. Anderson caringly and carefully proofread the prepared manuscript. Any errors that remain are mine. A number of people encouraged me along the way to publish my journal including Steve Dryden, George F. Thompson, Lisa Alexander, members of the Washington area nature and history writers group, and numerous faculty and students where I have lectured on campuses across the country. I also was stimulated to think about doing some sort of nature book by my friend and colleague Frank Kaczmarek, author of *New England Wild-flowers: A Guide to Common Plants*. He is a talented nature photographer and biologist whom I first met when I spoke in a class he taught at Mitchell College in Connecticut. Frank has since moved to northern New England so could not contribute his stunning photography to my journal. Many of the photographs are mine that I often took as much to recall the details of a flower or a bird as to illustrate a book. But I hope these, too, will encourage you to head out with your own camera or iPhone to snap a bee or bud or bird or two. The patience and careful observation needed to get a decent nature shot in many ways resemble and require the same sort of loving attention that characterizes the written descriptions of older nature writers like Louis Halle, whose classic *Spring in Washington*, inspired me directly.

My family, and especially my wife, Caryn McTighe Musil, has encouraged me at every stage and shared a number of the walks and rides and rambles that I record here. We have shared a common love for nature and for social justice for over four decades and been constantly renewed by both.

Washington in Spring follows a simple chronological order through the springs of 2012 and 2013. It reflects what I wrote and felt at the time on each day that I was able to get outside, take notes, and write. Each day or entry seemed to take on a shape and a meaning all its own—little essays that you can pick up or put down as you wish. But I think you may feel, as I did, as we wander around greater Washington together through two full springtimes, an opening, a blossoming of feeling and of love for the beauties of this earth. It is my hope for you. Now it's time to head outside.

— Robert K. Musil
Bethesda, Maryland

Introduction

Captain John Smith, the dashing, daring adventurer and explorer of Jamestown fame, walked right where I ride my bike on the C&O Canal, not too far from my home. I can see him and his men, pulling up the two-ton barge they have sailed from Jamestown, up the Chesapeake, along the Potomac, all the way to Little Falls. Even without Gold's Gym, they are well-muscled, bearded, sweating in heavy English wool on a warm day in 1608. They stow the barge, making their way slowly on foot, through the underbrush and beneath rocky, low cliffs toward the Great Falls of the Potomac River, about ten miles upstream. They have had friendly contact with the Native Americans here and are looking for resources for the East India Company—fish, game, minerals. There is even talk of gold. Along the way, the fish have been so thick that when they jump above the bay waters the men try to catch them in their heavy iron skillets. Sturgeon, shad, bass, and more are countless as the leaves. Captain Smith keeps careful notes of the journey; he has a flair for PR and prose, as well as adventure. He is, in effect, the first American nature writer and popular author with an eye for the environment and natural resources. He and his crew make careful, colorful maps as well. His become the first published accounts of what the Washington area is like in spring. They will not be the last.

John Smith has begun a tradition of exploring, observing, noting, drawing, and publishing accounts of nature, of flora and fauna, in the area that now includes our nation's capital. Greater

Washington and vicinity is still worth exploring, whether by foot or bicycle (with a little help from that later invention, the car). It is an area rich in fish, game, birds, woods, waterfalls, cliffs, wetlands, and astonishing springtime beauty. Each year, millions of families and foreign tourists make an almost obligatory journey to see the Japanese Yoshino cherry trees that surround the Jefferson Memorial and the Tidal Basin. It is a photographer's delight. They fan out to the Capitol, the White House, to George Washington's home at nearby Mount Vernon, and beyond. The nation's children, and sometimes Mom and Dad, get their first, lasting touch and taste for American history. But awestruck visitors usually do not know that they are literally following in the footsteps of historical figures like Captain John Smith and later well-known nature writers, many now forgotten.

George Washington, too, walked where I explore nature along the canal. He first surveyed it as a young man in buckskin and suggested how and where what would become the C&O Canal should actually be built. You can still see portions of the original eighteenth-century Washington-designed canal today. President Grover Cleveland, an early, leading conservationist, fished near the Pennyfield Lock of the C&O Canal toward the end of the nineteenth century. He would spend the night across from the lock at the Pennyfield farmhouse that has since been torn down. But 120 years later, you can see a photograph of him with his rod and reel, sitting there in a rowboat—properly dressed in a suit and stylish straw hat. You can even spend the night in the restored Lockhouse 22 near where he fished. It has been a good spot for anglers and a favorite of top birders for over a hundred years. It was where I first went birding along the canal some forty years ago and got my earliest glimpses of brilliant Scarlet and Summer Tanagers, iridescent Indigo Buntings, migrating spring warblers, and much more.

President Theodore Roosevelt, of course, was the leading naturalist among our presidents. He was a member of the

Audubon Naturalist Society (ANS) that still exists today. He invited ANS members into the White House to see the first moving pictures ever made of birds, wrote numerous serious books on nature, and kept a life list of birds he saw around the White House grounds that in those days were open to the public. He provided his records to a friend, fellow birder and member of the ANS, Lucy Maynard, for the second edition of her popular book, *The Birds of Washington and Vicinity*.

Writing a popular guide to the birds of Washington was suggested to Lucy by one of the most famous nature writers and bird experts of the Progressive Era, Florence Merriam Bailey. She was the nation's first campus environmental organizer at Smith College in the 1880s and set off the now widespread obsession or sport of birding with her popular 1889 book *Birds Through an Opera Glass*. It introduced Americans to watching birds through binoculars instead of shooting them to be collected and studied as had been the practice. Florence Merriam Bailey taught nature and birding classes throughout Washington, published the first real field guides to the birds, wrote regularly for Audubon and popular national magazines, and wrote a detailed introduction to Lucy Maynard's *Birds of Washington*. It describes how, where, and why to look for birds in Washington from Lincoln's Cottage to the National Zoo to Chevy Chase Circle. Florence did this all this by street car and on her bicycle. I simply retraced her steps.

Another great naturalist and writer, John Burroughs, helped inspire Florence Merriam Bailey. He was the national star attraction when she organized her first environmental event at Smith. Burroughs' career and writing spanned from his days in Washington during the Civil War where he was friends with Walt Whitman, and, as his beard lengthened and whitened, ran through his friendship with Teddy Roosevelt, John Muir, and Florence Merriam Bailey. Burroughs gives detailed descriptions of the Rock Creek area in spring in the 1860s and was among the first to suggest it would make an excellent, huge, wild, urban national park—which it remains today.

But I have Rachel Carson, the great naturalist and writer of the twentieth century, to thank for leading me to write this book. Rachel Carson is best known for *Silent Spring*, her powerful indictment of the widespread use after World War II of deadly pesticides like DDT, aldrin, dieldrin, and other "miracle" chemical sprays. They were deployed extensively during the war, saving the lives of thousands of civilians and American GIs in Italy and in the South Pacific from typhus, malaria, and other scourges. But in wartime, their dangers were either ignored or little understood. When our troops returned, toxic chemicals were soon turned loose at home to control fire ants, gypsy moths, and mosquitoes in a new war against insect "pests." Soon, robins, ospreys, eagles, and other birds were disappearing, unintended victims of overkill in this newly declared home front battle. *Silent Spring* also revealed that DDT and other pesticides were harming humans. Rachel Carson was already the best-selling nature and science writer of three previous books on the mysteries and magnificence of the sea shore and the ocean. So her voice was heard.

In my book, *Rachel Carson and Her Sisters: Extraordinary Women Who Have Shaped America's Environment* (Rutgers University Press 2014) I set out to show that Rachel Carson did not act alone, that women had been leaders in conservation and the environment for a century before Carson published her first bestseller, *The Sea Around Us*, in 1951. Rachel Carson was motivated to write and finally to work with what became the modern environmental movement because of her love of nature, her wonder at it, and her delight in tromping through it—often right here in Washington DC—to find and look at birds.

I have walked then, as you can too, in the exact footsteps of Rachel Carson, who birded along the C&O Canal and in other wonders of wider Washington. She, too, was a member of the Audubon Naturalist Society (ANS)—that of Teddy Roosevelt,

Lucy Maynard, and Florence Merriam Bailey. Rachel often went on jaunts with her pals from work at the U.S. Fish and Wildlife Service—Kay Howe and Shirley Briggs. Shirley Briggs founded the Rachel Carson Council, which I now head, carried on Carson's work against pesticides after Rachel's death, and wrote about birds and nature in Washington as well. Rachel Carson also was friends with and birded with the best-known of all modern bird artists and authors—Roger Tory Peterson. His field guide, first published in 1934, replaced Frank Chapman's and Florence Merriam Bailey's popular guides to the birds of the eastern and western United States. Revised, improved, and reissued after World War II, *Peterson*, as his new guide simply became known, sold millions. It introduced a whole new generation of Americans with more leisure time to finding and enjoying birds and the environments, or ecosystems, in which they live. With the spread of family automobiles, newer highways, and a larger middle class that could visit or camp in the natural wonders of the United States, the seeds for a new environmental consciousness were sown. Both Rachel Carson and Roger Tory Peterson testified before Congress, fought DDT, and inspired millions with a love of nature. But they followed the spring birds and deepened their love of nature right here in Washington.

It was while researching and writing *Rachel Carson and Her Sisters* that I finally became moved to write the book you are reading now. Rachel Carson's good friend, Edwin Way Teale, another popular twentieth-century nature writer, had inspired my wife Caryn and me with his 1951 book *North With the Spring*. A generation after him, on spring vacation, we planned a return trip home from Florida to Washington following the trails that Teale had trod. As Teale moved slowly northward at the pace of spring migration, he kept a journal and described what he saw, the warblers and the wonders of redbuds, azaleas, and forsythia as the blossoms and birds moved northward with him. As it turns out, Edwin Teale introduced Rachel Carson to his friend, Louis Halle, who had written a successful 1947 book called *Spring in Washington*. Rachel and Louis Halle met and even birded together along the Canal. Halle was a State Department official and author of a serious Cold War history who rode his bicycle to Foggy Bottom and took spins along the Potomac and in Rock Creek Park at lunch time throughout the spring of 1945. When Louis Halle met Carson, he thought that Teale's friend, Rachel, was a novice seeking advice for her writing. At first, he did not realize, much to his later embarrassment, that his new birding friend was already a well-received author whose blockbuster best-seller, *The Sea Around Us*, would soon appear. I was amused by the story, but also intrigued by Halle's book, a small naturalist classic that was reissued in 1958 and can still be found today.

Again, I had already birded and enjoyed the spring in the spots where Halle had pedaled before me. Because I also have taught the Cold War, environmental history, and politics, I had even read Halle's history book. So I was delighted to find that, like me, he sought refuge from the office and from the outer world, what he called "the hive," in the glories of nature and Washington in spring. I loved his charming, idiosyncratic, slightly rambling mix of nature writing, philosophizing, and his feel for an older Washington that you get while reading *Spring in Washington*. As I was working on my longer, heavily-footnoted academic book on Rachel Carson, Florence Merriam Bailey, and others, I, too, began to roam and ramble, to keep a journal, to find refreshment, solace, and serenity on the walks and bike rides I took to get a break from academic writing.

I also had one further model, mentor, or inspiration, if an unlikely one—Susan Fenimore Cooper. Sue Cooper, as she was known, was, as you may guess from her name, the unmarried, devoted, and dutiful daughter of the American pioneer novelist, James Fenimore Cooper. She edited and made editions of her father's works, but she also wrote a successful novel, was highly educated for her time in both literature and in science, and was America's first truly popular nature writer. Her 1850 book, *Rural Hours*, describes the town of Cooperstown, which her father and grandfather founded, and the countryside around it. She kept a journal and carefully recorded the nature—birds, trees, flowers, gardens, woods—that she saw. Susan Fenimore Cooper offers keen observations on village life, the declining Oneida Indians, and more. *Rural Hours* became a big best-seller, four years before Thoreau's *Walden*. Years later, Susan Fenimore Cooper joined with Florence Merriam Bailey and countless other women to fight the slaughter of birds—egrets, herons, even hummingbirds—that were providing extravagant feathers for women's hats. The slaughter was stopped, our first environmental laws were passed, and the conservation movement was born. But Susan Cooper, like Florence Merriam Bailey, Rachel Carson, and others after her, was motivated by a love of nature that came from her keen observation of her surroundings, her wandering in wonder and in awe. Only when she began to notice deprivations and declines in birds and trees and forests did she turn to activism toward the end of her life at the dawn of the twentieth century. I have been engaged in environmental campaigns for decades now, but they, too, grew out of my own deep love of birds and butterflies and the bounty that surrounds us everywhere in the United States. But nowhere more than in easy distance around my suburban Bethesda, Maryland home, smack in the middle of greater metropolitan Washington. My hope for *Washington in Spring: A Nature Journal for a Changing Capital* is simply that you will want to roam, explore, and feel the wonders of springtime as I have, as have those who have gone before us and led the way.

Thus, I set out—like Sue Cooper nearly 175 years ago, or John Burroughs 150 years ago, or Louis Halle 70 years ago, to record and write about what I love in nature, what I feel and think and gain from searching out a titmouse or a trillium. Since Louis Halle wrote at the end of World War II, Washington has grown immensely, but mostly in the suburbs, as has America itself.

Greater Washington now has over five million people, tangled highways, and some of the longest commutes in the nation. It should be no surprise that my ramblings are often in decidedly suburban, almost urban, Bethesda. But even here I have watched eagles soar, seen Cooper's Hawks tear up starlings, tracked and watched a silent, ghostly Barn Owl in a sycamore down the block. Foxes have trotted in my yard and along the sidewalk toward Suburban Hospital. And in spring, I grow delirious from the profusion of flowering trees and shrubs—Yoshino cherries in nearby Kenwood, redbuds, weeping and Kwanzan cherries, crabapples, dogwoods, and much, much more.

I will take you to places that writers have gone before—through Rock Creek Park with John Burroughs, along the C&O Canal with Rachel Carson and her friends, riding along the Potomac through Dyke Marsh with Louis Halle. And, of course, we will visit Little Falls, where in my mind's eye, and I hope in yours, we can still see Captain Smith or George Washington surveying. In all this, I am an amateur, in the sense of one who loves what he sees and tries to share it all with others. *Washington in Spring* is neither a book for experts, nor a field guide to birds, butterflies, wildflowers, trees, or turtles. There are plenty of excellent ones elsewhere in the bookstore, online, or even as an app. Those I found interesting and useful are in a bibliography in the back that will help you find your own way as you read and muse and wander into springtime. Florence Merriam Bailey may have said it best to the readers of her *Birds through an Opera Glass*. She explained that "this little book is no real lion, and that they have nothing to fear. It is not an ornithological treatise...it is above all the careworn indoor workers to whom I would bring a breath of the woods, pictures of sunlit fields, and a hint of simple, childlike gladness, the peace and comfort that is offered us every day by these blessed winged messengers of nature."

I started this journal in the early winter and spring of 2012, a critical election year, but one where the more important history, the story in the background, may prove to be that 2012 featured the "winter that wasn't." The late winter and spring of 2012 I record is extraordinarily dry and warm. And it was followed by a summer of heat that broke all records around the nation. In 2013, the reverse was true. Winter was far colder than in most recent years and spring came ultimately some two or three weeks later. The cause? Global climate change.

But I want to reassure you that this is not a book primarily about global warming. Those who are interested in climate change and the science and politics that go with it can take a look at my *Hope for a Heated Planet* and numerous important books on environmental policy and politics. This is not one of those. It is my escape, my balm in Gilead, my joy in letting go, in finding Florence Merriam Bailey's "childlike gladness...peace and comfort." But a mild word of warning. Susan Fenimore Cooper wrote with joy, but occasionally noted that there are those who cut down woods simply for profit. Later on, she noticed that fewer robins and other birds were nesting near her home. Louis Halle found comfort in nature, away from the matters of state and of the "hive" that so preoccupied his working life at the State Department. But he also noted the black skies and soot of coal-burning locomotives, the trash and detritus of modern life beginning to intrude on Roaches Run and the other inlets near the National Airport. Our knowledge of nature and our record of it owe much to amateur naturalists, birders, botanists, environmentalists. They note the decline of birds, the earlier arrival of spring, the changes in species, and in ecosystems. Placed alongside more thorough, scientific observations, we gain a picture of the American environment and the global one over extended periods of time.

We have now entered a period in human history when our actions, what we burn and drive and manufacture, determine the future of the nature that we see everywhere about us. Smith Island in the Chesapeake Bay, named after our intrepid captain and carefully mapped by him, is now slowly going underwater, graveyards and all, thanks to sea-level rise brought on by global warming. The Sharps Island Lighthouse, once on a tiny island nearby in the Bay, is now more than halfway submerged. It will not be too long before it is gone.

Frankly, I have written this journal to avoid thinking such dreary thoughts too often. I try to transcend them. I deeply believe that immersing ourselves in nature, enjoying, studying, rambling through it, even in the suburbs, can lighten our hearts, enliven our imagination, refresh our sense of wonder. I share a sense of fresh discovery with each bird, each butterfly that I see—even with old, childhood favorites like the robin or the Monarch.

I love the sentiment of Florence Merriam Bailey's close friend, her fellow birder and popular author, Olive Thorne Miller. She was chastised by the noted ornithologist William Brewster for having discovered a new bird species, but writing about it in a popular magazine, instead of a proper journal. Brewster was miffed because he never deigned to read popular stuff and so had announced his find of the same species in *The Auk*, not realizing that Olive Miller had already described it in two different magazines! Miller wrote, "to me everything is a discovery; each bird, on first sight, is a new creation; his manners and habits are a revelation, as fresh and as interesting to me as though they had never been observed before." Explaining her choice of a magazine rather than a scientific journal, she says simply, "my great desire is to bring into the lives of others the delights to be found in the study of Nature." I share that goal; it is my great desire for you as well.

Nevertheless, here and there, I could not help but note that the sights of spring that I have savored so much are now changed and threatened as they have never been before. I profoundly want you to enjoy the glories of spring in Washington. Like you, I suspect, I do not respond well to guilt or grim grumblings about our future, or our fate. But I hope, as did more noted writers before me, that once you come to explore, learn, and love nature more and more, you also will not wish to simply stand by and watch it be destroyed. But most of all, like Florence Merriam Bailey and Olive Thorne Miller, I wish you fresh eyes, fresh discoveries, and the childlike gladness, peace, and comfort that will be yours as you wander and wonder at the glories of Washington in spring.

— Robert K. Musil
    Bethesda, Maryland

Chapter One

Warming Up Toward Spring

January 10, 2012
Untypical New Hampshire

Historians and journalists will note the start of 2012 as a critical election year for a divided nation. The newspapers show reporters jammed outside the window of a diner in New Hampshire to interview a Republican candidate in the quadrennial ritual of campaigning among plain folks who seem sent from central casting for a sitcom about small town life in a disappearing American idyll. There are complaints that the photo ops lack the requisite snowy backgrounds of the Granite State in January. Spring has come early to New Hampshire, as it has to Washington. Spring is an astronomical fact—the vernal equinox, when the sun shines equally day and night—that can be accurately measured. On our calendars it is around March 21st. But spring is also a botanical event that lacks precision—it is when the crocuses, daffodils, and hyacinths appear or when the cherry blossoms cheer up happy hordes of camera-toting tourists around the Tidal Basin and the Jefferson Memorial. Spring is also a concept. For the literary and romantic, it is when young men's fancies turn to love or the poet e.e. cummings perceives a "perhaps hand." It is Walt Whitman on the death of Lincoln, T.S. Eliot on April, "the cruelest month, mixing memory and desire."

What I know is that springtime in the nation's capital is glorious. Whatever its botanical, political, or poetic correctness, I notice that it is unusually early this year. The day before yesterday, as I stepped out of my Bethesda home for my neighborhood constitutional walk, there was a snowdrop under the azalea at the end of my flagstone walk. Today there are three of these small, drooping white floral bells that I associate with the saving of my daughter's life by Dr. Eli Miller down the block at Suburban Hospital. At age thirteen, Emily had a ruptured appendix that we thought until too late was a mixture of teenage ague and angst. Dr. Miller pulled Emily back from sepsis and sutured her up. When she was safe in her room recovering, we took the small bunches of snowdrops blooming on McKinley Street near the hospital as a sign of hope and miracles. It was February 11, 1991. Today, I think of Emily and say a prayer of thanks for Eli Miller. But this year the snowdrops are a full month earlier.

I see them elsewhere on my walk, poking through pachysandra and ivy and lifting my spirits. Like the weather, like e.e. cummings, and like the public measuring politicians, I am confused. Is it winter or is it very early spring? Temperatures in the Washington area have set records for highs; it has been a balmy Christmas and New Year's here. Temperatures have been in the 50s and 60s. There are a few azalea blossoms near my door, a few small cherry trees blossoming both in my neighborhood and my daughter's in nearby Chevy Chase. Last night, my wife Caryn and I stood without coats looking at the full moon and listening as Canada Geese honked over our heads in a cacophonous, barely visible "V."

I follow primaries and politicians. I can speak knowledgeably about foreign affairs and nuclear weapons, taxes, energy policy. It has been my job here in Washington for some three decades. But I have come to believe that the best news, the real history, and the happiness whose pursuit Jefferson spoke about so long ago, is to be found in the blooming of a snowdrop, the honking of a goose, the finch I witnessed last week chased by a Cooper's Hawk in bursts of frantic, feathered flight.

The Joys of Juncos

As I finish my stroll and turn the corner onto McKinley Street, I glimpse for a nanosecond another small, arrow-like hawk, perhaps a sharpie, or even the rarer Merlin. Too small for a Cooper's, and no whirring sound like a tasty Mourning Dove, so awkward on the ground, so streamlined in the air. The hawk is gone as I peer over the neighbor's picket fence across one of the few real backyards left with the traditional lawn of grass. Birds are everywhere, reassembling, popping out of hiding from the shrubbery. Chickadee. Titmouse. And then a small dark bird. I see others on the lawn. One flies up to the rooftop gutter; I note the tell-tale white stripes on the tail, notice the light breast and pale beak. A junco!! I have looked for them since Thanksgiving in my own yard beneath the feeders, but have only seen a few White-throated Sparrows to mark the avian arrival of southward migration. No juncos. But here they are! A small flock of Slate-colored Juncos (now officially "Dark-eyed" to the professionals at the American Ornithological Union). They began a lifetime of birding for me and Caryn. We were fleeing our intense involvement and growing sense of gloom with the election of 1972 as young anti-war activists in support of Senator George McGovern. We headed for Canada in the summer—not permanently like the draft exiles and military resisters I helped in my day job—but to camp, hike, and escape the headlines. Our goal? Spot a moose. Needless to say, we spent many a lovely wooded traipse, at dawn and at dusk, without spotting a single oversized ungulate. But resting one afternoon at our campsite, we did notice an influx of birds—including little ones with white tail stripes that we had never seen before. We trudged to the visitor's center, inquired, and ended up with a $13 gorgeous, but very large, heavy hardback book, *The Birds of Canada*. It still adorns our shelves. In it, we learned that what we had been watching (without binoculars) were juncos, also known—long before the crossover country hit by Canadian singer Anne Murray—as "snowbirds."

I watch my first neighborhood juncos (they are late—another sign of warming trends) with real excitement, eager to tell my wife. My frantic following of and fears about the election of 2012 fade as fast as the flash of a hawk. After our first juncos in Canada, we bought binoculars, lighter field guides, and began to observe, to notice, the panoply of nature that surrounds us everywhere. We followed birds into fields and forests, to the seashore, through bogs and fens, muck and mire, and mosquito swarms we never would have dared before. We began to notice connections between their habits, haunts, and habitat, their very existence, and what we now call ecosystems. Thanks to the juncos, things began to appear that had been there all along, but that we had never noticed in our rush to save the world. We became aware that often the real story of our time was right beside us, or soaring above us, not on the evening news.

In our corner of Bethesda, near the Bradley Hills Elementary School and Suburban Hospital, between brick colonials, ranches, ramblers, and small, classic Cape Cods slowly transmuting into mightier, or at least more expensive, mansions, I have seen red foxes lurking beneath my feeders, greeting me at my car, and trotting down the street toward Suburban. Caryn and I have heard the hoot—and then tracked it down with flashlights—of a ghostly Barn Owl perched in the moonlight on the huge old sycamore down the street. I've gazed at length at Red-tailed Hawks, a gigantic goshawk on a neighbor's plastic children's shed, and more. Nature unfolds each day, each spring, around me, even in the manicured suburbs where teams of Latino lawn men keep things neat and tidy. A couple of weeks ago, as the year was turning, I saw on my walk, for the first time in my quarter century in Bethesda, a pair of mature, white-headed, magnificent bald eagles circling overhead, soaring in the sun. They could easily see the houses, yards, trees, shrubs, and struggling morning traffic on Old Georgetown Road down below. No one else seemed to notice.

January 12, 2012
Living with Black Vultures

After cool, steady, dreary rain all day Wednesday, spring has again come prematurely to Washington. This morning, it is already near fifty degrees with bright blue skies and low clouds. They create views through leafless trees in the slanting early winter light that are hi-def sharp, contrasting, deep. It is quiet. At first I mainly note the squirrels. I muse about race relations between the common, bigger grays and smaller black ones that share sumptuous offerings here in the suburbs. Remembering my first eagle sighting the other day, my pulse quickens a bit. I stop and slowly lift my small binoculars toward a large, dark, circling bird. Eagle? Hawk? Vulture? I twist into focus while holding my breath. It is all black with feathered wings. A vulture. But the size, shorter tail, white patches beneath a flatter wingspread, dark head, and lack of gruesome red "turkey" face reveal a Black Vulture. It is not the more common "TV" that everyone has seen floating and rocking over fields and farms on family road trips. TVs are almost as big as eagles and, as they search for roadkill, rock in the air on wings held on the point of a widely-spread chevron or "V." I am mildly disappointed not to have an encore from my eagles, but have an odd fondness for Black Vultures, compared to TVs, impressive as they are, especially at roadside. The northernmost range of Black Vultures stops somewhere around Delaware; I was unaware of them growing up in New York, or even when first birding near Philadelphia. Then I spotted a few, considering them exotic and rare, on birding trips from Germantown to the Delmarva Peninsula. Then, when we moved to

Washington near Rock Creek Park and the National Zoo, I saw them every day as I walked and birded around the zoo. Today, I see them most gathered around the bridge at Riley's Lock along the C&O Canal where I bike with binoculars. Once I slowly wheeled my Trek across that bridge through a roost of dozens of Black Vultures staring up close and spookily at me from the railings. It was actually a bit unnerving, reminding me of passing similarly, but by car, through an equal number of curious and intimidating baboons who seemed to believe they owned a bridge in South Africa's Kruger Park.

The noted writers and bird watchers, Rachel Carson, Louis Halle, and Roger Tory Peterson may have seen the ancestors of these Black Vultures as they birded along the canal in the '40s and '50s, but perhaps not. In his classic *Spring in Washington*, Louis Halle describes numerous year-round Turkey Vultures circling over the Kennedy-Warren apartments on Connecticut Avenue, not far from the National Zoo. Yet he only mentions one sighting of a couple of black ones who migrate in from around Mount Vernon in the spring. Black Vultures were once quite rare in the Washington area. They are not even mentioned by the most popular bird and nature writer of the turn of the century, Florence Merriam Bailey, in her introduction to Lucy Maynard's 1898 *Birds of Washington and Vicinity*. Florence and her brother Hart, head of the US Biological Survey, and a buddy of Teddy Roosevelt's, lived and birded around the White House and farther afield in the Washington area. The National Zoo was one of Florence's favorite birding haunts. In the 1920s, she and her husband, Vernon, built a large brick home at 4838 Kalorama Road in my old neighborhood near the zoo. There is a complete checklist of Washington birds from 1898 in Maynard's book. But the Black Vulture (*Coragyps atratus*) is listed only as an accidental visitor.

Even earlier, John Burroughs, the famed nature writer who inspired the young Teddy Roosevelt and later became his good friend, only mentions turkey buzzards, or today's Turkey Vultures, (*Cathartes aura*), in his lyrical descriptions of Washington's nature and bird life in his 1871 classic *Wake-Robin*. Upon departing office in 1909, Teddy Roosevelt also provided a full list of all the birds he had observed in and around the White House to Lucy Maynard for her 1909 second edition of *Birds of Washington*. Roosevelt frequently birded with Hart Merriam and others, was a member of the DC Audubon Club (now the Audubon Naturalist Society), and regularly telephoned the Merriam home for counsel on difficult bird identifications. But the Black Vulture is not on his list either.

Birds live in, are adapted to, and prefer certain climates and ecosystems. Our climate has been shifting throughout the twentieth century with slow, almost imperceptible warming trends. Cardinals and mockingbirds and other "southern" species were unknown in my early boyhood on Long Island. Now they are common. In the early twentieth century, the Black Vulture was a southern bird. Now it is a common resident throughout Washington. It has moved north with the spring that stretches up the East Coast earlier and earlier and more to the north each year, and whose weather I am enjoying today. Scary bird, indeed.

Confusing Christmas

As I pass what I call the "grössmutter's house" on Park Road, a modestly-sized, yet elegant and historic-looking home at the triangle of Custer Road, I come to a muddy driveway and small trees alive with birds chattering in the southeast sun. Blue Jays scream, nuthatches "yank" up and down the trunks, a Song Sparrow hops delicately from a puddle under a car, and robins poke hopefully, ears cocked at the moist, puddling ground before it dries again. I am in a suede jacket and an old college cap, comfortable as the temperature rises into the 50s. But I am a bit confabulated and confused since I have now passed some remaining Santas and plastic snowmen, nude Christmas trees lying prone at curbside, and other scattered signs of Christmas barely past. Robins are, of course, the beloved harbingers of true spring. But these days, some are resident year round, while others return in greater numbers, it seems, in honor of tradition. Heading home, I see a crow pecking and pulling at a squashed squirrel in the street. Perhaps it is the roadkill that the Black Vulture had within its sights. At a glance, I can't tell if it is a good old American Crow of lore and legend whose raucous "caw" is so well known, or the smaller Fish Crow, more common toward the shore, whose nasal "car" was heard and described by Florence Merriam Bailey over a century ago. My home used to be surrounded by flocks of American Crows that boldly devoured much of the feed I left for other, smaller avian appetites. But since the West Nile Virus arrived just before 9/11 and decimated many of my Carolina Chickadees and Tufted Titmice, American Crows are no longer found near 8600 Irvington. They have been replaced in the literal pecking order, it seems, by more Blue Jays, more Common Grackles, and the lone, longing cry of a single resident Fish Crow.

I pause again as I catch movement up the block. House Sparrows in a bush and three Hispanic women unloading vacuums, buckets, cleaning gear from a van. Bethesda is a Spanish-speaking neighborhood after nine a.m. Domestic cleaning services, the lawn men, nannies with strollers, trash and recycling collectors, all, in my experience, incredibly friendly, hard-working, fast and efficient. But like nature itself, they seem little noticed, taken for granted. Those ahead do not see me or the bevy of a half-dozen Mourning Doves huddled and snoozing in the sun on the bare snags of a small, dead tree where the "cleaning ladies" are striding into the house with a mix of resolve and resignation. Behind this scene, the United Methodist Church with its classic brick architecture, save for an undersized pencil point of a steeple, is framed against the sky, a few clouds, a cedar, and a few other evergreens at the end of the block at Huntington Parkway. Along the way home, cardinals "pink" and pose against holly and forest green for a few final holiday cards as my mind skips back and forth between Christmas, winter, and these unusual, early signs of spring.

January 13, 2012
Hawks at the Capitol

It is still balmy and sunny as I drive Caryn to National Airport for her trip to Cleveland for a National Endowment for the Humanities NEH project meeting and a stay with her sister, Sheila. I plan to go later on a tour of the inside and views from atop the Capitol dome arranged by son-in-law, Chip Unruh, Communications Director for Senator Jack Reed of Rhode Island. Only those accompanied by a member of Congress or sponsored by the Vice President's office (Chip used to work for Joe Biden) get to trudge up over two hundred steps above the guided tours of the Rotunda and the Capitol Crypt far below. You get three stops along the way to catch your breath, recover from any vertigo, and to learn about the various domes both planned and ultimately built. Today's dome dates from the Civil War; the inner ceiling is painted with marvelously colorful, symbolic, and outsized patriotic renderings in classical garb of the *Apotheosis of Washington*, Benjamin Franklin beside his electric generator and a revelatory rainbow, and finally Columbia overthrowing tyranny. It is an ideal day—sharp cerulean, cloudless skies, cool temperatures—for stepping out onto the balcony atop the dome. From afar the balcony shows as a tiny ring just before the final columns and the small statue of Freedom portrayed as a woman at the pinnacle, 288 feet above the ground. When I finally saw Thomas Crawford's great work—first assembled and hoisted up by slaves in 1863—being cleaned and restored down on the Capitol grounds in the early nineties, like everyone else, I was stunned by her nineteen and a half foot height; her mighty 15,000 pounds of bronze.

As it turns out, Caryn's plane is cancelled because of snow in Cleveland, even as we still enjoy early spring. Caryn joins me, our daughter Rebecca and Chip, and a few friends and relatives of theirs. Before we arrive at the dome, Caryn and I reminisce about our first sightings of swarms of flying, seemingly white objects around the dome while lit at night. They were Common Nighthawks, wide, gap-mouthed members of the goatsucker family, related to Eastern Whip-poor-wills; they feast on insects, in this case, those attracted to the lights upon the Dome. More recently, heading to a farewell for our old army friend, Congressman John Spratt of South Carolina, we stood by the ramp at the small white shack on the Senate side of the Capitol, watching with incredulity and amusement as a red fox jumped and twisted in the air, mousing at the security checkpoint. The Capitol police assured us that they enjoyed the occasional nature programs at their feet, assured us, too, that they were visited regularly by eagles from the Potomac.

As Caryn and I cling to the small balcony high atop the dome, we look down at scale models below—the Supreme Court, Library of Congress, the miniature Crystal Palace of the Botanical Gardens, the more distant Beaux Arts façade of Union Station, and, further off, a radio tower, and the basilica dome at Catholic University— that make us joke about Washington as Paris. Then, suddenly, we gasp. Even here, at the center of L'Enfant's planned, splendid city, with the seat of government literally at our feet, nature is on display. A single Red-tailed Hawk sails slowly by at eye level, almost close enough to touch. Then there is a pair of them; we watch them float and dive and swirl in the now gusty, colder wind. For a moment they are the main attraction here, but also a cautionary reminder. We build monuments, pass laws, ignore dangers, not only for ourselves, but for every living thing. Mankind is not alone in its majesty or mayhem. I know that Jefferson and Teddy Roosevelt and writers like Burroughs, Merriam, and Halle have all spotted red-tails in the District. And magnificent eagles—once endangered nationwide by chemicals and entirely gone from the Potomac—to be found only in the paintings inside the dome—can now, thanks to *Silent Spring*, once again be seen by security guards and sun-drenched tourists, not just by the noted Americans of yesteryear found in yellowing books, celebratory ceilings, and standing stolidly in Statuary Hall.

January 14, 2012
Keeping Watch

A cold front, without the snow, has moved in from Cleveland and the Middle West. We drive to National Airport again in the same sunny skies, but now Washington winter, if delayed, seems to settle in. There are winter ducks, Bufflehead, bobbing in Roaches Run. The fully bloomed daffodil near the Monocle we spied after yesterday's tour seems distant now. But there is no frozen water and the temperature, despite crunchy ground and hysterical weathermen talking of Arctic blasts, is still a pretty normal thirty-five degrees. But the first two weeks of January have already, thanks to global climate change, set a record for high average temperatures. Two years ago at my daughter Emily's wedding in Bethesda, there was record ice and snow. Only the long, slow, carefully measured trends of temperature, of the comings and goings of birds and flowers, of watersides and beach fronts rising, of species and seasons inching northward, really matter. Washington, Franklin, Jefferson, Roosevelt, and many others prided themselves on husbandry, agriculture, science, invention, natural history, the careful recording of explorations and environment. They measured. They kept lists. They would have wondered and written about the well-noted shifts in temperature and territories for today's flora and fauna. I like to think they would have been worried and been working on solutions. Worried, too, perhaps, that far beneath the dome, so few have seemed to notice.

January 15, 2012
Dr. Martin Luther King and Birding

I get a late start today on my walk. It is Martin Luther King's birthday. Church has put me in a spiritual place. Our interim minister, an African American woman, Laverne Gill, has shared a sermon with her old, close white friend, a mental health administrator, Patricia Hansberry. They talk with great wit and passion—a bit like Oprah or The View—in a two-woman conversational sermon. Laverne tells how while she was the minister for Chautauqua in upstate New York and miserably ill, she needed a kidney transplant, or a lifetime of dialysis. At the time, Patricia gently probed what was troubling her. When Laverne finally, reluctantly, shared her innermost secrets and fears, Patricia simply said, "I'll give you one of mine." No hesitation. No going back. They have shared secrets, sisterhood, serenity ever since. We are bathed, too, in music—"Precious Lord," "Lift Every Voice," "What a Morning." Our jazz star, Lena Seikaly, sings Ellington. Many recall Dr. King. We sing "We Shall Overcome." I weep. There is much to mock here with aging, mostly white baby boomers reliving the past, perhaps. But not with the presence of these two women—ebony and ivory—who have so given of themselves.

I started birding after Martin Luther King was shot in springtime. I had not made any connections before now. But when Bobby Kennedy was also killed, at the end of that spring, some sort of hope within me was dashed, my moods were darkened. It was a little later, with Caryn and friends from the staff of the first national peace group I ever led, that the birds sought me out. They connected me to my boyhood on Long Island when things seemed simpler; they connected me to worlds far beyond politics and war that I never knew nor noticed. With their shorter lives and struggles to survive, they reminded me not just of death but also of new life. I had read Emily Dickinson at my grandfather's knee and written about her many times. "Hope is a thing with feathers," took on new, deeper meaning.

And so I walk my neighborhood, expectant as always, for some revelation right in Bethesda. Eagle, vulture, hawk? This afternoon all is silent, as if in respect, or prayer, for Dr. King. Again, it is sunny and clear, just above freezing with a slightly stiffened breeze. I hear only my own footsteps and the light scraping, scuttling sound of the few remaining leaves on the ground puffed about by a gentle wind. I am left to savor this morning's tears and the tissue of lives that share kidneys instead of killing. I hear one lone caw of an American Crow not far from yesterday's feast of carrion. Some old-time crows, it seems, have returned after 9/11 and the West Nile Virus. I walk on. There is nothing but my thoughts.

Then, as I near the corner of Charlcote Street, with a small, grey clapboard house across from the grey stone mansion I watched entrepreneurs from El Salvador so lovingly erect, I sense some movement. There is a brief, happy sort of chuckling sound. I stop. Glance up. It is a robin, black in outline, silhouetted against the sun that is already near setting in the winter afternoon. As with the juncos in my youth, I have not noticed the scene, the scrambling above my head, that I am not alone, that life goes on. First, I see a few more robins. As one skims to a different branch, I notice a few more, and a few more, until there are dozens. They have been here all along. A large woodpecker sails in along with a Mourning Dove, a few titmice, a nuthatch navigating nose-first down a shaggy trunk. There are starlings, invisible to me before, pecking at the lawn. I round the corner to get a better look, wondering, as always, what brings these bustling bursts of bird life all together? Now with the northwest sun at my back, Technicolor sets back in. A school boy would easily know that these russet-breasted thrushes, sitting, talking, flapping, occasionally sailing, and gathered as a group, are the beloved robin. I note that as I turn onto Charlcote that breezes are blocked, the sun is strong, the temperature more modest. Some particular, precise arrangement of trees and dwellings has let the sunlight in, stilled the wind amidst the mostly cold, deep shade of oaks and tulip poplars. The birds have led me to this brief bower of bliss. They have sought it out, found it somehow, long before I noticed. It is a small, golden corner, a brief touch of sunlight and of spring, that, for a moment, we share together.

January 24, 2012
This is Global Warming?

I have been housebound most of the last ten days as winter finally sought out Washington. First it was near and below freezing temperatures with gusty winds that made it feel as frigid as Chicago. Then an inch of snow or so, plus some freezing rain that is a big deal in today's Washington. Severe weather alerts, events cancelled, weathermen chattering along with teeth. I forget to leave time to scrape ice and crunchy snow off the car, tiptoe down my walkways, wrap scarves twice around my neck. At American University where I teach global climate change and American environmental politics, it is, ironically, the opening of the "spring" semester. We get acquainted, talk climate science, and, as always, an average-looking student, making the mistake of slumping against a wall in the back corner (yes, it is a guy...), asks innocently, "If it's getting warmer, how come it's so cold this winter?" tossing a glance at the wind out the winter window. I happily pounce like a Cooper's on a starling. With the class clamoring back and forth (I jokingly forbid the two science majors from speaking), we pick our way through measurements, trends, historical data, the difference between climate and weather and why "one swallow does not a summer make." By the end of my late evening class, the roads are clear, the air offers light, misty rain. Winter has ended once again.

January 25, 2012
Spring in Winter?

Today's temperature peaks at about 54°. It is sunny with light, streaky cirrus clouds, clean, crisp air. I am lured outside again. A light windbreaker replaces thick coat, hat, gloves, scarf—the Charlie Brown look, dressed by Mom, lacking only galoshes. It is the smells of spring I note this January day. Moist ground, decayed leaves, fecund earth. A few very small, potholder-sized patches of thin snow are left in the corners of shaded driveways, clumps of trees. Near them in the sun are shoots of crocuses, daffodils, onion grass, and other green growths I cannot name. It is after school and I see grown boys tossing footballs, batting tether balls, or just running around like colts in Kentucky. Windows are open and the football group, trying to look like men, is decked in collegiate sweatshirts that are soon shed while rap admired by white kids blasts out the window. I actually like it. The voice sounds like LL Cool J of TV's *NCIS -Los Angeles*. Silence returns as I turn onto Maple Ridge, flaring my nostrils, sniffing the air with bear-like shuffles and pauses. I am caught in reveries of camping—something about the freshness of the air, the faint aroma of freshly-cut wood. I stop as I see that the Pepco utility men have been here, trimming trees away from the wires, leaving oddly distorted shade trees and ornamentals and a long line of small, light-colored wood chips along the street-side apron of green.

I fear that the suburbs will never have old, half-broken, rotten trees as in a true woods or forest where the cavities hold nests, hide owls, and host ants and bugs for woodpeckers. Then I hear the crazed chuckle of a Red-bellied Woodpecker as it lands above me and starts in on the maple that the men have mangled. Above the neat cuts and pruning, there are broken branches, holes—woodpecker heaven. As if on cue, my red-bellied is joined by a downy and then its larger look alike, a hairy, that seems giant in this unusual side-by-side view. Soon nuthatches are at the bark, sending out funny kazoo-like calls. As before, I catch a glimpse of one robin, then two, then, many, many more. And suddenly some rarity right here on Maple Ridge! I pull up my binoculars to examine a white, robin-sized bird. My brain has already whispered "pigeon" "dove" and then it goes wild—Rock Ptarmigan, some mutant, stray Snowy Plover, or a giant Snow Bunting. This rare bird is with the robins, is shaped like a robin, is digging and hopping and looking for worms like a robin. This all in a second or two before my rational self decides this must be an *albino* robin. There are a few, pale cinnamon patches on the breast, a yellow bill, but the rest pure white with black feathers occasionally marking a hand-drawn outline. This is surely some sort of omen. When I get home, I will search for lore. I will settle in to read my recently arrived, red-bound book from 1883 called *Avifauna Columbiana* by Elliott Coues about the comings and goings of the birds of Washington. Tomorrow will be warm again. I think of my new students and how I have told them that "one swallow does not a summer make." I want real winter—to settle in so I can burn some logs and write. And I want spring, an early spring, to throw open the windows, to watch weird white birds—and, perhaps, to prove a point.

January 25, 2012
Tree-hugger

I am surprised by a front page story in the *Washington Post* that tells how we have been moved into Zone 7, along with the South, in the horticultural zones put out by the Department of Agriculture. The story notes early blooming daffodils and snow-drops in the city. (It is always a bit warmer and earlier than Bethesda which is about ten miles north and has less heat island effect). But the writer goes on to state that the Department of

Agriculture went out of its way to say that the new maps for gardeners are not a tool to measure global warming! The headline and the story give the distinctly misleading impression that the northward climb of the southern gardening zone with its camellias and crepe myrtles and southern plants is not related to global warming. I write online in response, trying to explain that warming average temperatures over the past decades are indeed related, as are shifts in the habitats of animals and plants. But I feel like I am spitting in the ocean.

I am reminded of the mountain ash tree in our backyard that was healthy when we moved here in 1987. Steadily hot summers were evidently not to its liking and so it died. We left it alone for some years for the woodpeckers to drill neat holes in and then to nest. They were followed by House Wrens and by Carolina Chickadees. For years, it was a delightful diversion, a source of nature study for the kids. Now they are grown; the mountain ash is gone. I have seen no others and there are far, far fewer white birches and other northern trees throughout our neighborhood. In the meantime, the two tulip poplars we planted as saplings are now majestic shade trees that create, with other plantings, deep shade in our yard. I revel in a small woodland area with moss and rocks and wildflowers including John Burroughs' wake-robin or trillium. For him, in Rock Creek and throughout wooded Washington, its blooming announced the coming of bird song and true spring.

As I walk today at midday, in continuing mild temperatures, bright sun, and leafless trees, I am struck by how many trees there really are in the suburbs, of many kinds, and what a gift to us they are. As I make my rounds, there is an assortment of maples—sugar, Norway, red and silver; of oaks—white, red, scarlet, southern red, even a chestnut swamp; and evergreens—white pines, blue spruce, and others I cannot name. The slightly newer areas have ornamental cherries—Japanese, Kwanzan, weeping—along with redbud, fruitless Bradford pears. Come spring—along with native

white and pink hybrid dogwoods, azaleas, forsythia, and more—
they make Bethesda a floral festival. But we also have old-time,
mature, less noticed, scarcer trees—smooth and rough-barked
hickory, elm, ash, box elder, beech, walnut, black locust,
sycamore, sweet gum. By fall, my classic suburban section is lit-
tered with falling nuts and seedpods and aflame in foliage.

But today, it is pruning and cutting time. In winter, the
Pepco crews can see the limbs near transformers, wires, and poles.
Pepco has had a horrible record of power outages in winter, or
even in the thunderstorms so frequent in summer that steadily
knock down limbs and trees, killing light and power in my home
and elsewhere. So they are cutting. Homeowners, too, seem to
have ordered in more work trucks and cherry pickers to thin the
woods that surround our houses. Few seem to have read or remem-
bered Joyce Kilmer's "Trees" or read the websites from the EPA,
the Arbor Foundation, and others who so lovingly explain how a
few well-placed shade trees can cut air conditioning bills by 40
percent, save money, save energy, and, through transpiration, cool
the air within a few feet of their trunks by about 9°F. They give off
oxygen, absorb carbon dioxide, and delay global warming all at
the same time.

And so I am a both sad and angry as I see not only the under-
standable pruning near power lines, but come upon two mature
shade trees felled, dismembered, and left in piles. I am hurt most
by the loss of a huge, once proud tulip poplar, the tallest of trees
in the Northeast, now lying at my feet. Similar specimens adorned
Caryn's childhood home in the earliest suburbs of Philadelphia.
We planted ours when we first moved in not only for shade, but
as literal reminders of our roots. I examine the ruined remains
carefully. This tree is nearly four feet in diameter; it has, by my
rough count some seventy or eighty annual growth rings of
decreasing thickness as its youthful growth spurt slowed. The
deeply furrowed bark has moss and lichens that reveal the north-

ward side—how cool and shaded it once was, and no longer is, beneath this giant. This poplar was probably planted as a sapling when the house that has had it cut down was built in the early 1940s as Bethesda expanded along with the federal government and World War II. I can see no excuse for the felling. There are no signs of disease, borers, carpenter ants—no weaknesses of any kind. I have begun to muse too much whether there is such a thing as horticultural homicide, or what the penalties should be. I should describe, not judge. I want to inspire, not scold. But my grandchildren, if still alive, will be in their dotage before a tree like this, if planted today, can once more grace the land.

The First Sputters of Spring

I try to shift my mood, to shake off these thoughts that are why audiences chant almost in unison when I ask them on campuses what comes to mind when I say the single word "environmentalist." They answer merrily, knowingly, as one. "Tree hugger!!" they all respond. Yes. I guess I am. But I perk up when I hear the spring-like sounds of a quartet of Blue Jays whose odd calls sound like gurgles or gargles, not their regular, raucous scream. They fly, flashing blue and white as they pass. I am taken swiftly back to childhood and my favorite backyard birds, the mini-tragedy of the first dead baby bird I ever saw, half-naked in the grass, pink flesh with a few blue feathers against the green. It was a Blue Jay fallen far too soon, before it could fly. I have cherished them ever since. Now I am coming close to home, striding more purposefully and feeling in a better mood. I am at the neighbors' picket fence on our corner when I see a small brown bird scratching and hopping under a bush. I am usually not patient enough to sort out all the sparrows—but I always hope. Perhaps it is an unlikely white-crowned, or maybe even a rarer, chubby Fox Sparrow that jumped back and forth happily for a time one year amidst the oak leaves beneath the boxwood in our yard. Alone. Striped. Spot on chest. Grey cheeks. Longer, notched tail. This one is a Song Sparrow. That's the species that sings, according to birding lore, a rousing "Hip, hip, hooray, boys! Spring is here again!" My songster flies to a finial on the fence, as if posing for a photo, throws its head back, opens beak, clears throat, prepares to sing...Out come a few squeaks, only the first vague hints of the opening of hip, hip, hooray! Spring seems not quite here after all. It's like rejoining a choir, voice out of shape, or drinking too much milk before a solo, or maybe spring training when a baseball hitting a bat still stings the hands. My Song Sparrow's eyes gleam, he gathers himself up, he tries again (it is the male who sings). The beak opens, trembles, and out tumbles a slightly clearer, longer set of squeaks and a couple of short, squawky notes. They sound something like hip, hip, hoo... and then trail off. He has not trilled, but I am thrilled. My songster is as close as a canary in a cage; he is as happy as, well, a lark. I am witnessing the exact scene recorded by Louis Halle in *Spring in Washington*, written on almost the same day, two generations ago while I was still a toddler in Manhattan.

Halle muses that spring begins, if you watch carefully, long before the vernal equinox. On Sunday, January 28, he notes that the Potomac is still frozen. There are winter ducks at Roaches Run, but a cardinal is singing "his full spring song, two musical syllables going downstairs into the cellar. But, in contrast, "The song sparrow tried the first few notes of his own song, experimentally, but never got beyond them. He reminded me how early it still was for spring." It was certainly early for Louis Halle. He records subzero temperatures, ice and snow. He has journaled about a brief thaw. I am witnessing something entirely different. I am comforted by the rotation of the seasons, the resurrection of nature, the bursts of life unconcerned about the doings of mankind—a single, brainy species. But as much as I imagine happily sharing a brisk morning walk or bicycling by the bronzed gulls with Louis Halle or sharing the exact same, hesitant hoorays of the song sparrow, harbinger of spring, I know that since 1945, everything has changed.

February 1, 2012
The Crocuses Are Early

It has been a week of unusually warm spring weather now. January has set a record. It reaches sixty-eight degrees today in bright sunshine with only a few low clouds. I spot more and more snowdrops popping up through lawns as I walk through my virtual spring. As I near the Methodist church on Custer Road, I see what the *Washington Post* has already recorded. Crocuses! There are a few dozen purple ones just opened overnight in front of 8209. Each year, I am amazed that flowers seem to leap from the ground in full blossom where there have been none before, or beneath my notice, only negligible nubs. Although I have not kept precise records over the years, I am aware that, on average, the first crocuses—a sign in my mind of true spring—usually do not pop out until the first week of March or so. Spring in Washington this year seems at least a full month early. I see other signs and overnight appearances. A profusion of yellow star-like blossoms on three small circular shrubs, daffodils with full buds about to burst upon the scene, and my first tiny yellow wildflower by a driveway. I have been so taken by the first flowers that I have barely seen or heard the birds. I have been simply soaking in the light, the warmth, the decidedly unexpected and abnormal birth of springtime in Bethesda.

February 2, 2012
Political Birds and Religious Flowers

I am out early this morning. Caryn delivers the grandkids to pre-school on Thursdays. The streets are busy with the cars of commuters and well-dressed suburbanites hauling recycling bins and trash cans for curbside pickup before driving off to downtown deadlines. There are nannies, too, with strollers, or hoisting squirming kids into vans and mini-SUVs. It is cool and hazy, having rained overnight. Things are damp and rich—the feel of fall. It is fifty-two degrees and rising. The morning mist, the sounds of Spanish, the early spread of flowers—all call up Berkeley and the Bay Area. There, it is eternally spring or fall. Maybe we East Coast establishment die-hards really do have things all wrong. But who could work? Who could write amidst such balmy beauty?

But Washington does have its charms. A Red-bellied Woodpecker calls a clownish "Brr-riick" before I realize it is a Democratic bird. If you listen closely, it is really campaigning, calling out "Ba-rack! Ba-rack!" Now that is a sign of spring! In Washington, "primaries" are not the designation for the longest wing feathers on a bird, but rather the ritualistic electoral rites of spring. Now I see crocuses near a neighbor's yard—the only one of a far right-winger for blocks around. Just a few, short weeks ago it shone from afar, like an airport, with huge, garish, lit up plastic displays of Santas, stars, snow globes, snowmen, Disney trains, even a complete, cheesy Jesus and Holy Family, mixed in together with the commercial stuff. Not very conservative this plastic potpourri of the Saturnalian and the sacred. But this morning God has indeed shown up, even if oddly early, as dozens of tiny, purple-clad crocus choristers sing their hallelujahs. Further on, a small, bent, old, gnarled, and oft-pruned cherry tree is pushing out its first pink petals. No lines of tourists will drive here in droves—as they do to the Tidal Basin or to Kenwood—to see this venerable, tiny tree, still clinging to life. They should. It is a sign.

As I turn into the green swath of the cut-through to Charlcote, where there is a bank of forsythia in shade waiting to burst forth, I am given another sign. It is some distant cousin, a descendant, of Louis Halle's sputtering Song Sparrow. It is too far away to be the one from my neighbor's fence. But this one is singing! I can watch it easily and up close as it moves a bit around the forsythia stems, hops down to pick amongst the leaves, comes back, poses, and lets forth a complete verse, clear and proud, of "Hip, hip hooray, boys, spring is here again!!" I am in ecstasy. If this keeps up, I will need to name the little fellow, as Caryn and I did Hadley the Hawk, a resident Cooper's who was a regular in our yard one year. (Note the gender-neutral name since neither of us can tell a male from a female Cooper's, even at close range, as it dines upon a dove.)

Now that I venture outdoors more when the trees are bare, I start to see not only the ubiquitous, leafy nests of squirrels, but those of hawks and maybe other raptors, too. High up in a very tall, thin cherry, reaching for the sky, I see a tell-tale pile of sticks, lying on a branch and snuggled against the trunk. Cooper's? Red-tailed? Who knows? As I ponder through my binoculars (the nest is at the height of a house) I see another in a tree yet further back. I will have to look and read and ask some pro what kinds of nests these are that are all about. It is the juncos all over again. It is as if these hawk homes had never been here at all until I was led to stop and look. I picture myself in residence for a week at the College of Notre Dame in Baltimore on its small, historic campus, hidden next to Loyola, on the way to Hopkins, in the tonier part of town. My host, a dean, shares a secret that few are privileged to know or will be told. We tromp up to the tower of the old Victorian main building, open only to guided guests. The views alone are worth my winded state. But then, beneath us from high up here, atop a big white pine, invisible except from above, is a Red-tailed Hawk, sitting on her eggs. This will be a nativity scene worth the waiting and the wonder.

Cheering Robins

I hurry home now. As I get nearer, a close-up robin cheers me on. This is the first red-breast amidst the migrants and the winter residents that I have seen who speaks to me directly, who celebrates the mood of spring. "Cheer, cheerily! Cheer, cheerily!" he happily instructs. It is fifty years since *Silent Spring* when Rachel Carson saved the robins for moments such as this. Robins have been our favorite bird since the English colonists misnamed this stunning, friendly thrush in a nostalgic nod to the small, bluebird-sized robin of the British Isles. Our first popular nature writer, Susan Fenimore Cooper, in her 1850 *Rural Hours*, described the near delirium, the celebrations and commentary each year when the robins returned to the wintry village of Cooperstown way up in New York State. Here in Washington, the great nature writer, John Burroughs, whose career spanned Walt Whitman and Abraham Lincoln through Teddy Roosevelt's day, first eagerly noted robins in his rambles recorded from Civil War times in his 1871 *Wake-Robin*. "You hear their piping in the meadow, in the pasture, on the hillside. Walk in the woods, and the dry leaves rustle with the whir of their wings, the air is vocal with their cheery call....How round and genuine the notes are, and how eagerly our ears drink them in! The first utterance, and the spell of winter is thoroughly broken, and the remembrance of it afar off." I think of Florence Merriam Bailey, whose *Birds through an Opera Glass* started millions of us birding with binoculars instead of blasting away with guns. Florence helped found the DC Audubon Society to which Roosevelt and, later, Rachel Carson and Roger Tory Peterson belonged. She taught classes on birding throughout the Washington area and was the authority and author for the foreword of her friend Lucy Maynard's 1898 *Birds of Washington and Vicinity*. Both Florence and Lucy were welcome inside the White House when birding was then possible for the public throughout the surrounding grounds. Roosevelt even kept a detailed list of the birds he watched. Florence recalled the same robin notes I have just heard as a "red-letter day" when the calendar moved toward spring. "As I look back, one of the brightest is the day when from a tree opposite the Treasury the first spring carol of the Robin arrested my steps and magically transformed the noisy city streets into a quiet countryside, as a sudden burst of sunshine illuminates a dull landscape."

A half century after Florence Merriam Bailey and Lucy Maynard, Louis Halle again had the same sensation, though in mid-March, not a freakish February. "It was no longer a matter of listening for an isolated cardinal or song sparrow at dawn: for now, at dawn and dusk alike, and at intervals during the day, the robins stationed in the treetops filled the atmosphere with their uninterrupted caroling, *'cheer up cheery cheer up cheery cheerily cheer-up...*, *and then the rapid succession of call notes as if the birds were near to bursting with their passionate vitality.'"* [Italics in original] I find myself standing stock still, trying to capture, to keep, a keen sense of gratitude for those who have gone before, whose footsteps I try to trace. They have savored and saved these moments, have written and acted so that my heart, too, can sing without a silent spring.

February 6, 2012
Changing Worldwide Weather

I am still enjoying mild Washington winter or early spring. The last few days have been more "normal" with temperatures around 40 or a little above, with bright sun except for cloudy skies, light rain, and snow flurries over the weekend while Caryn battles a rare fever. But my reveries and writing are haunted a bit by reports in the news of the opposite effects of an unusually early, warm Washington spring. Elsewhere, people are dying—freezing to death in frigid temperatures, massive snow falls, icy rains. I was first aware from a student in my American class on climate change and American environmental politics. His mother is ill and he is going to Anchorage, Alaska, where he grew up; he politely warns me—or rather asks my indulgence—that he may not make it back for tonight's Monday, once-a-week class at 8:10 p.m. I assure him his mother and his concerns for her are more important. Then I read that Anchorage's only main highway south has been blocked by an avalanche! I will see if he makes it back, but I doubt it.

In Eastern Europe, there are record snows and low temperatures, Ukraine is worse, protesters against Putin in Moscow brave subzero temperatures to demonstrate for democracy. I look at a photo of ice around Lake Geneva where I have often been, and take in a stupid AP story, and a telling one, about what fun it is to have frigid winter back in the Netherlands since the canals have frozen and they can put on a legendary country-wide ice-skating race that has not been held since 1997 since the darn water just won't freeze. No mention, analysis, concern for other Europeans dying or of climate change. I see, too, that the drought continues in Texas—the worst, including the Dust Bowl—since accurate records have been kept beginning in 1895. The entire Texas rice crop is at risk. It will drive up prices everywhere and lead to more hunger and misery in a global economy still suffering from recession.

I start to envy Louis Halle and Florence Merriam Bailey, John Burroughs, and other Washingtonians who drew inspiration, took refuge, and were restored by nature, thinking it unchanging and eternal. I seek similar insights, similar in-dwellings of the spirit. But my mind and soul are split, multi-tiered, and modern. Nature and the future are essentially in our hands. How we perceive what is around us, the seasons and the sun, the flora and the fauna, the fun, the foibles, even the ferocity of our fellow man— all matter, matter immensely. I take hope that our new power, new global knowledge can still be turned to the good. But then I am an optimist, a Romantic, a Victorian, a progressive Christian; I have been wrong many, many times before.

Sunset in the Suburbs

I need to shake off such wintry wallowing and whining—head for the sun. Get outside. As Caryn was sleeping off a fever in late afternoon yesterday after some morning rime on the windshields and a few, small snowflakes trying futilely to stick, I head out to clear my head, unkink my joints, and get a grip. I walk quickly, think a lot, notice little. It is an hour or so before the Super Bowl; the suburbs are silent. Slowly things begin to sink in. High in the trees the robins I have been seeing are chuckling and chattering, settling in. Again, a Song Sparrow sings and I take heart. Caryn had seen the silhouette of a hawk in the backyard neighbor's tree so I scan above me, seeking swift, deadly signs of hope. I spy yet another set of sticks that marks the nest of some accipiter that I have missed until this year. But this is not a walk of raptors; it is one of rapture. As my eyes have been lifted up, it is the early evening sky that stirs my soul. Dark clouds are backlit by the waning sun, the trees stark, sharp, and silhouetted, as if snipped and scissored by some craftsmen's practiced hand. I stand and stare, seeing now some romantic artist's scene— Hudson River Valley School or Thomas Moran or Thomas Cole. There is golden light and ominous, dark clouds that blend or bump side-by-side the lighter, whiter, greyer ones with patches of blue and streamers of orange and pink strung in between. The scene shifts somehow to a sacred ceiling—the Sistine Chapel, perhaps, with a Michelangelo-made hand of God. The colors of the sky are more subtle than I first observed. The blues fade from aqua and azure to cerulean, pale blue, pale silver, and almost white. The clouds seem more luminous, less ominous, as they show subtle shadings of sable, obsidian, or jet, then charcoal grey and old, patinaed pewter, true grey, and whites well-copied off ivory or an eggshell. I do not wish to move or think, just feel. It is silly, here in the suburbs, in February 2012, to think I am in some enchanted, sacred scene, sharing secrets with the artists, or with saints. But all the same, I stay awhile, as if this is all there is.

February 7, 2012
A Quick, Lone Hawk

Today is simpler, with work to do and little going on outside. I take a break and head out to walk simply to stretch, not really to see if the saints of nature will speak aloud to me. Same as before. Mild winter day. Low 40s. Brilliant sunshine with little wind, quiet, bright blue skies. I am being efficient once again. Red-bellied Woodpecker. Check. Song Sparrow. Check. A few more crocuses and tiny garden flowers I cannot name. Check. The tree murderers are back. Check. And two different sets of Hispanic rug installers—is there a special day or special sale that I have missed? I am simply walking, and by my standards, walking fast. Even so, I have some sort of hawkish feeling. Not to go to war, but to see one live. Caryn saw one briefly, unidentified out the window the other day. I have now seen nests, so somehow I think I deserve to see an occupant. Arrogance or superstition can often reign supreme. As I come to the oblong small island that once held a small sculpture garden where some roads converge, I pause and look carefully at the large white pine that is on one corner. There were reports in the paper of Great Horned Owls in New York City. Why not here in Bethesda? I look below the pine for pellets or other signs of hunting owls. Nope. Not here. I imagine, then, that there must be a red-tailed's nest high atop the crown of the pine, unseen, as at the College of Notre Dame. I glimpse a possible humped hawk shape in a far-off tree. My binoculars regretfully reveal that it is no buteo, but a bunch of leaves that betrays my hopes and chuckles at me now.

Another clump appears nearby in the huge maple in the sun. Fool me once, shame on you. Fool me twice, shame on me. But I lift my trusty, portable Swifts nonetheless. And what to my wondering eyes appears? A brownish head, a cold, staring eye, a beak as hooked and hawkish, as lethal, as a Harrier jet. Light streaking on the chest, white breast, longish tail. Some thirty feet above me, perched and poised, is a hawk of which sort I am not sure. I think red-tailed, because that is what I have been thinking and what I want. But I cannot see the tail real well from where I stand. And truth be told, unless I see the pinkish tail in spread of flight, I am never sure of what I've seen. I circle slowly round the tree. My hawk seems totally unconcerned. It sits just one block in from the passing sights and sounds of Old Georgetown Road. My hawk is oblivious of traffic reports, of the news of tumult in our world, of the few passersby below. I circle a little more, less cautious now since I seem beneath its notice or not good enough to eat. From behind, the bird is a light brown with a few pale scattered spots. The tail shows no pink or salmon or cinnamon or the other shades displayed by a red-tailed, depending on the sun. On closer look, the tail is brown and rounded at the end with two black stripes on it, barely visible. I am embarrassed, yet excited. It is, of course, a Cooper's Hawk, the suburban hunter who seems to have been spreading—feeding on doves and starlings and sparrows and other succulent victims drawn to the seed that hangs in feeders in many yards.

February 16, 2012
My First Confusing Crocus

I have been writing or teaching when not battling a computer virus that seems to constantly outwit the geek service at American. It has been closer to true winter, though not much. Some light snow stuck in patches barely covered the ground for a few days. The earth has been mostly crunchy as temperatures head below freezing at night. My fewer walks are quiet, gray, given to thought, broken only occasionally by robins or a Song Sparrow or the sight of some new flowers that have dared to come out early. This morning it is another cool or cold morning rain with the thermometer right near freezing. The drops are viscous, almost sticky, trying to turn to sleet or snow. They feel a bit like oobleck, the gooey stuff that falls from the sky called up by Dr. Seuss' horrible magicians; they tamper with nature simply to humor their paying patron, the king. By midday, it is truly rain. Bartholomew Cubbins has saved the day! I spot the very first crocus in my own yard, a single yellow one pushing through the mulch. I am confused, with contradictory feelings. I feel a rush of panic as real spring approaches; deadlines will loom along with the daffodils and dandelions. I miss real winter where one hunkers down, works hard, puts on a few pounds, gets some snow days, snuggles by a fire. But I am beginning to long for easy warmth and sun and lengthy rides along the C&O Canal, peddling past Dyke Marsh, peeking around Peirce Mill, or meandering through the marshes at Huntley Meadows. When the semester is over and my speaking schedule slows down, I can become again the master of my fate and trace the tracks of Burroughs, Bailey, Roosevelt, Carson, Halle and all those who have fired my desire to see Washington in spring.

February 20, 2012
I Declare It's Spring

The vernal equinox is thirty days away, but I am ready to officially declare it spring in Washington. It's an insider thing inside the Beltway, being a *cognoscente*, as when I called John Kerry as the Democratic candidate in 2004 while Howard Dean was still ahead and had not yet done "The Scream." The ground has still not frozen; the days are sunny and near fifty. It is supposed to top sixty-five degress Fahrenheit. at the end of the week. But spring is in my mood and the merriment of the birds. There are steady signs now. The robins are working the lawns for worms, giving off long whinnying calls from the trees, flicking their tails flirtatiously when they land upon a branch—some likely spot for bearing a springtime brood. I see a pair of House Finches dashing in and out after each other from among the bedroom branches of a pine. The male stops to sing in the sunshine, thrusting out his chest, as if Ezio Pinza pouring out, "this nearly was mine." The red is so deep and rich in the slanting late sun that I wonder if he is the more deeply stained Purple Finch after all. I have always had to puzzle out the difference, often falling back on the simple, if somewhat shaky, supposition that Purple Finches aren't too common and are more likely found in woods.

As if to confirm my subjective seasonal shift, small daffodils near many doors and driveways have split open their buds and nod contentedly in the breeze. Most look like what I think of as narcissi. One beauty stands quite alone with slim, short leaves, its blonde head radiant with the glow of sunshine. There are more crocuses and snowdrops everywhere I look, including a small bunch I have neglected ever seeing before behind the sun porch on my house. And perhaps the most significant sign is the sudden darting out from beneath a bush of my old friend Peter Rabbit who lives in the lane by Mr. McGregor on the cut-through to Northfield Road. I had stopped to admire and measure a young white pine like one, now fully grown, we planted years ago in the yard in Philadelphia.

February 21, 2012
The C&O Canal

It is sunny and sixty degrees Fahrenheit. I pump up the tires on my Trek and head to the C&O Canal. It is my first bike ride of whatever season it is supposed to be! I head to Lock 10, the nearest one, since I am short on time. I have ridden the canal for many years, in every season. But this is where I began a quarter century ago, with different binoculars, a different bike. Before that, I came to the C&O when we first moved to Washington with John Ginaven and other birding friends who visited from my old peace group in Philadelphia. We were new at it and still adding lifers of fairly common birds that thrilled me at first sight. Scarlet and Summer Tanagers, Indigo Buntings, and more. The C&O Canal has been a birding and nature hot spot during its operation since after the Civil War when Florence Merriam Bailey popularized collecting birds through binoculars rather than through the barrel of a gun. The railroads drove the canal out of business; coal from Cumberland was hauled by rail, rather than by the picturesque, but painfully slow, canal boats with their cantankerous mules. The C&O hung on until 1924 when it finally shut down and fell into deep disrepair. The New Deal and a force of Negro Civilian Conservation Corps workers rebuilt the first twenty-two miles from Georgetown, inching slowly toward the northwest to just a few miles beyond Great Falls. When the Depression and the war were ended, hikers, fishermen, birders, naturalists returned in numbers. Among them were some great ones, and, before the days of Google and of Gmail, some of them would write. Rachel Carson and Roger Tory Peterson came here often along with lesser known, but talented birders and writers like Louis Halle and Shirley Briggs. Even Whitaker Chambers, the avid anti-communist of *Witness* fame, led Alger Hiss down the path to perjury charges with a Prothonotary Warbler they both had seen.

I wheel across a small wooden bridge by the stone lock house and head southeast toward the District. In full spring, this section of the canal will have family flotillas of Wood Ducks in their small, multi-colored, wide-eyed splendor. There will be herons, turtles, troves of warblers, and other woodland birds. But today things look fairly barren, almost bare. The Potomac is the premier vista. It runs close by the canal with eddies and swirls, small islands, wooded floodplains, and its rocks. Though less than ten miles downstream, the nation's capital, with its contemporary concerns, seems a century removed. A few miles in, I pause for a

quaint reminder of why this is. The woods and water to my right
have moved in closer now. The larger river is blocked from view
by a long, small island across a small, slow stream. Wooden steps
lead to the water's edge and an old, odd contraption. It is equal,
in its Rube Goldberg design, to the beams and bolts, levers and
gears that manipulate the heavy oaken gates that guard and guide
each lock and the laden boats of coal that once slipped through.
A small, hand-pulled, wooden ferry, its pulleys, cables, chains
intricate as a clock, deserve display in the Smithsonian, or some
other reliquary of equal reputation. The cables lead across to
Sycamore Island where stands a small old clubhouse, with some
new additions, and canoes stacked and spread like a Boy Scout
camp. By the gangway to the ferry is a single wrought iron lantern
atop a post with a simple sign nearby. Montgomery Sycamore
Island Club. Founded 1885. Dedicated to the Preservation and
Enjoyment of the Potomac River. Private Members Only. I
imagine scenes from Renoir's *Boating Party*, or somber WASPs
with muttonchops and mustaches like those of Grover Cleveland.
It is unbelievable that such a club has hung on here right by the
towpath up into our time. All that stretches out before me is now
a national park. Not a nickel is needed to relax or row or ride the
rapids. But such private preserves once served to save the sights I
now enjoy for free. Somebody's great-grandfather, muttonchops
and all, was looking out for me.

And so, I head on down toward Little Falls. Soon two Red-
tailed Hawks circle and sail above my head. It is too far away for
them to be the pair I nearly touched from my human perch
outside the Capitol dome. But they are equally wonderful and wild
as they cast a cold eye for some creature to catch and claw and
eat. Nature is not all Disneyland or delightful dabbling ducks.
There are dangers for us humans, too, as huge signs soon
announce. Where the river has become wide, there are three large
white, slightly rusty barrels floating. In what seems a placid part

of the Potomac, they hold aloft signs that say DANGER DAM AHEAD. Equally old, and just as unnerving, are two huge wooden, white painted signs on each bank of the river, perhaps twenty feet per side. Their eighteen inch high, red block letters command attention. STOP. DAM AHEAD. DEADLY UNDER-TOW. GET TO SHORE. There are other warnings posted all along the river and canal. Most are for campers, climbers, kayak-ers upstream along the Billy Goat Trail, near Great Falls, where rocks and ravines create roiling white water rapids. On average, some seven people a year drown in the Potomac. They slip and fall or, seemingly safe on solid rocks, they are surrounded and sub-merged as water roars in from further on upstream. No sign, it seems, can properly prepare you when storms and surges or spring thaws send walls of water rising, rushing across the rocks.

Captain John Smith and His Men

I feel new respect for the explorers, adventurers of old. On my Trek, I am easily traversing a ten-mile stretch of the Potomac that was first navigated and noted by none other than Captain John Smith, of Pocahontas fame. Weighed down by heavy English clothing in a thirty-foot, two-ton barge laden with provisions and with arms, Smith and his crew of fifteen men alternately rowed, sailed, and slogged their way in two separate trips in 1608 and 1609 from Jamestown to the top of the Chesapeake, including the Potomac. Along the way, fish were so numerous that they tried to catch them with their frying pans. Smith and his party were not birders or naturalists, but noted nature all the same. They had been sent to find the Northwest Passage that would create a simpler, straighter voyage to the riches of the Orient. And they were to report on any resources that they found while laying claim to the country to outdo the rival Spanish. The result is John Smith's *Map of Virginia*, 1612. It is an account of his exploits and explorations, including the first maps ever of the greater Washington area, much of Maryland and the Chesapeake Bay. He notes birds and fish, fauna of all sorts, including some bison and some bears, along with descriptions of landscape, natural formations, and friendly Native Americans all along the way. Captain Smith reaches the very spot where I am now. It is the rocks that catch his eye; those in the falls had "divers tinctures." They glisten with silver and golden bits of glitter that could mean riches when gotten to England for assay. A landing party is sent out to explore for minerals further up the river, reaching as far as the Great Falls. They meet more Indians in canoes "well loaden with the flesh of bears, deer, and other beasts whereof we had a part."

George Washington Drew Here

I continue on, an explorer's mood and Jacobean English engraving mental maps and musings of my own. I imagine myself in puffed sleeves, a breastplate, a pointed sword like John Smith's knightly garb when his portrait is presented to us in his famous later years. But civilization soon intrudes as I pull up sharply near Lock 6. I am cast forward over 150 years in time. There is George Washington, tall, stately, staring at something farther on. He is dressed in frontier, huntsman clothes, all leather and belts, as if straight from the pages of *Last of the Mohicans*. He holds a powder horn, and some unusual instruments and scrolls are at his sides. I had forgotten that Washington was a surveyor when he was younger. He explored and mapped the Potomac Valley before he bumped into the French near Pittsburgh and set off the French and Indian Wars. A careful draftsman, Washington's drawings are beautiful to see. But here his portrait points out to tourists at Lock 6 that Washington championed the Patowmack Canal. Part of it, the predecessor of the C&O, the signage tells me, ran from the spot where I am standing "to the Abner Cloud House at mile

3.1." More signs point out that the lockhouse here was built in 1829, a year after the July 4th groundbreaking for the canal at ceremonies at Little Falls. It was the great flood of 1924 that ruined the canal and really put an end to its already declining operations. There have been many floods since, including a big one in 1936 that washed things away and set the stage for the CCC to build it all again.

But you and I are able to pedal along after Captain Smith, Colonel Washington, and the Civilian Conservation Corps, to follow in the footsteps of Rachel Carson and of Louis Halle, because of the intrepid intervention of Supreme Court Justice William O. Douglas, whose picture is here at Lock 6, too. Known mainly as an outspoken civil libertarian, Douglas was a conservationist who organized a march of notables to save the C&O Canal from being filled in and paved as a highway to speed 1950s tourists to scenic highlights along the way. He dared the editorial board of the *Washington Post* to join him on a hike along the entire 180-mile length of the canal from Georgetown to the coal country of Cumberland. The city editors never made it that far, but they were soon convinced. A national park was born. The sights and strides of Smith and Washington were saved.

March 9, 2012
Washington and Rachel Carson's Mother

Temperatures reach seventy degrees Fahrenheit in Bethesda on March 1. There are now daffodils in my shady yard. But my speaking schedule is sprouting now as well; no time for rambling walks and wistful reveries. I will follow George Washington toward Pittsburgh through the Alleghenies, again on an easier path. The first national highway, US Route 40, headed west through northern Maryland and the mountains of West Virginia running just below Pennsylvania's Mason-Dixon Line. Now it is

Interstate 68 that whisks me toward a week at the historic college, Washington and Jefferson, founded in 1787. It is also the place where Rachel Carson's mother, Maria McLean Carson, was a brilliant student at the Washington Female Seminary, a rare, elite education for young women of the time. Maria McLean made honors in the class of 1887 and was even able to take some courses at then all-male Washington College. She became a teacher and a devotee of Anna Botsford Comstock and her nature-study movement. But as soon as she married, as was required at the time, she was forced to quit her job. All her learning, her science, her love of nature, were poured into Rachel, her brightest, youngest, favorite child.

Despite speaking and meeting with the president, faculty and students, energy experts, and the head of the Rachel Carson Institute, my highlight is the evening sky. The nights of March 6 and 7 are clear and crisp. A full moon shines and sets historic buildings to shimmering. I am using an office in the oldest building from 1787 that reportedly has a female ghost. I wonder if it is Rachel's mother, grieving that her female prep school has been torn down for a new LEED-certified science center. The president tells me that her huge Victorian mansion also has some ghosts and bats for those who think that academia is too stodgy. But visible with the moon is a rare display of all the nearby planets—Venus, Jupiter, Mercury, Saturn, Mars. I rue that I have left my binoculars and spotting scope safely settled in the closet in my study. Still I gaze and gape in wonder. Washington, Jefferson, Maria Carson, and her daughter Rachel, would have loved a scene like this.

Chapter Two

Early Spring in Washington

Friday, March 9, 2012
Above Great Falls

Spring waves me on as I descend from the late wintry gusts of Pennsylvania and West Virginia. I drove to Washington and Jefferson College through swirling snow, crossing the ancient Alleghenies, worn down with time, at a height of some three thousand feet. Maryland slopes down toward sea level with fields and farms filling up with green. There are large quilted squares of land recently sere and beige and brown now showing off chartreuse, apple, and spring green. As I reach Bethesda, spring has come for real. There are small cherry trees in bloom, flowering forsythia, budding redbud trees, and northern magnolias bursting with blooms that are raspberry-stained cups of china. A dozen white daffodils are lined up beneath the azalea leafing out at my front walk. As I get out of the car, a Cooper's Hawk is chased across the yard by a new, small gang of springtime grackles. The Lenten roses stand upright and in bloom. I see two long-lost, endangered honey bees lazing in and out. I sort the mail and skim the piled-up *Washington Post*. Careful watchers of the Tidal Basin report that the peak of the Japanese cherry blossoms that brings the annual migration of *homo sapiens* to this spot is only two or three weeks away. March

24 will be a remarkably early start postulates the *Post*—without a hint of causes or of consequences. But I have had my say on climate change on the campus I just left. The damn *Post* article is a feature after all. It is spring break for us perennial students. Time to take the Trek back out along the C&O Canal.

Like Captain Smith and his men searching for the glitter of gold, I head north toward Great Falls. But instead of hiking the nearly ten miles on foot, I drive out MacArthur Boulevard across the nineteenth-century, one-lane bridge toward the entrance of Great Falls. Then I cruise down a winding, wooded road just over a mile to the entrance gate with a friendly ranger at the window. I park and ride in by the old Tavern at Great Falls, an eighteenth-century white brick building, now a museum, that stands beside Lock 20. It is shadier, cooler here in the woods along the canal where Captain Smith and his men have searched for gold.

I am greeted as I slowly ride and gawk along the way by the crazed, cackling laugh of a Pileated Woodpecker. It is a sound only heard where there are big old trees that this crow-sized woodpecker likes to pound upon. I have a few in my neighborhood—pileateds in the fall favor the red, grenade seed pods on my specimen southern magnolia. All else is still. A few Mallards dabble and do their feeding headstands in the shallow water of the C&O. Then I see a small bird flit from branch to branch. It lands somewhat upright, briskly bobbing its tail. Usually, when the trees are all leafed out, I hear an Eastern Phoebe before I see one. It is a friendly little flycatcher, tame as a tabby. Here on the canal they can be seen near lockhouses, around bridges, just about any place to sit and flick that tail. Phoebes put me in a vacation mood. Caryn and I have had many a phoebe neighbor nesting near our rented cottages and cabins. They are far different than their shy woodland cousin, the Eastern Wood-Pewee. If you don't keep a list of birds heard, but never seen, you should consider it. The phoebe has a white breast and that restless tail. The peewee, if you see it, is mostly brown with white stripes, or wing bars, on the side. It's a flycatcher, too, though it rarely seems to move. It gets its kicks by calling over and over a long, drawn out "pee o' wee" in a sort of Southern drawl—slow and descending a couple of notes as it slides steadily down the "weeee..."

But my first real sign of woodland spring in Washington is spread before me, tiny white flowers, almost invisible at first, amidst the crushed, wan remains of oak leaves that trim the towpath. I would have missed them, even cruising slowly, if I had not stopped to watch a phoebe. They are spring beauties, no more than an inch or two in height. Their small, quarter-inch, five-petalled stars are subtly streaked with pink. They peek out from the forest litter in little groups of one and two and three. I look at them on bended knee as if a professional photographer or, perhaps, a pagan at my prayers. None of my beauties move; they are rooted to the soil. But the more I look the more pop up and multiply, marvelously, like Disney animation. Two more there and there and there! There are many hundreds I see now as I slowly bike on down the path. I hope that walkers see them—if they go slowly, observantly enough.

Further on I now can see the river. I stop again because a fellow with a camera is taking pictures of some scene. It is piles of wood—debris drifted downstream and piled artistically upon a rock. But behind it, all unnoticed, are four small, dark ducks bobbing against a current. My naked eye says Ruddy Ducks like those that frequent Four Mile Run, along the Potomac in the city, where Louis Halle would ride. But my trusty binoculars bring them closer and magnify the light. Being an optimist, my mind always goes for broke. Little tufts behind the head, could they be Tufted Ducks? I have seen so few and they are so uncommon, I calm down a bit. That simply cannot be. What I have before me are Ring-necked Ducks that are good enough for me! The bird books say they are common in wooded ponds, but I have never seen them here. Ringed-necks have a somewhat inconspicuous white stripe that arcs up along their shoulder, contrasting with a greyish side and solid black above. The male's head is slightly misshapen and pointed toward the back. In good light and with glasses it shows a dark, deep purple. But now it just looks black. The far less common Tufted Duck is not, of course, truly tufted after all. It sports a single feather tailing from its head that, trust me, can be difficult to see. But who said birding should be easy? Identification can be hard. It's why the early, old-time ornithologists like Elliott Coues who, during the Civil War, wrote the first good book on birding in DC, shot their species, and studied them at home.

Grover Cleveland Relaxes on the Canal

Soon I come to a birder's paradise, or at least it will be in migration. Pennyfield Lock, or Lock 22 of the C&O Canal, is named after a father and son who were lockkeepers here. George Pennyfield, and later his son, Charlie, lived in the lockhouse from 1890 to 1910, over a hundred years ago. The lock was built in 1832 and like other ones, in their prime, saw some five hundred canal boats pass by each day. The lock is not far from the edge of a large lagoon. A path at its side runs down to the river, with woods on the left and the muddy, marshy lagoon on the right. Be sure to wander down here in season; there will be birds galore on either side. I saw my first Summer Tanager here some forty years ago. Right now the birds are few, but a noisy, cheeping, chirping, high-pitched racket is intense. I cannot see them all; I never have. But I know spring peepers when I hear them. Their avid amphibian echoes are all around me, drowning out each other. These tiny, tan and brown, and less than one inch chorus frogs are, for all intents, invisible. Someone must have wired the lagoon with speakers, like a theater, with its locomotive wheels and rumbles, advertising Dolby's surrounding sound.

I watch a single Great Blue Heron standing in the water, watching and waiting to spear a snack. Despite the high-pitched peepers, it is a serene, simple scene that has brought out countless human fishermen long before my time. The most famous, out of many, was President Grover Cleveland, who angled at this site. His photo is on the Park Service marker in front of me. It says he "sought refuge from the pressures of the White House by coming here on fishing trips." Cleveland shows his signature large moustache, is clad in suit and tie, and wears a suitable straw hat. He sits partially in shadow with his rod and reel in a small row boat, the lockhouse to the rear. It is hard to imagine, but for this photographic evidence, that an American president could relax undisturbed here, unhurried as a heron. Teddy Roosevelt, our better known naturalist president, must have been here, too. He was an avid birder who kept a careful White House count and bicycled around on short trips like this with his expert ornithologist friend, C. Hart Merriam, the head of the US Biological Survey. But Cleveland was a conservationist, too, as his fishing trips attest.

In 1894, during his second term, he signed the Yellowstone Act, the first federal legislation ever designed to protect wildlife on government lands. Yellowstone had been a fabled spot, rumored and written about for years. But in 1892 when an expedition that included famous artists, photographers, and writers returned to Washington, they besieged the Congress. In a remarkable early example of environmental lobbying, they buttonholed members and distributed copies of their lavishly illustrated report for all to see. Cleveland welcomed the bill, but he was not done. Like TR, he had been governor of New York and worked on reform legislation with the Republican Roosevelt before either became president. In 1897, not long before Roosevelt went to the White House upon the assassination of William McKinley, Grover Cleveland set a conservationist precedent for TR by creating additional federal forest reserves containing more than twenty-one million acres.

As I return, I see three deer by the waterworks where the fields are always trimmed. They are often here in mornings or now towards evening. I put my binoculars on the cell phone tower beyond the field to see what birds are making use of this new, handy, hardy tree. Ubiquitous as ever and willing to nest in man-made structures, a small flock of starlings has taken roost. But hoping for bigger stuff, I decide to see if eagles are on their nest. Just over 5 1/4 miles from the Great Falls lock, there is a barely visible aerie in a tree across the river. It can only be seen from the canal in early spring before the leaves come out. I have watched it for years and seen eagles and eaglets come and go. An eagle's nest is re-used each year and gets bigger over time. They are eventually huge, ram-shackle affairs, some dozen feet in width, often weighing tons. This one is so far away, it looks, even with binoculars, like a robin's nest nestled in the crotch of a neighbor's tree. I find the spot each year just past mile marker 18 and near the repair of serious erosion in the towpath. It has long been marked by a cautionary belt of meshed, Day-Glo orange fencing. I am momentarily confused, since the brilliant plastic now is gone. But the nest sits where it always has—in the huge, slightly right-leaning fork of an ancient tree whose top looks like a slingshot. The nest is empty, but will not be for long. I will return and watch. And when I do, herons and egrets will be roosting in other trees nearby. There must be fine fishing all around to create such a rookery. I slowly breathe a sigh. My day is nearly done; special sightings are somewhat sparse. But on the cusp of springtime when things are fairly still, one pauses and takes in what is offered—my old friend phoebe, a single heron, some ringed-necks in a pool, or a portly president, seeking refuge in a rowboat.

Mergansers Out of Water

All the signs of fishing here, including Ring-necked Ducks, should have been a sign that nature is not yet done with me. I try to stay open and observant, or I will never see. And sure enough, their fishing done, two seemingly huge white birds catch my eye. As with the ringed-necks, I am totally confused at first. There is a pair of ducks with long, toothed bills. Mergansers perhaps, but large enough for geese? It is their rotund shape and huge white sides that throw me off at first. I don't often see winter riverine ducks like this standing on a rock at water's edge. It is a pair of Common Mergansers whose male, when half submerged in water, shows only a little white and seems far sleeker at a distance. But now I see the bright red legs and dark green head, separated sharply from the white neck and chest by a clean, straight line. His mate is reddish brown with a comb of feathers sticking backwards from her head. I rarely see mergansers and never close on land like this. They were truly common once. In the 1940s, Louis Halle would see them in the Tidal Basin when traffic there was sparse. I watch my mergansers for quite a while. I may never see the likes this close again. Like synchronized swimmers, they stretch and preen and move in unison. Their simultaneous moves seem as natural and unpracticed as an old married couple making their way carefully across a crowded street.

A Soulmate

I do not really believe in spirit animals and such. But as I finish up my ride, I am greeted by a soulmate. I hear the crazy calling first, a frenzied whooping noise, as if celebrating life. The pileated swoops in beside me no more than forty feet away. This normally wary bird now seems as friendly as a phoebe. It stays still for a time, letting me admire its black and white formal wear, its red Phrygian freedom cap prominently on display. I am grinning from ear to ear, wishing my new friend well. He pounds his chisel bill against the trunk like Michelangelo at his marble. It looks like vigorous nodding, telling me that there is food and freedom enough for both of us in this simple patch of woods.

March 17, 2012
Spring Breezes and the Easter Bunny

I have been speaking in Seattle, amidst cold, endless, splashing rain. Before I left home I could see spring unfolding all about me. My first bees, ubiquitous Cabbage White butterflies, chalk-blue periwinkles popping out in shady yards. While I am gone, Washington reaches eighty. The town is all abuzz with talk of early, early spring. Today I walk slowly, breathing, basking in the beauties broken forth before me. A pair of goldfinches buzzes and lands. Their heads are turning gold. Soon gone will be their antique, burnished look of winter. They will sport gaudy black and gold and gladly sing some tee-de-dees in gilded, undulating flight.

The air is warm, but gentle. I am determined to simply feel. No notes, no noticing for me. A tender breeze touches my cheek. It is a zephyr, as in Chaucer's day, when springtime was sent by gods. In just a week while I was gone, full spring has opened up. Magnolias now are everywhere. Magnificent magenta is the color of the day. Festive falling petals coat the plainest paths and porticoes. They turn them into pleasure domes and bowers of bliss as if an Indian wedding has just been celebrated. Cherry trees of every sort stand by in pale pink contrast. Some weep freely with tears of joy at the freedom and fecundity of earth. Robins happily flip leafy beds, whether for grubs or worms, or mud for nesting, I cannot yet be sure. The bees are out to pollinate or simply poke around. There are tiny, tiny dark ones I have never seen before. And honey bees and bumble bees on every flowering bush. The Cabbage Whites are everywhere, maybe one or two per block. They defy all logic, any rhyme or reason that I can tell, as they drunkenly dart about. Their restless roaming is as unpredictable as the flight of a whiffle ball I see lying on a lawn. No other butterflies have yet to strut their stuff. It is St. Patrick's Day and President Obama has quaffed green beer at the Dubliner downtown.

But here the green is everywhere; it is nature that is on parade. A large, dark bird is spotted overhead. Of course, no eagle, but a man can always hope. It is a Turkey Vulture circling and then I see that there are two. I stop and watch and more appear, a kettle, as they call it at Hawk Mountain, of some dozen vultures soaring on a thermal of warm and rising springtime air.

Then waiting for me on the path by Beatrix Potter-land is my first real rabbit of the spring, not counting the earlier one I flushed; the Easter bunny is checking out his route, ready soon to spread delight to children far and wide. He sits stock still, backlit by the sun. His ears show various veins of red against a fleshy pink. The coat is a soft and rich light brown, the tail is made of cotton. His nose twitches, trembles, sniffs. This small statue is full of coursing life, a potpourri of Christian symbolism, St. Patty's Day, and ancient pagan rites. It is indeed some form of worship as I watch and wonder on my walk. But soon the moment passes. My rabbit darts away despite my breathless stance. I have tried hard not to scare him; I am puzzled at his flight. And then from round the corner, unseen or heard by me, a neighbor and his eager dog come strolling into view. I marvel how the Easter Bunny has scampered off and simply disappeared. There is some sort of mystery or magic in his ways that is worthy of worship in these surprising springtime days.

March 25, 2012
Cherry Blossom Time

Last weekend, around the equinox, the weather was cloudy, cool, and grey. Caryn and I headed out to our favorite, secret springtime spot, the Kenwood neighborhood in Bethesda. We discovered it when we first moved to Bethesda and tired of daytime traffic tie-ups near the Tidal Basin at cherry blossom time. Kenwood is a leafy, pricey part of Bethesda with curving roads and a country club. Bethesda was just beginning to grow when Louis Halle was lamenting pollution around the birds and beauties of the Tidal Basin and beyond. My 1941 brick colonial home had just been built and the single high school (now there are three) was still brand new. The murals at the farmer's market show countryside and farm stands. But the Kenwood neighborhood, its gracious homes and cherry trees, was already there between Little Falls Parkway and River Road. The Kenwood-Chamberlin Development Company had the foresight to plant some 1200 Japanese Yoshino cherry trees along the streets—the same kind as those more famous ones downtown. Caryn and I marvel over the huge ancient ones, survivors from 1920 that can still be seen.

But there are even older specimens, city elders, who seem as ancient as Sequoias, that line the Tidal Basin and now are blooming at a record early date. Caryn and I have often strolled around the basin at dawn or in the evening dusk. I have loved the postcard picture spots, the paddle boats and pink-stained panoramas for as long as I can recall. I even own a watercolor of the Washington Monument awash with painted spring. I have hundreds of handsome photos I've snapped of Jefferson or Roosevelt, of marbled steps and Mallards floating by, of gnarled old trunks, their blossoms bouncing in the breeze. It is odd to think that as visited and venerable as the cherry blossoms are, they were not here when Teddy Roosevelt or Woodrow Wilson was, let alone when Washington and Jefferson were still alive, admiring and recording what they saw. John Burroughs and Lucy Maynard and Florence Merriam Bailey never saw the Japanese Yoshino trees in bloom. They had not yet been planted.

As late as 1883, the best observation of birds and nature at the site where the Cherry Blossom Festival now is held was in the swamps and duck hunting grounds along the Potomac. Elliott Coues and Webster Prentiss wrote *Avifauna Columbiana* for the Smithsonian Institution in 1862. Coues was a young doctor stationed in Washington during the Civil War and found time to notice nature amidst the human horrors of the war. Later, he and his boyhood friend Webster Prentiss, also a doctor, thoroughly expanded and updated *Avifauna Columbiana* for a second edition in 1883. But the bird-rich swamps along the Potomac also had malaria and yellow fever before being all filled in. Dr. Coues' book has a wonderful fold out map with hash marks along the river where can be found the marshes "of wild rice, marsh grass, wanquapins, etc., which afford feeding grounds for vast numbers of reed birds (*Dolichonyx oryivorus*), Rail (*Porzana Carolina* and *Rallus virginianus*), Blackbirds (*Ageloeus phoenicius*), Marsh Wrens (*Cistothorus palustris*), etc." Given the disease, the marshes will have to go. In 1882, as Coues is writing, Congress has already taken steps to improve the Potomac Flats as they were called. "In a few years...these marshes will all be reclaimed and their present *locus* occupied by a beautiful park diversified by picturesque lakelets, bridges and groves of ornamental trees." The marsh birds will eventually be gone, but along the Anacostia River and the Potomac between Analostan Island (now Theodore Roosevelt Island) and Greenleaf's Point, Coues says there are large numbers of ducks, "especially abundant in the months of February and March, just previous to their spring migration. At this period many are shot for the market by gunners, and sportsmen can have fair sport on occasions in shooting from floats located above or below Long Bridge [now the 14th Street Bridge]". Similar sounds of gunfire could also be heard in 1882 along the way to what is today the National Airport (though Homeland Security might look askance at all the shooting). Roaches Run and Four-Mile Run are also favorite feeding places for "Summer Duck, Teal, Rail, etc." A judiciously placed blind and decoys, says Coues, "will at times afford good shooting." There are also several fine Woodcock brakes nearby and on the high banks nearby some colonies of Bank Swallows. Gravelly Run receives and discharges the tides and its borders along its entire length are a "swamp of tangled weeds, shrubs, and small trees." This makes it, Coues says, "a favorite resort for Green and Blue-Winged Teal, Summer Duck, Green Heron, Wilson's Snipe, Woodcock," as well as more common marsh birds.

By the 1940s and the time of Louis Halle and *Spring in Washington*, things are much improved. The malaria and sludge from sewers in the spring are mostly gone, though now with heavy rains you can still sniff the stench of storm sewage overflow that sours the waters of the Potomac near the beautiful boathouses in Georgetown at the foot of the Aqueduct Bridge. This huge, old structure made from massive blocks of stone was there in Coues' time. Now it can be reached from Georgetown or from the C&O Canal or at the terminus of the Bethesda Crescent Trail for bikes. Atop its stony buttresses, views of the river with scullers, ducks, and cormorants are still sweeping and serene. But whether the shining glass cliffs of office buildings that shimmer behind the view is progress, I leave, dear reader, up to you. The end of the Aqueduct Bridge on the Virginia side, according to Doctor Coues, was once a charming place, a tiny, tiny village with the name of Rosslyn.

There are fewer birds now than there were for Coues or Halle. The Tidal Basin that Halle saw was filled with grebes and loons and mergansers. They are gone today. And for our 1940s chronicler, the clash of nature and modernity was not always welcomed. Railroad locomotives, which were euphemistically called steam-powered, actually burned huge amounts of coal. Halle writes that "from the airport to the outskirts of Alexandria...the age of smoke and machinery has blackened the land... All along the Virginia shore locomotives were belching black smoke that flattened out on the west wind...blotting out the sky from Roaches Run through Alexandria...The railway yards and the highway have been constructed over marshes that persist, but ink has replaced the marsh water and the reeds have turned black." It is still a paradise for the blackbirds, Halle tells us, and for egrets in summer, along the fresher margins of the river. Roaches Run, a shooting spot in Elliott Coues' day, is now trapped between the National Airport on one side and the railroad tracks on the other. "Ducks and gulls and herons have remained faithful to it," Halle explains with some admiration and some regret, "despite low-roaring airplanes and smoke-breathing locomotives. They are accustomed to these dragons and these pterodactyls, regarding them not. The government pays conscience money here, posting the lagoon as a sanctuary and scattering grain, like Ceres herself, for the wildfowl."

At Four Mile Run, Halle records there are still river and marsh birds and the fattest frogs "amid a talus of steel drums and other jetsam that has tumbled from the brink of the airfield above." Halle rides further on along the river toward Mount Vernon to find more idyllic scenes like those at Dyke Marsh. It will take until after Rachel Carson's time before the steamy soot and blackened waters are sufficiently all cleaned up. But the electricity that powers trains and burns the trash comes from coal fires, too. The birders, backpackers, and bicyclists—we call them environmentalists today—have all turned out in demonstrations, in lobby days, and silent candle vigils to close down the last of the coal-fired utilities that once ringed the Capitol. It still churns out carbon dioxide that is changing DC's climate far faster than Coues or Halle or Carson ever could have known.

March 27, 2012
Springtime Planets

Just two weeks ago what once was an occasional wedding scene with magnolia blossoms scattered along some doorsteps and driveways is now a blizzard of small petals of pink and white. They swirl and blow and cover the streets like a massive ticker-tape parade. Petals track into the house, sneak under the garage door, fill up the curbsides with confetti. Nature is celebrating wildly its champion resurgence. Even the sky has joined the jubilee. Since I was in residence last week at Washington and Jefferson College, I have been studying the heavens like the Magi or some astronomer at Mt. Palomar. Just at the vernal equinox, the moon was full and five planets could each be seen. Venus and Jupiter are large and bright and difficult to miss. They are posed near the moon as in a scene from Art Nouveau. Saturn is nearby along with the sci-fi planet, Mars. Even tiny, far-off Mercury can be found hiding nearer the horizon. That day, I joined an astronomy class for sophomores who need to take a science; they all had seen the evening show. My job was made far easier as we talked of global climate change and how it really works. The size and composition of the earth, its position and distance from the sun, the reason for our atmosphere, the fusion source of solar energy, and where the light beams go. How growing amounts of carbon dioxide and other greenhouse gases can trap invisible, infrared rays that should head back to space. But it was the beauty and the wonder of the shining, passing planets that had really caught their eye. Once seen and felt on a sensuous spring night, the daytime stuff of science is so much easier to bear. The moons of Jupiter—Europa, Io, Ganymede—the rings of Saturn, the Martian red, the craters of the moon soon open wide the eyes, the head, the heart.

Even last night in Washington, the bright planets were still artistically on display. Both Venus and Jupiter are beauty marks at the silver smile of a crescent moon. No wonder then that all is festival down here, on foot, on Earth. Nothing now can hold spring back. The planets, the moon, the sun have had their say.

Redbuds

As I walk around, it is the redbuds, small southern trees, that light up every path. Invisible, unremarkable plantings until this week, they shine with tiny raspberry lights strung all along each and every branch. They blaze out, one or two per block, their small, flower-laden branches splayed at unruly, crazy angles. It is as if the sun has touched these marvels; they have been jolted back to life, electrocuted and survived. Their blossoms spring straight out from the branch where they stick in little clumps of dark pink cotton candy. Up close, the redbuds are things of beauty. Each of the many, many blossoms is like a tiny orchid or a miniature pink lady's slipper shrunk down from its size out in the woods. There is a pod of pink, two small wings at the side, and a fragile, fringed petal at the top. These glories are joined by early azaleas that stand on the sunny side of the street. The large cupped purple flame azaleas are first, with a few pink and red ones not far behind. The cherry trees and Bradford pears are fading now, but popping out as each one fades are big Kwanzan cherries with bright pink double tufts of blossoms near dogwoods showing white and pink.

Arousing Spring

But this stunning visual array is rivaled by a parfumerie of scents. Aromas from a few old-fashioned purple lilacs and hyacinths gently fill the air. But on almost every block, or along a path, near fences on the way, the spring is redolent with the romantic, potent potion sent forth by neighborhood viburnum. Like the redbuds just a while ago these backyard bushes were ordinary, unremarkable, a simple clump of sticks. Now they are covered with white powder puffs of fragrant blossoms. At the tip of each branch is an orb of tiny flowers which, when deeply sniffed or smelled, is practically orgasmic. Despite the suburban houses, Pan or Bacchus or satyrs must surely live nearby. Spring is prodigal, full-blossomed, full-throated now. No more half-hearted, tentative tweets from Song Sparrows warming up. "Hip hip, hooray, boys, spring is here again!!" is shouted from every beak. Robins cheer, woodpeckers laugh and whoop and pound. Wrens and chickadees and titmice are searching nesting sites and calling to their mates. They will recruit reinforcements, new rioters in the weeks that are to come. From south of here, moving mile after mile each day and night are migrants who will soon add new nests, new colors, new calls, new celebrations to Washington in spring.

April 5, 2012
Wildflowers in Washington

There has been a gorgeous gibbous moon. It is almost the full Paschal moon that each spring marks Passover and Easter. I cannot resist patrolling the C&O Canal, an advance guard, a point man on recon, for the early, stealthy movements of springtime migrants. The neighborhood is bursting with azaleas, violets, dogwoods, a new, delightful deluge of petals from the Kwanzan cherries. Here and there the Voice of the Naturalist phone hotline and website from the Audubon Naturalist Society report an early warbler moving into the Mid-Atlantic. I am afraid that I will miss the early birds and their miraculous cousins, the early wildflowers. Each year they land and reappear along my bike path as if on weary wings.

It is cool and sunny, no more than sixty degrees, with slight, slender cirrus clouds smeared lightly or daubed delicately against a bright blue scrim. No puffy cumulus cotton balls, no dark, foreboding rain-filled ones. I can ride all day. The canal is full and reflects the half-leafed out branches from above. There are a few fading redbuds as I start out on patrol. An occasional bending, reaching, sometimes vine-covered, native dogwood lights up the path. All is quiet and free of hikers, bikers, strollers, dogs. It is too bare-boned nature, too early spring, too cool for picnics, woodland walks, or kayaking in the canal. At a glance, there is nothing here. Azaleas in nearby neighborhoods or the National Arboretum offer more spectacular scenery for sauntering in spring. But I am on alert for sneakier, subtler signs of the springtime invasion that is to come.

Heading north from Great Falls, I enter shade at first. In only a few weeks there will be geese and goslings, downy baby ducks, and bunches of basking turtles. But now there are simpler, smaller signs. My friends the tiny spring beauties are the first to show. They seem to have doubled in size from my last ride here, but they still are only a few inches tall with tiny blossoms, such stuff as fairies and dreams are made of. Mixed in are taller, stouter weed-like plants with tiny white clusters pasted on top, with much bigger, heart-shaped leaves that embrace the stems. These are garlic mustard whose leaves when crushed and sniffed give off a tiny garlic smell.

Then my first wild blue phlox appears—a small, single, lonely figure standing in the shade. I brake to a halt and stand and stare. I have loved phlox as long ago as I can remember in my mother's garden. But when I first saw and understood that such beauty had started in the wild—unwatered, unweeded, unworried—a deeper reverence was revealed. The phlox start to multiply. There are small bunches and then more. The wild phlox which show shades of white and pink and blue are joined by blankets of Virginia bluebells—large throw rugs of color in the floodplain forest. They seem placed near large trees and their roots, as if seeking water. But I decide I cannot really see a pattern to their placement. I settle for now on the hand of God. Perhaps later I will have a good long conversation with a botanist from the park. The swaths of blue are soon joined by outbreaks of breathtaking orange and yellow. I halt again to puzzle out the presence of these perennials. They are erect, perhaps a foot tall, with flowers that explode out of tiny, tight bead-like buds the size of capers. As they open, there is more orange visible, once in full bloom, a head of yellow petals. Two sides of my brain struggle for dominance. One simply soaks up the wonder of these wildflowers that have been put here who knows how or why. They are not showy or tall like sun flowers or sneezeweed that show up in summer and early fall. But they demand attention now when rich, bright colors are so rare. My left brain is fighting to take over, to categorize, to name, to sort. Sun flower, sneezeweed, sea oxeye, some sort of aster, something like... And then my images, intuition, imagination, and inventory all seem to merge. These are golden ragwort—one of the inglorious bastard names that show up in the science books. They line the path on the canal or sunnier side. Cherokees used the root and stems to make a tea for treating heart trouble and preventing pregnancy. Other Native Americans used these lovely plants to aid childbirth, treat urinary problems, and lung diseases like tuberculosis. I should eat some just in case. But I don't have time for tea and the water in the Thermos on my Trek is filled with broken ice.

As I admire the floral welcome that rises up before me, blue to the left, yellow-orange to the right, I am pulled up short once again. Another puzzler. Smiling up at me from the canal side is a single stalk with small, complicated, daisy-like white petals. But there seems to be dozens of flat, delicate tiny blades in a blossom the size of a dime or nickel, symmetrical as a sundial. I take a photo and stare, smiling back some more at these few small, happy faces. Daisy fleabane! A great name for a character from Dickens, or maybe Henry James. Folklore holds that, when dried and hung indoors, fleabane, as its name suggests, will somehow organically keep away the fleas.

I lurch lazily along, slightly swerving like a five-year-old learning to ride, so I can watch for wildflowers and listen for birds while not driving off into the canal. A small white wildflower, the first and only one I will see today, catches the corner of my eye. It is one of my favorites, the cute and comical Dutchman's breeches. Hanging just above the brown and green woodland floor is a tiny pair of white bloomers, pantaloons, or perhaps some undergarment drying on the line, blown upward in a V, as if by wind. When I come back there will be more of these, but never many. Just small, hidden clusters for us cognoscenti. A true wild-flower, small and delicate, almost totally unknown to those who stroll and jog and bike on by. I am sure it is the name I like as much as I do the flower. It shapes one's imagination, the two little pants legs that mark these pure white blossoms with a tiny golden tip. What's in a name? Suppose it had been "Pulled white teeth" or some such moniker that takes the mind and musing to an awfully different place.

There are other wildflowers coming, but not yet in full bloom. May apples, small green umbrellas that spread and make a ground cover, are up now. Soon, come May, each will have a small, off-white, waxy rounded bell beneath. Colonists and Native Americans used extracts from the roots to treat constipation, fevers, even syphilis. The most toxic part, the rhizomes that run beneath the ground, contain, according to my biologist and photographer friend, Frank Kaczmarek, podophyllotoxin and alpha and beta peltatin. These unpronounceable organics now are used to produce modern, anti-cancer drugs. But for now, I prefer to think of umbrellas for the fairies.

The Wisdom of Butterflies

As I ride on, I see my first serious butterflies of the season. They are medium-sized with black stripes on a very pale background of greenish wash. They fly low and relatively straight, as if they know where they are going. No flighty, drunken weaving like the little garden whites and sulphurs nearer home. These are Zebra Swallowtails, though the tails are not too visible in this early springtime batch. Later broods will be larger and have something like a tip or tail at the bottom of each wing. Perhaps it is the way they run ahead, not the stripes, that makes us call them zebras. Each time I draw closer on my bike to one alighted or sailing just above the path, it dashes ahead and lands again, like a kingfisher fleeing, always ahead of me, as I close in on its branch. The zebras will be here for quite some time; I know they are drawn to mud after rain and to the dung

from saddle horses that trot by on warmer days. Now I see a few early
Tiger Swallowtails sipping from bluebells and dipping lazily about. A
childhood favorite that will show up later on verbena, butterfly bush,
and butterfly weed within my yard. I feel about these lovely yellow
floaters as I do about the robins. Familiarity breeds contentment.
The only other large butterfly I have seen this spring was basking in
the sun, slowly, occasionally flapping, stretching its wings as it sat in
the dirt of a garden border along my regular neighborhood walking
route. Unlike the cabbages and sulphurs, the zebras and the tigers,
this Mourning Cloak was a very special sighting. Amidst a bird-walk
after the second Lincoln Inaugural, a single one caught the eye of
John Burroughs while he moseyed near Rock Creek. He notes, "saw
a small, black, velvety butterfly with a yellow border to its wings."
Like him, I was not sure what this beauty was. The outside or under-
side of the wings when folded up was a deep purplish black with a
fringe of dipped white paint across the bottom. When my Mourning Cloak let down its wings, the sun gave rich warm color to the
mahogany inside. Living near wet areas (a storm drain and run off
from lawns is right nearby), the Mourning Cloak is the longest-lived
butterfly around, with a span of upwards of a year. Younger ones are
fringed with the yellow that Burroughs saw. With age the tail band
turns slowly into ivory or bone. I have come upon an old, white-
bearded, Burroughs of a butterfly, a grandfather, let's say, that has
wintered over in Bethesda. I am looking at a wise, wonderful old survivor, a shaman, who sits and slowly takes in sun and scenery and
spirit from our suburban spring.

A Talking Crow

There is wisdom out in nature if we could but learn it once
again. Call it silly or superstitious or unscientific, if you will. But
it is not so long ago, in human terms, when flora and fauna were
the stuff of fables and of feeling, of stories and of song. I hear and

then see a lone, loud American Crow cawing from a snag. It is raucous and untiring, like a car alarm set off by chance. It throws its body into screaming, croaking sounds. A showboat, an egotist, an operatic bird. My peaceful path is fractured by this awful, awful noise. And then I see a Red-tailed Hawk fly by me, fleeing in frightful flight. It hightails it for the woods and river, not to be seen again. Suddenly everything, once more, is still. My crow gives a slow, smirking turn of the head, a double take, like Jack Benny or Jackie Gleason, after delivering a withering, comic line. La Fontaine from French class leaps into my head with talking animals from long ago. "Maître Corbeau sur un arbre perché, tenait en son bec un fromage..." Of course, the wily fox comes along, smells the cheese, flatters the crow, and asks him to sing with his beautiful voice. The crow sings, the cheese falls, and our fox trots off with the prized, delicious morsel. Are crows and foxes both smart? You bet. Can they talk? Have I not just witnessed it? Can we learn from botany, birds and butterflies? I think so. If we look, linger, listen. I move along taking in patient herons, huge, horrible-looking Turkey Vultures hopping about on a tree above my head. They settle in, as if satisfied with a meal of some mushy, rotting flesh. Political reactionaries should love them. No need to pay for park personnel to clean up around our trails. Valuable vultures, indeed! Their skinless, wrinkled red heads and hook-like beaks prove that beauty is indeed only skin deep.

Brother Skink

Soon I slow and stop to see some sort of salamander sitting on a log. It disappears, as if by magic, in an *augenblick*, the twinkling of an eye. I stay stock still, send forth Franciscan warm vibrations, the benevolence of Buddha, some tidings from Thoreau. My small reptile slowly creeps back up satisfied, it seems, that I am, indeed, a brother. I have not seen one like this before, as thick as a snake, a full eight inches long from stem to stern. It is brown with subtle stippling, but its head is plated, shining, wide. Through binoculars it could indeed be a snake with legs, or a small dinosaur still evolving. Almost half is body, more than half is tail, a vine, or rope, or stick-like creature, the color of a log. It is a lizard, not a salamander. I have found a broad-headed skink, a creature with a marvelous tail—a built-in device, a diversion—which if caught by some hungry predator, simply breaks off and grows back once again.

What to Save?

By now I have reached—at a bicycle pace that averages no more than that of Justice William O. Douglas' brisk historic walk—Lockhouse 22 at Pennyfield Lock. It is the place where President Cleveland fished, Rachel Carson birded, and I started in some forty years ago. I have since learned that Cleveland used to stay here overnight at the Pennyfield farmhouse near the lock. It was still a farm when Louis Halle came here at wartime's end. Over many, many years, I have watched it slowly sink into disrepair, dishevelment, a dump. Finally, to our disgrace, it has had to be torn down. The lock and lockhouse have been spruced up again, but history is gone. The price of saving such a place could be no more than a single new McMansion like those that abound outside the park. Or an hour or two of warfare we pay for in some place far away. Are we the smartest animal? At times it is hard to tell. Pure science has not saved us. Perhaps there is something here in nature that, if we learn to listen, will.

April 13, 2012
John Burroughs and Rock Creek Park

The large-leafed trillium in my shade garden, where there are jack in-the-pulpits and false Solomon's seal and a riot of ferns, has me thinking of John Burroughs. He was once the most famous nature writer in America. As a young man, he was published in 1860 in the then new *Atlantic Monthly*, edited by anti-slavery poet and writer, James Russell Lowell. By 1871, Burrough's first collection of essays, *Wake-Robin*, was published to instant success. The essays are about the coming of spring. But many an environmental history major has been fooled into thinking the title refers to our feathered friend, the robin. Wake-Robin is an old-fashioned name for trillium, the three-leaved wildflower that blooms even as the plant emerges. Chapter Five in *Wake-Robin* is called "Spring at the Capital." Burroughs, born in the Catskills, took a job in Washington in late 1863 during the Civil War, became friends with Walt Whitman, and roamed the woods reflecting on the birds and flowers and the start of spring. Decades later as a bearded, older, famous man, he was friends with Teddy Roosevelt. But when he first arrived, Washington was a much wilder place.

In the spring of 1868, about which Burroughs writes, he walks past the reigning boundary of the city up Meridian Hill, today miles away from Maryland. Many years after Burroughs, Meridian Hill, along Sixteenth Street, became an elegant neighborhood with an appealing late nineteenth-century park. It turned dangerous and sour in the sixties and seventies, but now, given gentrification, is elegant again. But when Burroughs writes, there are cattle lowing, bluebirds calling, and flickers, or "high-holes," whooping up a storm. Ten minutes' walk from here, he says, is "real primitive woods." Outside the city limits, the "great point of interest to the rambler and lover of nature is the Rock Creek region." The creek is a large, rough, rapid stream...marked by great diversity of scenery." It is a wild gorge with overhanging rocks and high precipitous, wooded headlands. It is Burroughs who first suggests that such an area, with its wild and rugged scenery, should someday make a great, unparalleled urban park. "A few touches of art would convert this whole region from Georgetown to what is known as

Crystal Springs, not more than two miles from the present State Department, into a park unequalled by anything in the world. There are passages between these two points as wild and savage, and apparently remote from civilization as anything one meets with in the mountains of the Hudson or the Delaware."

In 1881, Professor Lester F. Ward, quoted in Elliott Coues' *Avifauna Columbiana*, writes of the same area in similar, glowing terms in his *Guide to the Flora of Washington and its Vicinity*, published by the National Museum or Smithsonian. He, too, suggests a park. "Rock Creek is most beautiful and picturesque, often rocky and hilly with frequent deep ravines...the whole region is an ideal park. No one can see it without thinking how admirably it is adapted for a national park." Ward recommends a parcel from Oak Hill Cemetery, about a mile and a half wide, up to Military Road. But a mere twenty years after Burroughs, he must warn that because of destruction and development, time is running short. "Not only every botanist, but every lover of art and nature, must sigh at the prospect, not far distant, of beholding this region devastated by the ax and the plow. The citizens of Washington should speedily unite and strenuously urge upon Congress the importance of early rescuing this ready-made national park from such an unfortunate fate." Ward mentions Peirce Mill and other landmarks still visible today. Since the anniversary of Lincoln's April 15 assassination is near at hand, I decide it is a good time to start out on foot, like Burroughs, and head north in Rock Creek Park. Burroughs describes the second inauguration and then goes that afternoon for a hike through the woods. So I will try to imagine Rock Creek when John Burroughs and Florence Merriam Bailey were alive. Peirce Mill is where I start.

A Royal Pair of Wood Ducks

The stone mill and nearby barn that sit at creek side where Tilden Street crosses over are carefully restored with federal funds bolstered in these penny-pinching times by donations from the Friends of Peirce Mill. Across the street is a similar stone historic house, now a home where I have been to fundraisers held for friends of the environment, of history, and of politicians who support such things. The day is again cool and bright, perfect for a lengthy ramble in the park, into its pastoral past. Behind the mill before too long, stones in the creek create a small spillway as the water wends its way southward to the Potomac and beyond. I spot a Mallard floating happily around like a child held up by an inner tube.

As I put up my binoculars, I catch my breath at what I now behold. I am rewarded like all those before me since prism binoculars were invented and Florence Merriam Bailey, who also birded here, suggested we look at birds through an opera glass, rather than shoot them like her more famous brother. I see a single male Wood Duck sitting, shining, sunlit on a stone. There is cinnamon on chest and tail, with darker wings and white. But it is the head with bright red-orange and yellow bill, a large red eye, a cream-colored horse's bridle strapped all around that catches your attention. Swept-back dark blue, purplish feathers with bold white streaks fall back from his head to form a helmet. Our Wood Duck has a profile worthy of some ceremonial guard, or even, perhaps, a prince. The back is green; the sides are cream, with white showing underneath. A vertical black and white stripe slashes downward from behind the slightly speckled cinnamon chest. It is America's most handsome duck, a sight that made Louis Halle wonder why we needed zoos with exotic ponds when such glories stood outside. I try to soak in every feather, each brush stroke of nature that has caused the Wood Duck to be captured again and again by colorists, carvers, cameras, then placed proudly in a den.

I am always torn that, with birds, it is usually the male who is the singer, the show off, the one with the sizzling wardrobe. I am reminded how and why things seem to have evolved this way when I finally notice the female Wood Duck. She has been there all along as I trained my mind and eye upon her mate. Now they swim as a pair, a couple who soon will trail downy ducklings in their wake. She is an understated beauty, a natural, with no need for show. From afar, or with the naked eye, she blends into the background, a somewhat small and brownish duck. Through binoculars, or perhaps a telephoto, she is all elegance and equanimity. Her head is held aloft with a longer, curving neck than handsome hubby. His head is almost neckless, hunched directly upon his colorful, velvet, medieval garb. Her neck shows white below that matches her most prominent part above. It is an unmistakable white eye ring with a short streak streaming toward the back. Set upon a pale slate blue, it makes her wide-eyed, open, alert, all-seeing, while gliding gracefully along. She, too, has a helmet, but formed by stylish, shorter swept-back hair. Her back is brown with dotted brown below. The only color to match her mate is a tiny patch of blue, her speculum, sitting way back upon her wing. They form quite a royal couple, this pair, our Catherine and William, posed here beside a mill.

A Walk in the Woods

There are a number of bicycle trails throughout the park. In 1898, Florence Merriam Bailey described Rock Creek as one of a number of good birding spots you can go to by "wheel." Old photos in a park brochure show 1890s-style men posing with their bikes not far away from here. But I walk along in Burroughs style, a roughly five-mile trek on foot. I start beside Rock Creek then head up a long, steep hill; it is the bridle path along a ridge toward the equestrian barns and National Park Nature Center over a mile and a half away. Then I wend my way back down toward Rock Creek following the path that runs back along beside it. My way rises and falls with the ridges. Sometimes I am near the water and rugged rocks, at others peering down from far above. It is early spring flowers I hope to see and perhaps a good bird or two. As I start my ascent into pine-oak woods, a Red-tailed Hawk circles right above me, a traveler as if I have entered some other time and place. Along the way, there are spring beauties, a few hepaticas, star of Bethlehem, chickweed and star chickweed, buttercups, but no bloodroot, a single white, wildflower star, that Burroughs could see everywhere.

I pant a little as I tramp uphill, or, occasionally, I trudge. I am in the wild with fallen trees and rotting, moss-topped logs. There are holes for woodpeckers in lots of places, round ones for the flickers or "high holes," bigger rectangular ones chopped out by the pileated's hatchet bill. Ravines and rivulet ditches fall downward, without water, toward the creek. It is awfully dry, things are not that lush. The path is dusty; my shoes are soon a coated, off-white brown. The main plants are the garlic mustard that is everywhere in Washington woods in early spring. A few plants were brought in 1860 as some restaurateur's idea. Burroughs did not mention them, but now they dominate the scene. They look just fine in empty woods, but they spread like mad with tangled roots and squeeze out gentler, native plants. I will try to appreciate them; they clearly are here to stay. But like starlings, or English Sparrows, they are a good idea gone bad. These alien invasives sneaked across our borders without ever checking in.

A Record March

The forest floor is dry as well, with leaf litter and often dried-up moss. The flowers are few and in the shade, near a tree stump or a tiny hillock, where they can find relief. There are some lovely little bluets here and there and not much else. It is a drought I'm seeing in these woods, no roaring rivulets or muddy spots to jump. The Northeast record spring has had some ill effects, it seems. The first three months and the month of March have shattered record highs. According to the National Oceanic and Atmospheric Administration (NOAA), temperatures for the lower forty-eight states were 8.6 degrees above normal in March and 6 degrees above normal for the first three months. This beat the old record by 1.4 degrees based on accurate records going back to 1895. And records like this are typically broken by a mere one- or two-tenths of a degree. What is unusual about all this is that scientists have now begun to say that such extremes are really related to global warming caused by us industrious humans. But it takes a chain of careful observations, calculations, and causations to connect the dots.

Most weathermen and reporters still don't mention climate change, because no single event is directly linked to warming global temperatures caused by the burning of fossil fuels. But the melting ice caps, rising seas, stronger hurricanes, tornadoes, and other storms, the uneven patterns of heat and cold, floods and drought, are related after all. Melting ice in the Artic means rising warm air, more absorption of heat in the open Arctic Ocean since the ice that reflects the sun is gone. This helps to move the placement of the jet stream, once routine and steady. The changes in the jet stream then affect our weather fronts and cyclical events like El Niños and the warming La Niña pattern we now are in. The result, says Jake Crouch, climate scientist at NOAA's National Climatic Data Center in Asheville, North Carolina, is the more frequent extremes and new weather records such as we are seeing. More directly, Jerry Meehl, a climate scientist who specializes in extreme weather events at the National Center for Atmospheric Research (NCAR) in Boulder, Colorado, says of the warm winter and early spring that has everybody talking, "It's a guilty pleasure. You're out enjoying this nice March weather, but you know it's not a good thing." One scientist, speaking of the shattering, or better, the wreckage of the old temperature records, says it is the weather equivalent of a baseball player on steroids. The old records are just obliterated. What I am seeing in Rock Creek Park is part of a trend that has produced since April of last year the hottest twelve-month stretch ever. Overall, 7,775 weather stations nationwide have recorded new record high temperatures for the month of March.

A Pileated Saves the Day

I come to the woods to be refreshed, renewed, not to think like some scold or write a screed. I try to amuse myself along the way and chat at the equestrian center, when I reach it, with an African American family out riding for the day. There are some signs of progress here. I talk with the ranger at the nature center and walk its lovely woodland trail. As I descend, my mood has brightened up a bit. The path towards home is by the creek; it is rushing still. I see more flowers. I feel refreshed. I will enjoy this unsettled spring. Up ahead along the trail, I see a young couple stop and stare. My old friend, the pileated spirit bird has descended at their feet. They point and shrug and look amazed as I look at them and this avian apparition through my magic glass. Our crow-sized woodpecker does an easy loopy loop to the side of a nearby tree. It struts it stuff, displays its cap, its bold black and white body against the bark. I reach the man and woman, about thirty years of age. They ask excitedly if I have seen the unbelievable bird that appeared to them at their feet. Feeling a bit like Burroughs once again, I happily explain what they have seen. They will want a book, a website, an Audubon app, some more that they can learn. I spill it all and wish them well, as happy as a lark. Once more a bird has saved my day and spoken to the souls of those I meet along the way.

April 15, 2012
Spring on the Potomac

Sunny, warm, the new normal spring. Who can stay inside? I lash my bike onto the car and head off for the Potomac. I pass and pause at Roaches Run and Four Mile Run and Gravelly Point, some hallmarks in Halle's book. But they are empty of ducks and birds or his other signs of spring. I head south past the airport, through heavy traffic and happy families ambling about in Alexandria. I pull off at Belle Haven Marina and picnic grounds to start by bike to Dyke Marsh and beyond. There are people parking, pulling in and out, almost everywhere. Big family picnics are spread beneath the trees. Our Washingtonians are more diverse, more modern, with sportier, scantier dress than those in scenes from Roosevelt's day. They resemble, though far more democratic, some painter's scene of the Tuileries or by the Seine. Soccer balls and scooters, bikes, and baskets full of food are everywhere on display. It is indeed a dandy day, as I sail along the trail.

Dyke Marsh

Dyke Marsh is all along the Potomac here, though woods and wetlands intervene. Some 485 acres in all, it has some of the best, most easily reached freshwater marshes near a major city that can be found. The bike trail is punctuated by marshes that feature boardwalks that rumble as bikes roll over. I stop and hold onto a railing and simply breathe more deeply of the slightly swampy, warm, fresh air. My childhood flashes before me as I hear the first "brr, burreee!" It is one of a handful of early nature memories imprinted on my brain and in my soul. A lone, male Red-winged Blackbird is perched singing in the marsh atop a puffed-out cattail. They sang in the weedy fields behind my home before all Long Island was built up. And I heard and saw them from boardwalks just like this in Oceanside where I would go with Mom to look for the first tightly swirled green and red spotted buds of skunk cabbage in early, early spring. Robins, Blue Jays, and cardinals are the beginner's birds we know. They populate the bird books, both old and new, that now I read for fun. This marsh and a magnifi-

cent red and yellow striped shoulder on a pure black bird offer me
something deep, primeval. I cannot say exactly what it is. I feel it
in my bones. I take a longer stop at a small cove with benches and
with logs. There is a pointy shore and a few small islands that look
like they could move. I see one lone, lingering winter loon, or at
least I think it is. Its shape and bill are silhouetted. I do not have
a scope. There are Double-crested Cormorants floating and flying
and fishing right nearby, so I cannot know for sure. An angler with
a sportsmen's vest is trolling down the way, an unsuspecting kin
with birds. I clearly have stopped at some ancient fishing ground
where the Piscataway lived, and Captain Smith passed by, trying
to scoop up plentiful fish with his trusty frying pan.

As if to underscore or prove the point, I spot an Osprey's
nest. It is piled atop the roots of a giant, fallen tree. I focus in and
sure enough, there is my first Osprey of the spring! Its black and
white head mark it off from the bald eagle that all Americans can
name. And then I see another one, holding, pecking, tearing at a
fish it has landed on a branch to claim. Another soon sails by
holding a fish, held tight with awful talons, dangling to its death.
From a different angle, I see another Osprey nest, more spectacular than before. It is huge and wide and sprawling atop the crotch
of an ancient tree. It seems to me an eagle's nest. Maybe once it
was. But the Osprey sitting on it rules out our nation's bird. But I
am watching an American miracle all the same. Rachel Carson's
classic *Silent Spring* was spurred by the death of robins written
about by a friend. But it dealt with other birds and humans, too,
all doused with DDT. Along Dyke Marsh and the C&O Canal
and other spots I haunt, Rachel and her friends and birders
watched the Osprey's near demise. Louis Halle, Rachel Carson,
and the famous bird guide author and artist, Roger Tory Peterson,
all lived and wrote and birded here. Like almost every birder and
amateur naturalist my age I know, I started out with Peterson's
Field Guide to the Birds. I did not know then that Florence Merriam

Bailey had preceded him, or that he had helped Rachel Carson kill DDT. Peterson had followed careful studies of the decline of Osprey in New England and had witnessed the sad spectacle of empty nests himself. Ospreys, eagles, peregrines, and other fish-eating birds of prey dined, at the top of the food chain, on pesticide-laden fish. It affected their reproductive systems and led to eggs whose shells would crack. No bird babies could be born. And so those famous writers and scientists who birded all through here testified to Congress. They called for tougher regulations and restrictions on miracle chemicals that were killing off our miracles. I did not see many bald eagles or Ospreys in the 1970s when I started in to bird. It is easy to forget that they were nearly gone. But I still thrill and praise my elders when I see a black-and-white, bent-winged Osprey soar and dive and snatch its prey. They are a sign, I think, of resilience, resurrection, of what a few good, prescient people, well-organized, can do.

As if listening to my thoughts, the National Park Service provides another sign for me. This one in actual words and pictures. It tells about Dyke Marsh and credits Miles Abbott Jackson, of whom I have never heard. He is described as a birder, skilled naturalist, and advocate for preservation who wrote, "There are few if any other areas in the Central Atlantic States so accessible to the budding and blooming naturalist, where such a variety of flora and creatures wearing fur, fin, feathers or unadorned skin can be found in such a small area...all in all, a naturalist's paradise within seven miles of the nation's capital." It does not say that Jackson, born in 1920 and a graduate in zoology from Swarthmore College, was an army colonel who served in intelligence in World War II and Korea. The son of a wildlife artist, Miles Jackson is the only American ever to win both first and second place in the same year in the Federal Duck Stamp Contest for wildlife artists. Jackson initiated the annual Christmas bird count at Fort Belvoir, not far from here below Mount Vernon, when he was stationed there in 1941. He also has a preserve named in his honor there, the Jackson Miles Abbott Wetland Refuge. Abbott also wrote a column on birds for the old *Washington Star* and fought to save Dyke Marsh and Huntley Meadows. But for me what should also be on the sign for everyone to see is his role in studying eagles in our area and the effect of DDT upon their shells. Along with Peterson and Carson and Halle and all the others, it is why you and I and the eagles and the ospreys can still find refuge here today.

Swallows at Belle Haven Marina

Along the way back, I note slightly moister woods near water here with some jack-in-the-pulpits popping up amidst the May apples on the shaded woodland floor. The May apples, or mandrakes, are already in full May bloom with waxy, white, large jingle bells attached beneath their leaves. I stop along a tiny bog, the only one I've seen. Tadpoles scatter each time my shadow moves across the water at my feet. Large marsh blue violets droop near a rotting log at water's edge with some white wildflowers I do not recognize. I end my ride at Belle Haven Marina and wander around a bit. I see my first spring swallows, barn and cliff together. When we have played the game of which bird we resemble, I often think of Caryn as a swallow. The Barn Swallow is a dark-haired, dark-eyed beauty, elegant and slim. It makes its mark with blues and blacks and purples, none easy to be seen. The Barn Swallow is an active soul, almost always on the move. It swoops, glides, dives, swirls, and rushes all about. It gets more done than I can ever contemplate. But then it comes to rest. A wire, a rope, a hawser on a yacht will do. It doesn't seem to matter. But when it stops, it sits serenely still. No bobbing tails, no preening wings, no fluttering at all. It is at peace, at one, with where it is right now. Then off it moves and flies again, its fierce life force restored. If I were Carl Linnaeus, this swallow would be Carynensis.

I need to move on, too. My day is growing short. I watch some larger terns; they're Caspian or Royal, too hard for me to tell. I smile at a small Pied-billed Grebe, coming out of winter garb, diving near the boats. I read the names of boats docked here and start to smile some more. As a nature buff, I should demand these carbon hogs all transmute into canoes. But there is love and humor here, an escape from office life that Louis Halle called the "hive." I see guys waxing, polishing, tying, roping, engaged at water's edge as much as I. There is a huge speed boat from Virginia called *Valhalla*, the endless search for gods. But my favorite is a smaller, more standard motor boat. It has a terra cotta top. On the stern, similarly shaded letters lovingly script its name. I glance at my watch and laugh out loud at where my time has gone. The owner and I are one in sneaking off like this. His pleasure craft is called *The Other Woman*.

April 18, 2012
A Gift at the Front Door

I plan to get outdoors to sense, to smell, to see springtime that signifies hope for me. But I am distracted within my own indoor hive—e-mails, phone calls, writing, chores. A thud and rapping at the front door jangles my concentration like a telemarketing intrusion. It must be one of many UPS or FedEx packages, I surmise. What could it be? A gift? Some catalogue clothing? An antiquarian book that will describe the spring or birds of yesteryear? My heart and hopes go out to antiquarian books, small leather messengers, whose words and drawings speak to me in sepia tones of what has been and what yet might be. I hear the muted roar of the departing delivery truck as I open up and glance through the glass storm door. My heart and breathing stop. A young Pileated Woodpecker has descended out of nowhere onto the weeping cherry tree just ten feet from my eyes.

Our cherry tree was planted in honor of Caryn's father some twenty years ago in spring when he died amidst the splendid, beauteous weeping of ancient cherry trees near the hospital in Bryn Mawr. Now it is mid-sized, but stressed and struggling in the fiery summers and unsettled seasons that mark the climate we have now. An aging bulge protrudes where the branches start above the trunk. Sap oozes from its splits. There are insect holes and cracks and crannies where the pileated has been placed for me to find. Even as I am frozen without motion at my door, my mind races at top speed. What are the odds of my being visited at home by this bird I have come to love, to see as some special sign or spirit—madcap, moving, and mysterious? Of course it is only hunting insects, but why here, why now, why me? I am wishing Caryn could be here near me to share this special sight. I am calling up old memories, old paintings, old books, new revelations in the woods. Whatever I was thinking, writing, doing will now just have to wait.

My visitor is a young pileated. It is somewhat small, not yet majestic. No larger than a Red-bellied Woodpecker, or perhaps a great big robin. The body is mostly black with white along the wing. The head is like a pterodactyl. Its red cap is peaked and prominent, contrasted by a white nape and chin, with a black stripe across its face. The long chisel of a bill is light black, or charcoal gray, with a yellow spot just behind it. My spirit bird pounds and probes the splits of my somewhat sickly cherry. Dust and chips fly, a tiny hole increases, it finds small things to eat. Then more pounding, probing, chips and dust. I see flashes of its tongue. This drilling, drumming, feeding ritual goes on for maybe fifteen minutes. My pileated has ignored grackles, cardinals, titmice, the roar of engines, cars. It is focused on just living, being, feeding on the springtime food it has found at the home of its new friend. It finally seems quite satisfied with the work, or play, that it has done, the meal my home has now provided. It flies off as suddenly, mysteriously, as when it first appeared. I feel my breathing start up again; it is deep and strong and slow. A smile is on my face and in my heart. I pick up the package at my feet, still staring at the cherry tree where this gift was left for me. I am deeply satisfied on this simple day in spring. May there be many more like it, I pray, before I turn and close the door.

May 2, 2012
My Friends the Birds

It has been very cool, cloudy, and, at times, downright cold in late April. The buzz over the winter that never was has subsided just a bit. Now folks talk simply about things being weird or no longer normal. I have been off talking about climate change on campus and in residence at Kenyon College in Ohio as their Edgerton Lecturer. We start out with rain and, the first night at dinner, I find myself in the middle of a friendly but spirited debate about climate even in this liberal enclave in a critical, could-go-either way 2012 election state. Before I leave, I head to a team-taught biology class with incredibly knowledgeable and committed professors. One is an expert on Atlantic sea birds—specifically the Leach's Storm Petrel, a small robin-sized ocean-going (pelagic) bird that nests on inaccessible rocky islands off the coast of Maine. I have seen Leach's Storm Petrels and Wilson's and other pelagic birds, but always from the side or stern of a bobbing boat or ferry. Never have I seen one nest. We talk happily of gannets at Bonaventure Island off Percé Rock in Canada, of puffins and the times this landlubber author got nauseous despite the Dramamine and peanut butter sandwiches. There is a strong, invisible bond amongst us birders, humans given to biophilia, that draws us hundreds, even thousands, of miles just to see avians nuzzle on a nest.

At the end of my stay, as the sky is clearing up and springtime in Ohio is really settling in, the talk turns to my writing and what

I call my nature book. Nature is always new and surprising, especially in spring, I say. After all these years, something is somehow revealed to me, as if from another, spirit world. As if on cue, near the entrance to the new "green" energy-efficient science building, we scientists—modern, skeptical, sincere—are startled as a Pileated Woodpecker suddenly lands beside us. It proceeds to calmly probe the lawn no more than a dozen feet away. It is not a mature, majestic crow-sized specimen like the one in Rock Creek Park. It is smaller, younger, like the one at my front door. I have not eaten mushrooms, no mescaline, no grass. This spirit bird has somehow followed me from my front lawn in Bethesda to Gambier's biological building. I have made new friends and colleagues at this venerable college, new allies in the attempt to alert the public that this spring is not only different, it is dangerous unless we change. But I cannot fully comprehend or grasp the meaning that my newest friend and ally, with whom I share some bond, is a crazy, cackling, cartoon-like red-headed woodpecker. In other words—a bird.

Bloodroot and Adder's Tongue

At home this springtime madness marches onward. Perhaps I travel too much and stay alone too long. I worry I have missed some April wildflowers and perhaps some warblers, too. Spring migration is underway. I fear I may miss it all. Over two weeks have slipped by and April is all over. It has gone cool, even cold and wet, as if to prove the changes in our planet are not simple gentle global warming, but unusual diversions, disruptions from what was once the norm. I had hoped to find more April wildflowers and perhaps an early warbler or two. Last year in April, I had some revelations riding along the C&O Canal. I'm sure they have always been there, but I had never seen a bloodroot, not even sure how I would know. So when I spotted a sole, small white flower at the path side, I once more jammed on my brakes. Without a wildflower book at hand I start taking photos as my mind raced fruitlessly in circles. This single specimen I had never seen emerges from a short, broad, tightly-bundled stem. It stands triumphantly as if it has escaped from hell to heaven. It has burst its winter bondage and is gloriously free. Its broad white petals with pale pink stripes beneath form a cup with a golden center. It is a cluster of spreading stamens, of many gilded threads. Each bloodroot flower is there for just a day or two. I did not know how fortunate I was to have it open to me as I was gliding by. The bloodroot is enchanting, but ephemeral. And once it breaks free from the clasp of its girdling, blue-green, toothed leaf, it only shows itself from midday until it closes up at night. The name, I only found out later, comes from the deep, orange-red sap that Native Americans took from the root and used for dye and for repelling insects. Bloodroot can also make a tea that reduces fever and can remedy rheumatism. There must have been many, many more when Indians roamed the woods. My wildflower book oddly cautions not to eat them since they are highly toxic. I had not even contemplated such an unusual idea. With or without its toxic alkaloid, sanguinarine, a bloodroot is a thing of beauty.

Further on down the trail, last year, I learned another lesson. I had been searching each and every April for adder's tongue, my favorite woodland flower. Like a yellow day lily, but in tiny, woodland, fairy size, the adder's tongue, or trout lily, emerges from a group of pointed, blade-like, or lanceolate, black-spotted leaves. That's the adder part, I think, but I prefer the kinder, gentler lily name. I first saw a few many years ago in Fairmont Park in Philadelphia while I was walking near a stream. Only a few inches high with drooping, curled-back petals, they seemed both beautiful and rare, as if painted by some botanist from another place and time. I searched each year with mixed success to find them once again. The Holy Grail of flowers, I could not stop my quest. I carried it to Washington in the woods at water's edge. But I always turned up empty, no matter how eagerly I scoured the ground. Perhaps it was my strong desire that made the search so hard. My love was lost, no longer to be seen. Then one day in April, while ambling, rambling, just moseying along, no purpose or goals in mind, just taking in the air, a tiny yellow flower appeared before me just sitting by the path. I was overcome with joy. My more modern self, the rational side, was just a bit embarrassed. The time of Wordsworth and his daffodils is long since out of date. A flower no larger than a palm print had altered my views of fate?

As could, of course, be predicted, such wildflowers and Wordsworthian moments became again too rare. I searched again and pressed too hard, too purposefully, in pursuit of trout lilies and loveliness, the visionary gleam. So just last year around this time, I rode out into April just to see what I could see. No notes in hand, no scouring of the ground. The rocks, canal, the sky, the air, the birds, the bowers were simply to be enjoyed. A small, rocky cliff loomed slightly up ahead. Some yellow patches smeared the rocks in streaks like veins of ore. Flowers, I think, my conscious self slowly began to say. I pulled out my binoculars to see what this could be amidst a bare outcropping where flowers do not grow. In several places, on cliff-side shelves, part-shaded, where soil had taken hold, they happily stood in hundreds, an apparition of adder's tongues all come to life, all safe from us below. Inaccessible, invisible, if you simply seek out beauty on familiar ground.

A Backyard Yellowthroat

It is in looking afresh at the familiar, perhaps askew, that new phenomena are found. Look carefully for moose; juncos suddenly appear. Ponder a slightly rotten weeping cherry tree, a pileated descends. It peers and probes and picks at something precious you have passed by at least a thousand times. The same is true, it seems, as I return to my routine and stare out at the familiar foliage of my yard. It is no pileated this time, but a different friendly bird that plops down on a chair rail on my patio. It is a small, yellow-masked intruder, a tiny burglar of a bird. I know this bird, have seen it before, but it seems truly out of place. It is as if I have built a small pond or wetland with weeds and tangled thickets, not a nice suburban spa. It takes a second or two for my mind to get it right. Yellow warblers of all sorts with black somewhere splashed upon them flash quickly through my mind like a *Peterson's* on speed. Hooded, Wilson's, Canada, Kentucky, Aargh! I know this bird. It says witchet-y, witchet-y, witchet-y when you are birding near a swamp! Of course, it is a Common Yellowthroat, often heard, as much as seen. But here it is, friendly and familiar as a goldfinch, just resting in my yard. It is a first for my years-long yard list, as prodigious, as prized, as the giant goshawk that sat majestically atop a plastic toy shed in my neighbor's yard next door.

The Cat's Meow

Then there are reunions with old friends, not oddities, who come around each spring. We should not single out our favorites, though hating grackles is allowed. Between a chickadee and catbird, I am faced with Sophie's choice. But I see the chickadees around the year; the catbirds have just arrived! How they find my home, the birdbath, bushes, trees, out of all the places they could go, I really do not know. They are gentle, wary birds, mostly seen down low or peering out from bushes before they make a move. Slightly smaller, slimmer than a robin, they dress in simple gray. I think of them as Quaker birds—they would not harm a soul. A black cap sets off their plainness. They slowly bob their charcoal tails. No rushing, flying all about. They show the patience of a

Job. A pair has come back to stay with me, I cannot tell the sex.
One after the other, each lands softly upon my bird bath to take
a drink, to hydrate, after their long, long journey here. Both birds
show off their one surprise, a rich, small patch of cinnamon
beneath the longish tail. Later on, I hear them meowing, the
sound that gives the name. Soon I hope to hear them do some
catbird imitations of the songs of other birds. They are cousins to
the mockingbird, though they offer fewer repetitions and skip the
show-off style. The mockingbird, in bold light gray and white with
wing bars, stripes and all, is louder, brasher, holds forth much
longer, sings proudly in full sight.

Robins' Nests

I should not be surprised that in springtime my birds are
building nests. I've had chickadees and House Wrens move in to
hollow old downy woodpecker holes in the mountain ash that
once stood out in back. Carolina Wrens have nested in the garage
next door. My neighbors had to leave the back door open until the
young wrens fledged. I've had House Finches under my awnings,
robins in my trees. Now I see one jamming mud and mulch into
its mouth. This robin repeats the ritual I noticed just last year. It
loads its bill and then flies direct as an arrow to a tree across the
street. The early Washington naturalist, John Burroughs, com-
plained in *Wake-Robin*, unjustly, I believe, that the robin's nest of
mud and sticks was beneath the status of our beautiful, most
visible, springtime bird. "Its coarse material and rough masonry
are creditable neither to his skill as a workman or his taste as an
artist. From Robin's good looks and musical turn, we might rea-
sonably predict a domicile of equal fitness and elegance." But how
would school children proudly bring in a robin's nest to show in
class if it were not made so well? They are placed not too far up
in nearby trees where young naturalists can see them. In a crotch

of branches about eight feet up, we can marvel at the chicks, watch feeding time, see them gobble up those worms. Every child knows the blue of a robin's egg, and many have sadly found one on the ground. If the nests were made of more delicate, elegant stuff like the gossamer of a hummingbird, or hung far up, some swaying pendulum like that of the oriole, we might not learn about birds at all, or care, as did Rachel Carson, if suddenly they were gone.

A Visit from a Veery

I am thinking of Rachel when, incredibly enough, one of her favorite birds arrives and strolls into my yard. We know of robins from *Silent Spring*, but there are other thrushes, too. All our older nature writers held the Veery in high esteem. John Burroughs, who also called them Wilson's Thrush, "heard the veery thrush in the trees near the White House; and one rainy April morning, about six o'clock, he came and blew his soft, mellow flute in a pear-tree in my garden. The tones had all the sweetness and wildness they have in June in our deep northern forests." I hope to hear them sing, but I am transported into wilderness even as they simply explore my suburban yard. I have the usual excitement and confusion when first I see them. Clearly a thrush, but a Wood Thrush in my yard? Where is all the spotting on the chest? I soon realize that this will be a tougher, though wilder call. Gray-cheeked? Hermit Thrush? Veery? I note there is little spotting and more creamy-yellow near the throat than on any thrush I can recall. The back is all rich, rusty colored, surely a classic clue. I also was confused because my Veeries are not big or robin-sized. In fact I first thought Louisiana Waterthrush when my woodland visitors wandered in. I had never seen a Veery at close range, no less within my yard. Perhaps I should pay more close attention to my forebears like Burroughs.

One hundred fifty years ago or so, presumably without binoculars, he caught the very essence of the Veery. "I see by his impulsive, graceful movements, and his dimly speckled breast, that it is a thrush...he offers a few soft, mellow, flute-like notes, one of the most simple expressions of melody to be heard, and scuds away, and I see it is the veery, or Wilson's thrush. He is the least of the thrushes in size, being about that of a common Bluebird, and he may be distinguished from his relatives by the dimness of the spots upon his breast. The Wood Thrush has very clear, distinct oval spots on a white ground; in the hermit, the spots run more into lines, on a ground of a faint, bluish white; in the veery, the marks are almost obsolete, and a few rods off his breast presents only a dull yellowish appearance. To get a good view of him you have only to sit down in his haunts, as in such cases he seems equally anxious to get a good view of you." Burroughs wrote this while sitting on a mossy log. I think I need one in my yard, near where my little woodland patch, with trillium and jack-in-the-pulpit, false Solomon's seal and ferns, fends off Bethesda heat. But the Veeries have not returned, unlike my yellowthroat that has!

No Rose without a Thorn

This spring invasion of my yard is proceeding all apace. A rabbit now greets me in the morning and lives somewhere nearby. On my walks rabbits show themselves on almost every block. My neighbor knows and loves it that there is a resident pileated visiting our block. The rhododendrons now relieve the wilting, tired azaleas with huge floral bursts of pink and red and lavender. The best I have is in our front; it pleases passers-by. It is a simple, hardy, native white, as if in the woods, not some hybrid type that struts its stuff in suburban splendor everywhere I look. I have only seen one other just like mine while on my daily walks. To call it white is not quite right. Seen up close the flowers are washed with a tiny hint of pink. Inside the blossoms with five petals that form a star-shaped cup are streaks of pink and golden wash. These native plants seem to fare much better with the stress of suburban life and gradual global warming.

The riot of rhododendrons is joined by a war of roses in many of the yards. Most now are knockouts, the bug-resistant bush that blossoms without work, without sprays or powders, or anything at all. Mine are on the corner in front of my specimen old magnolia; it is intoxicating, erotic when its plate-sized blossoms come out in the climax of the spring. But the roses underneath it are striking, a deep and vibrant pink. Yet there is no fragrance to them. Like disease, the aroma has disappeared. No Japanese beetles, mildew, aphids—no ambrosia, no arousal. I had a nineteenth-century print once with a young swain reaching through a flowering fence to hold hands with a girl. An angry father rounds the bend to drive him off with a switch and with a scowl. The motto underneath it says, "No Rose without a Thorn." I wonder if the admonition for us older, busy Washingtonians will hold for long if only knockouts thrive. "Stop and smell the roses" may soon draw merely a puzzled look or two.

And so I drink deeply from each fragrant hybrid tea rose I find blooming within my reach. There are some left by fences on my walk. Some yellow, some pink, but mostly red, deep red, crimson, carnadine. I stand on tiptoe or gently pull them toward me, letting the perfume carry me off to long-gone thornier times when roses meant romance. A similar state can be induced by sampling the aroma from an iris. No wonder young men's fancies turn to love at this luscious, almost lurid time of year. Like real roses, hyacinths, lilacs, and other blossoms stir the blood, create the blush and bloom of love. I fear that irises are also in decline. Most yards are smaller now as new custom homes, or expanded houses, fill up suburban lots. Fewer flower gardens or messy plants to take up one's time and space. Developer and designer plants are all the rage, no muss, no fuss, no fragrance, no foolish dreams.

May 4, 2012
Red Admirals and Beauty

Caryn and I are escorted by an advance guard of many dozens of medium-sized butterflies as we head west from Pennyfield Lock along the C&O Canal. It is a Friday and given our schedules and the weather it is our first, best shot at Washington's wave of spring migration. Caryn has taken a day off from her office, the world that State Department official Louis Halle called "the hive." As if to reassure us that we have chosen the more important path, the butterflies that lead us are not low-ranking sorts. They surround us, beside, behind, in front. They guide us forward into spring. We are safe with them it seems. Captain John Smith came up the Potomac with his men just short of here four hundred years ago. Our guards are of higher naval rank, perhaps dispatched from the Naval Surface Warfare Center that we pass by in getting here. They are Red Admirals, but not the Russian kind at all. As befits a species with this rank, they are a global power. These admirals are found around the planet in northern, temperate climes in open woodland, like that by our canal. About two inches, tip to tip, they are marked by bold red-orange stripes on their epaulets and coat-tails. The orange forms a sort of circle with a deep rich brown inside. The upper wing, above the epaulet, is jet black with a few small badges of white pinned on. It is a dress uniform worthy of such ceremonial patrols. The Red Admirals breed twice a year; the next batch will be larger, darker, even sharper. Their caterpillars feed on nettle leaves, the kind that scratch and irritate your hand. Then they roll themselves up in silk, all harmless, before the full admiral will emerge. Now they have led us on to beauty as we have stopped to see them close.

Since we have been quiet, watching, waiting amidst a bounty of butterflies, we are rewarded by a sight we rarely see. Just standing, waiting, in the middle of the towpath, is one of the East

Coast's premier birds. It has flown in just to greet us from some-where further south. Lighted by sunshine, gleaming brilliantly in blue, is one small Indigo Bunting, though colorful, sometimes dif-ficult to see. The Indigo Bunting is so striking that it is one of just three beautiful birds displayed on the cover of the popular *Birds of North America: A Golden Guide to Field Identification*. It is dazzling, but when staring at the trees, one had best learn its call. During nesting season, indigos sometimes sit on wires, but not here in the woods. Instead they sit and sing for long periods at a time. But unlike springtime warblers, insect eaters who seem impatient and are often on the move, the bunting has a broader, sparrow-like bill and sits and sits, stock still, to the frustration of us below. But when they move, you cannot miss this bird. They are truly, incred-ibly, iridescent blue. But sitting on the ground, just waiting? It barely can be true.

Bluebirds

If an Indigo Bunting lifts the spirits, imagine our feeling when we see another bright blue bird. When I get to see a Eastern Bluebird, I start right in to sing. "Zippity doo dah!" is the phrase that comes to mind. For younger Washingtonians, it's Disney's *Song of the South*, with its prettied up plantation, that we recall. "My, oh my, what a wonderful day! Plenty of sunshine, heading my way... Mr. Bluebird on my shoulder. It's the truth. It's actual; everything is satisfactual!" The bluebird is, indeed, a southern bird and once was truly common. But releasing English Sparrows and starlings more than a century ago to add Shakespearean birds to our humble shores proved a major ecological mistake. Now they are ubiquitous. Gentler native species, the Eastern Bluebird chief among them, have been pushed aside, their numbers in sharp decline. You can trace the rising tide of transplants in the natu-ralists of old. Lucy Maynard, whose *Birds of Washington and Vicin-*

ity was published in 1898, is typical of the time. Maynard was, with Theodore Roosevelt and others, a member of the Audubon Club of the District of Columbia, now called the Audubon Naturalist Society. The second edition of her book, stimulated by and with an introduction from Florence Merriam Bailey, contains a complete list of the birds that President Roosevelt, an ardent birder and published naturalist, saw and recorded on the White House grounds. These Washingtonians together watched the first motion picture ever of birds in flight at a 1908 meeting of the DC Audubon Club hosted in the White House by Roosevelt himself.

For those who think that the chirping, cheeky bands of English or House Sparrows they see on the street or begging for food at Washington cafes have always been with us, Maynard is an important antidote. "English Sparrows are generally regarded as an unmitigated nuisance, but in spite of their noise and filth, if they could be kept in check they might be tolerated in the city, where they give a certain life to the streets and parks and furnish some entertainment to children and house-bound individuals. It is in the suburbs and country that they are most objectionable, for they drive away from dwellings and barns the native birds that would naturally build about them, and their incessant, unmusical cries drown all other bird voices.... As they are such undesirable tenants, it is worthwhile in the country to make an effort to get rid of them. A shot-gun is occasionally effective in keeping them from getting a foot-hold on a new place...for they are quick to take a hint...Nests should be watched for and destroyed - an iron hook at the end of a long pole is useful in tearing them out."

Bluebirds, once as common as robins, now need our protection. Many attempts to provide them with nesting boxes, bluebird trails, and other life supports, have kept them in our midst. But for those of us who don't live near farms and fields, and that is most of us, a sighting stirs the heart. It is what Caryn and I each feel as on this shining springtime day suddenly, as if to start the

season properly, a bluebird is in easy sight. It stands on the muddy
shore of the lagoon to the left of the trail above the lock. It, too,
is in full sun, a stunning shade of blue. Slightly bigger than a
bunting, it has a robin's breast with white below the rose. When
seen in silhouette, the bluebird's posture is slightly slumped,
somehow lacking in self-esteem. A bird this blue should show off
and thrust its rose chest forward. But it is a gentle, murmuring
soul that is losing out to sassy sparrows.

An Eagle Snatches a Heart

It is quiet back along the lagoon side where we have seen our
bluebird. And so it is no surprise that at the water's edge, two
other birds come forth. These are sandpipers, birds that make you
think of surf and Ocean City. But these are woodland waders,
found near streams, and not in noisy flocks. The Solitary Sandpiper is, as its name implies, not the social type. To see a pair is
quite a treat as they probe the shallow water. Dark gray and white,
Solitary Sandpipers are best told by an eye ring and their bobbing
up and down. But from here the eye ring is somewhat hard to see;
they are feeding, not standing on the sidelines rocking up and
down. We watch awhile to be sure that two solitaries are what we
see. Satisfied, we move along and chat with birders on the way.
We birders are a plain and simple lot, decked out, if that is the
word, in khaki, green and brown with binoculars and birding
books, and perhaps a camera, too. The etiquette is to share your
finds and point out what lies ahead. Our comrades tell us there are
Orchard Orioles and tanagers that we can see today. I try not to
look too excited; I see Baltimore Orioles every year, but not these
other birds.

Then all is moot as a large, darker bird circles into view.
Hawk or Osprey, who can tell, it's partly hidden by the trees. I
suspect I am not alone in hoping, thinking, feeling, it may be a

bald eagle. But I am rusty and hesitate to make a rookie's call. But there is soon no doubt as it soars close by, with bright white feathers on its head and also on its tail. It is always thrilling to see an eagle, since for decades they were gone. It is a majestic bird with wide, flat wings, a piercing eye, and deep-hooked yellow bill that can tear up any meal. It has talons that can snatch and carry things I do not wish to name. Our little group of birders beams with satisfaction. We have come for springtime migrants; but it is the gliding grandeur of our national emblem that has snatched our hearts away.

Organizing and Egrets

I spy an American Egret (The proper name is now the Great Egret) further on in the lagoon. These, too, were nearly gone until women organized to boycott feathered hats and stop the slaughter of the millinery trade some hundred years ago. It was Washington's own Florence Merriam Bailey and many, many others who led the fight that first put value on things in nature instead of greedy trade. She was the nation's first campus environmental organizer while a student at Smith College in the 1880s. She wrote her senior thesis on the slaughter of the birds and invited John Burroughs to campus to help her sign the Smithies up. Before the year was out, one third of Smith belonged to Audubon; one half had joined her field trips. In 1889 she published *Birds through an Opera Glass* that set off the sport we have today. Here in Washington, she taught birding classes, wrote for *Bird-Lore*, and worked with Roosevelt and others to ultimately gain the Migratory Bird Act of 1918 that protected herons, egrets, and all the birds we see today.

Finding a Flycatcher's Nest

I am musing over history as I move on down the path. But it isn't long before I spot the *other* oriole, the orchard one, whose breast is all brick red. I have not seen one of these in years and truly am excited. These, too, are somewhat southern birds I never saw in New York or Pennsylvania. The first I recall was in the District almost forty years ago. It was near the Potomac, in a small grove of trees, a park near the bronzed bird statue noted by Louis Halle along the George Washington Parkway. An Orchard Oriole was thrilling then, no less today. It is a bird worth knowing. Its song is clearly oriole, as is its sleek, sharp-beaked silhouette. Although it is slightly smaller, and less gaudy in its feathers than its cousin, the famous, orange one from Baltimore, it is surely underrated. No sports team logo here, just rich, deep color and a preference for parks. It may always be known somehow as just that other oriole. But to me it is sweet and special, a secret friend of sorts.

The same is true of the bird that pops out next after making quite a racket. It is the Great Crested Flycatcher, a smaller bird, but one that insists on being known if you are new to birding. It sports a yellow breast and rusty tail, a gray chest and throat, a pale green head with a zany crest that completes the picture, except it does not rest. Like other flycatchers, who are less well-dressed, it snatches insects in the air after perching on a branch. It sits so you can see it and then it does its stunts. Today there is a pair of them; they're going back and forth. And then I see they're making all this noise from in and out, around, a hole above my head. This cavity is in a sycamore; it could almost hold a screech owl. But there is no doubt; it is another first for me. I'm watching Mr. and Mrs. Flycatcher preparing their brand new nest.

May 16, 2012
A Skink on the Movie Set

It is nice again and I am free to head out into nature. I see four deer on the approach road just before I wheel onto the C&O

Canal at Great Falls and the Tavern at Lock 20. It is now the tourist season. The canal barge and mules are back in action, using locks and ropes and gears. They are steered and led by guides in amazingly authentic nineteenth-century costumes. Odd shoes, pants held up with braces, bonnets, men's shirts with puffy sleeves, and floppy, outsized hats. Like Civil War re-enactors, they clearly are enjoying this. Those come here, too, at other times, with tents and guns, for fun, and for some real live action. I briefly stop and watch and slowly fade back into history. Part of the charm of the C&O is the setting—like a movie on location. In Civil War times, the Union had lookout posts along this way to watch for an invasion. There are some shallow fords where rebels could cross over from Virginia. They finally did and fought some skirmishes here just a little bit upstream.

As I am musing in the past, some movement underneath the bridge draws back my mind and brings me to the present. Then out pops my brand new friend, whom I just met this season. It is another broad-headed skink, or, perhaps, the one I saw before. But this one does seem smaller, though it crawls out on the wooden bridge and suns itself a bit. I can watch it, magnified, as if sitting in my hand. Same reddish-brown and scaly head, same mottled gray-brown body, a balanced, longer tail. I consider announcing my find for all nearby to see, but it might seem odd; the movie set and bargemen are the bigger, bolder view that got them here today.

The Great Blue Heron

I mosey on and am greeted by an older friend this time. A Great Blue Heron is in my path, holding its ground as stubbornly as a mule. This part of the C&O must be blue heron central. They walk and stand and fly and fish for everyone to see. I have photos of them up so close, now framed, that visitors think I must be Eliot Porter or use some nifty camera with a huge and hefty lens. I have never lost my fascination with these proud, primeval birds. And almost every passerby I see will stop and stare like me. This time it is the legs that get me first, with careful, cautious, deadly steps with backwards bending knees. I almost always see blue herons wading, hunting, or staring absolutely motionless at some unsuspecting prey. This one will soon step into the killing grounds of a canal chock full of fish. But for now it simply stands there showing off its plumes. These, too were prized a century ago and worn on women's hats. Now they're back with their rightful owner in gray and blue and black. The one that streams out from the head is really dark, dark blue. It matches with a broad blue eye line that forms a strong, striped face. And then there is that staring, yellow eye with black within the center. I wish I knew what kind of vision allows the Great Blue Heron to peer through muddy water and spot and spear its dinner.

A Taste of Goslings

As I am standing, staring, I spot some dinner, too. Although I do not hunt, I know some folks who do. Right there in front of me, swimming in the canal is a pair of Canada Geese with three little goslings in their wake. Each spring I look forward to the downy gosling broods. They range from tiny, creamy-headed puffy ones, to larger, awkward, long-necked gray ones that seem somehow in their teens. Each year I worry about the goslings, a tasty morsel for some critter here in Washington's wilder parts. Yet in many places, the geese have grown to be a nuisance. On golf courses, lawns, in parks, they waddle about and eat our man-made grass. Their signature, curled greenish-black droppings are left for us to find or step on as we pass. But the goslings now before me are far too cute and vulnerable to be held hostage for their clan. And since now there are just three of them, their siblings must have been eaten by some predator—from water, land, or air. I have seen them carried off on two separate spring trips out here—the merry month of May. Canada Geese are not endangered. There are plenty enough to spare. But I watched with a bit of horror as they were carted off to die. Both times the killer was a red fox—a favorite of mine. The first walked in my direction with something in its mouth. Then it seemed to see me and paused to take a look. No remorse, no shame, just idle curiosity as it stopped to have its lunch. That's when I saw that in its jaws, between its teeth, was a little yellow gosling. It saw I posed no danger and, not rushing, the fox stepped down to riverside where I could no longer see. The fox and little goose were gone forever. The image stuck with me. I never thought I'd witness such an awful act again, until the next middle of the month of May.

This time I was less horrified, more impressed, by another red fox within my path. Pretty much same time, same place, same stroll toward me again. But the victim was one of those large, almost grown, gray goslings. It seemed nearly as big as the fox. Its long neck dangled out one side of the mouth; its body and feet the other. It was quite a catch and seemed quite right. I was rooting for the fox. But when I count up little goslings now, I know their siblings' fate. I hope they do not share it. But then each time I see a predator, I know they need a meal. It isn't always foxes either; there are lots of hungry hunters here. Hawks and owls and eagles are among the dinner crowd who prowl from up above. Down below submerged beneath the water is one of the most horrible predators of all. Along the canal you see them now and then. The snapping turtles, in their armor, have jaws as if of steel. I fear them, too, so I can easily imagine the frantic, horrid scene when a gosling is pulled down underwater, mangled in the mud.

The Majestic Mallard

My imagination is getting grisly and so I'm glad to see a pair of Mallard Ducks just up in front of me. I have loved them since my boyhood on Long Island when on some roadside pond we would feed ducks just for fun. Like the robin and the Blue Jay, they are among the first birds that we can name. I try not to take such common, familiar ducks for granted. I have, of course, been disappointed when birding in some unexplored wetland, stream, or marsh. I spy some ducks excitedly, then murmur "only Mallards." The same is often said of cardinals and chickadees when birding off a list. My Mallards are just standing in the sun, their colors, feathers, features all proudly on display. They have been put here as if stuffed or carved or painted—a Smithsonian moment—for me to marvel at today. The orange feet are quite distinctive with a touch of water in the webs. These spectacular, showy paddles are usually flapping underneath as Mallards glide along. The male, or drake, is as dashing as they come. In full light, the head is emerald set off at the neck by a simple band of white. A fully yellow bill stands out from there; it makes a striking profile. This elegant, unique and richly-colored duck head is made for pictures, paintings, or those preppy summer woven belts that hold up linen trousers. Below the head, a chest of cinnamon, or well-worn, vintage burgundy, that has paled a bit with time. It's set off by a subtle back of gray with white all underneath. Within the wing you see displayed some medal or some honor; the ribbon, proudly worn, within white stripes, is of a brilliant blue. This is called the speculum; it shows the Mallard's lineage, no matter what the season. In August when the drake is dull and in eclipse without its emerald head, the speculum still stands out to mark the Mallard's true nobility. Even the tail adds a courtly clothier's touch or, perhaps, the royal baker. It is pure white, like wedding cake, with curled black feathers on it, as if a shaved, dark chocolate topping.

Turtle Land

As I proceed, I come to the land of turtles. In May they are everywhere basking in the sun. Along the canal, wherever logs or branches have fallen and are lying in the sun, you'll find a dozen turtles sitting piled up near each other. One May, Caryn and I counted over two hundred of them within a single ride. It's presumably a world record we still hold with local pride. These are mostly painted turtles and sliders, as far as we can tell. The painted ones show orange-red, especially below. The sliders are creamier, with stripes upon the head. As I approach, the little ones will sometimes plop down in the water. The older, wiser ones just soak up some more sun. The newborn, springtime turtles range in size from tiny inch or two long babies, to older toddlers topping out at three or four inches on the log. The older ones are perhaps a full foot long if measuring just the shell. There are some even bigger ones, the grandparents I guess. But learning turtle reproduction, gender, geriatrics is more than I can master. The turtles are always a hit with children. It's like going to the zoo. As any canoe full of family floats slowly by, with Mom or Dad doing the soft and silent paddling, the kids will point and squeal and stare with obvious delight. Despite some gentle shushing, there are soon far fewer turtles in their sight. Sometimes, I try to see with childhood's eye as I wander down the path. It is the simple things—the herons, Mallards, turtles, after all—that make the children laugh.

An Uncommon Blue

As May has moved along, smaller wonders have emerged. Near the turtles is a clump of yellow, larger irises, then smaller, Siberian purple flags. How they got here, how they grow are mysteries to ponder. How turtles, flowers, butterflies and birds all find their proper niche always piques my curiosity, my wonder, as I look for nature's riches. The smallest gem I find today is sipping at a patch of white along the towpath edge. It is a tiny, silver butterfly I think I've missed before. The white that it is drinking from is really large bird splatter; a feast sent down by herons. I focus in with binoculars to see this butterfly in some detail. The silvery surface is slightly woven, quilted, bumpy, as if hammered by some jeweler. There are tiny spots of inlaid ebony along the edges, too. The head with, thread-like antennae and proboscis has stripes of black and white. What kind of magic butterfly is this I've come upon today? It sits and sups in leisure, the course is *crème brûlée*. I watch entranced for quite some time, before I think there are wonders still in store. I gently stomp my foot to make this silver stunner fly. So off it goes. It flutters all around me, a gorgeous, powdery blue! My tiny butterfly must be magical if it can transmute itself from silver into some cerulean hue. I check my butterfly book. I have seen these blues before. What has shown itself in springtime is called a Spring Azure or sometimes in older books, simply a Common Blue. We do not live in England—a commoner is no shame. But surely this lovely creature deserves a better name. Like Common Loon or Common Merganser, what were our lepidopterists thinking? This is science at its worst—all shorn of wizardry or wonder. Imagine how we might perceive these tiny, common blues with names like "Magic Princess," "Lady-in-waiting," or "Silver-sided Cerulean Blue."

Barrister Owl

I am all alone today, a weekday without people. Things unfold that I have never seen before. The water and the woods are silent. Something strange is sitting on the opposite side of the canal, not moving in the sun. Because it is the daytime, my brain cannot conceive nor capture what is this feathery, foot-long stump I see. Then on top, a face, two discs with beak, appear; it is some sort of owl! A Barred Owl, a predator of evening streams and woodlands, is sitting, staring straight across at me. A Barred Owl is heard more often than it's seen and I don't come here at night.

Its hoot-hoot, hoo, hoo! (with the cadence, one-two, three *four*!)
is pretty distinctive when booming across the night. While
camping by a swamp I've watched them hunt by moonlight or
caught a glimpse of one sitting out in daylight on southern highways lined with pine. But here in Washington and sitting in close
view, I feel my heart beat faster. The brown and creamy barring is
surely diagnostic. The jet black eyes in facial discs set at a small,
slight angle resemble the Barn Owls I have seen. But they are
slimmer, whiter and more ghostly. As I am reassuring myself that
a Barred Owl is what I see, it turns its head completely round. It
could care less for me. Perhaps it has spotted something to lunch
upon today. Now it turns its head in profile. It looks like a British
barrister or judge, bewigged, before the court. Its aquiline beak
looks deadly. The talons I can't see. When it is finished looking
all around while moving not a muscle, it lifts itself into the air
without a sound, or beat, or ruffle. It disappears in silence, gone in
woodland mystery, as when it first appeared. It is how things out
here should be.

The Tug of Wood Ducks

In the quiet afternoon with ears attuned, I hear a gentle,
muted piping. Another sound I have not heard. I cannot place it
well. It comes again and goes away and comes again once more. I
turn my head now sideways like the owl who has vanished from
my sight. And then in dappled sunlight I finally see my sound. It
is a mother Wood Duck with eight small ducklings in tow. Her
swimming is quite easy, rhythmic. She simply moves her head
back, then forward, like a rower in a scull. She is carefully tugging
some invisible tether leashed behind that pulls along her ducklings. Then comes the airy, sweet, soft piping that holds her babies
close and calm. I'm calmed myself—I feel more gentle—by the
sounds and sylvan scene.

Some substance in the woods has elevated my urban mood. I ride along content and dreamy as the Washington spring unfurls. I count up all the turtles and watch them bask and dive. I smile at cormorants drying out their wings while standing on a stone. I follow more butterflies and watch them drink at flowers. I see pairs of kingbirds, a Great Crested Flycatcher on a cedar growing out of rock, a wild scene like out West. High above me on either side of snags that form a sycamore slingshot, I see a bluebird and a kingbird perched against the sky, sharing space to watch the wonders, or simply catch a fly? As I cruise by the lagoon above the Pennyfield Lock, I discover where all those goslings have been hiding to stay out of most harm's way. There are lots of them, some twenty, along with the adults. The attack approach by land is blocked by moats of water. They're feeding on some grass and plants with a mud flat to their front. No snappers lurking down below to jump from out of the water and pull them down below. The air sortie is easier, but the goose defenders are impressive. Most of the goslings here are big and gray and almost safely in their prime. I smile some more and cruise along incredulous at Washington in May.

Smooching Cedar Waxwings

As I turn toward home, the herons start to cruise away to roost in some safe, secluded spot. As the sun grows low, I see one standing quite serenely with its mouth a touch agape, facing west to the setting sun, as if in gratitude or prayer. It is cooler now, the hour when animals start to feed. A deer steps out some sixty yards ahead. I watch this doe pause briefly, then step into the water. She walks, then wades, then swims; her head is all I see. She too is calm and simply rises slowly, dripping, out of water. She walks up on the other bank and then softly fades away. As I near the tavern, I see some birds and stop on the platform that overlooks the river. The slanting sun adds golden tones to the old sycamore that has stood here for a long, long time. Some birds in little flocks are flying in and out. They settle in and show themselves—all golden in the light. It is a group of Cedar Waxwings. I can see their colors well, their yellow chests, with tawny, burnished golden tones above, a small black mask and sharply angled cap. There are small red dots upon each wing. But best of all, I think, is the waxwing's gray-black tail, dipped in gold, its brush to paint the sky.

Two Cedar Waxwings are sitting side by side, upright on a branch. I think it is a mother feeding berries to her child. But both male and female waxwings are feathered just the same. Could this pair be kissing as their bills come close together? Then I see that they are passing a single berry back and forth between them. One steps away a little bit and then they come together. Then the other backs away, comes back, with the berry still uneaten. They go on like this for quite a while; they pass it back and forth. This is no dining scene I'm witnessing up above me. Selecting mates, or building trust, or just lascivious fun? This definitely is a courtship—a berry, sunshine, and thou.

The larger birds at end of day are pairing up as well. I go to leave and in swoop two Pileated Woodpeckers, flying close in tandem before landing on a vine on the building near the tavern. They move from there to a larger tree and start to move together up the trunk, no insects on the menu. They clearly are more fascinated by each other than by finding any food. It's May. It's spring. And soon, they'll have a brood.

May 18, 2012
Muskrat Ramble

I am able to get off early to the C&O Canal. It is cool and mist clings close to the water. I see an animal swimming up ahead.

I used to see beaver and signs of chewing all through here, but not in recent years. I draw a little closer and bring up my field glasses. A brown, furry head and a bit of body swims near the edge and then across. I will need to see the tail to know which swimmer I have here. I suspect a muskrat which is typical now along the C&O. But I can hope to find the scarcer beaver as they had in olden times. My little friend swims back and forth, but never shows its tail. If a long and rat-like one then it is a muskrat. If it is round and wide and pancake-style then it surely is a beaver. I feel that split again between enjoying local wildlife and spotting, cataloguing, naming them. It swims some more as older scenes pass before my eyes, of beaver dams, and Lake Louise, and evenings in Maine. Then underwater slips my quarry. It does not come back out. There are no signs of chewed up wood or teeth marks on the trees. I sigh a bit and get back on my bike. I've learned to like and cheer for muskrats despite their awful name and tail. But there is a deep, deep reason we really look for beaver on any watery trail.

Meeting the Other Indigo

I glide along in the morning sun enjoying cold, crisp air when a tiny patch of blue ahead causes me to stare. I slowly brake so there will be no screech and look on down the path. It is the Indigo Bunting I saw the other day. I wish I could tell an individual bird apart from others that I see. It's why we have bird banding and modern, minute, micro-tracking devices to put upon some birds. But this is where I saw my indigo, right here past Penny-field Lock. But now, in an act of interspecies courtesy and friend-ship, he has brought his wife along. Both stand within the path; he introduces her to me. To see a pair of indigos in full sunshine is an amazing sight. If opposites attract, than these buntings take the prize. His iridescent, shiny blue seems even richer than before.

To call it indigo, like blue jeans, does not do him justice. Standing at his side, demurely, is his plain and simple bride. I assume the perky personality and pluck she has is somehow hid from human sight. She looks just like a sparrow. Plain brown, with streaks, is all I see. A slightly darker tail; a hint of cap upon her head. There is something heartening about this small, unlikely couple. They upset our preconceptions, turn stereotypes around. I am getting used to apparitions. I cannot make them happen. I must simply be alive, awake, attuned. Having shown his mate the visitor and finished up their courtesies, my buntings bid farewell, take to air, and disappear from off the ground.

Remembering Wrens

One small brown bird deserves another. A pair is on the left just up ahead. It is dark and shady here and they are in the woods. In, out, around a fallen tree they go, dead branches, twigs and sticks abound. I finally spot one with my eyes. It is some sort of wren. The tail is cocked straight up with little ladder rungs all down it. I know by feel that these are House Wrens; my yard has carolinas. But I look at the head to still make sure. Big eye stripe, carolina. Small buffy, barely a streak, a House Wren has appeared. But then I am not certain. Though smaller and less common, Winter Wrens could still be here. Their paths cross briefly with the House Wrens when May rolls into town. They also like woodpiles in moist and darker woods. Again I decide to give up listing and watch them jump around. The looks are short and fleeting. Who cares what kind they are? Caryn and I were in Canada years ago out hiking when we saw our first real Winter Wrens. For "lifer" birds it's best to have a partner. Check out each mark, each sound, each characteristic behavior. For now I'm happy seeing wrens outside my cozy yard. The mist, cool air, and shady woods have taken me afar. We once had House Wrens in our yard; they nested long ago in the hole left by some wood-pecker. I muse for just a moment about my boyhood home where the House Wren outside threw back its head and sang along as my mother played piano.

Such reveries are hard to find and often interrupted. So mine is now by a sound that makes me listen. I have been looking, musing, lost in thought, watching tiny woodland wrens. Over-head within the sun, no mist to hide him, a Baltimore Oriole rings out to catch my poor attention. I swear he's saying, "Look up here! Look up here!" like Steve Martin in *Three Amigos*. "I'm up here!" my oriole continues, impatient now that I am slow to turn, to watch him sing so grandly. He's right, of course; it is a fine display, one of Washington in springtime's finest. "Those small brown birds and branches are so commonplace", he says. "They simply will not do."

The Virtues of a Vireo

A white Great Egret glides overhead to add to the display. Its dangling legs have all black feet, not yellow like the Snowy. Again while watching, I hear another sound. It's like an alto robin, less cheery, less voluble, but happy just the same. It's some-what more repetitive; it sounds like a recording. "Cheer-y, cheerio; Cheer-y, cheerio!" it sings and sings. Its voice is slightly breathy. This is a Red-eyed Vireo, singing somewhere in a tree. Using echolocation, I tiptoe toward the shade while following the sound. There it is. No. There are actually two of them, pre-tending to be little robins in pajamas. The vireo is smaller, plainer, with white breast, not rich red. The back and wings are grayish brown and dull; it has a blue-gray cap. The vireo's best features are all upon its head. Beneath its colored cap, just above the eye, there is a bold white streak, marked off with a patch of brown. And then if you can see it, comes the part that gives the name. A bright red iris, as if caught in someone's flashbulb, lights up its tiny eye. I first learned from *Peterson's* that the Red-eyed Vireo is the most common woodland bird in North America. I still find this hard to believe, though I have seen and heard lots of them throughout the years. Robins are more common and more visible, of course; they prowl suburban lawns. You can find a vireo or two in woodsier suburbs, but deciduous forests and places like the canal are their true home. But I trust Roger Tory Peterson, perhaps our most famous bird artist and expert, who birded on this path.

Like millions of other birders, budding naturalists, I started out with him. His guides have sold in millions, have changed our view of nature, have become a household name. When I first began to bird, including here at Pennyfield Lock, I had no idea that Roger walked upon this very path. He started in New York, then moved to Washington, and summered in New England. His first guide came out before World War II with simple field marks on the pictures to show us how to look. When the war was over, he revised the guide; the timing was just perfect. Washington grew, the suburbs spread, and people had more leisure. Highways connected once exotic, distant birding spots and families took vacations. We wanted pristine sights and fresher air and water we could drink. Environmentalism arrived. And at the center of it all was Washington, DC. The C&O Canal was under threat. The Potomac was polluted. DDT was killing birds. Our future was in danger. And so right here at Pennyfield Lock, I'm following in the footsteps of those who rescued nature.

Modern Daddy Birds

As if to match the oriole that had called for me to look, I spot a Scarlet Tanager on the outskirts of a tree. This one is a beauty; I think it's the morning light. Bright red, black wings, an unmistakable, unforgettable sight. This one is some sort of modern Dad. While Mom is at the office, he is feeding a tanager young-ster who sits fluttering nearby. Now another bird is demanding my attention. It's loud and sort of raspy and not too nice at all. It's shouting "Creep! Creep!" at me as if I carried guns. This Great Crested Flycatcher is insistent that I watch him do his thing. He, too, drops into view right in my towpath's way; there's no mis-taking him! He walks a bit and pecks the ground and picks at veg-etation. There are little bits of straw-like grass along the towpath edges. He finally snatches some and flies away. At least he's stopped the racket. And then I realize that he's another modern, wimpy guy who's helping with the nest. I feel a little better. Perhaps he wasn't mocking me. But then I hear him once again, same words, same tone, same "Creep!"

A Warbler in Its Vestments

A gentler, sweeter sound soothes my wounded ego now. I seek it out and look up high against the clear blue sky. If this is what I think it is, my wings are all a twitter. I see some yellow on a branch and focus in real fast. There it is. A Prothonotary Warbler, at last! Another southern swampy bird, not one I knew up north. The first I saw was in a swamp at Harris Neck National Wildlife Refuge in Georgia, with live oak and Spanish moss, at what once had been a plantation. There were egrets and herons, wood storks, gronking all around, a rookery of sound. It was in this primeval setting that a swatch of gold appeared. Then blue wings and sweet singing etched the scene upon my soul. In Wash-ington, the prothonotary is a rare sight; you must know where to find it. Louis Halle waxed eloquent about this gorgeous bird so many years ago. I can hear Halle whispering in my ear. "Here is the home of that shining wonder among birds, the prothonotary warbler. I suppose the College of Prothonotaries Apostolic, in the Roman Church, wore blue and gold vestments. This is a bright golden warbler with dark eyes, blue wings, and blue tail. It perches on open twigs and branches overhanging water and throws its head back to utter its loud, plain, *tweet, tweet, tweet, tweet...* It's golden, almost orange body plumage has a deep velvety quality, like that of the scarlet tanager, which gives it a loveliness of texture beyond its loveliness of color when seen in direct sunlight." Even in Halle's day, there were only two colonies in Washington—one at Dyke Marsh, the other here at the canal. I watch and listen, linger longer as if traveling back in time. The prothonotary has transported me. Its call is soft and kindly. It is singing "sweet, sweet, sweet, sweet."

A Vivid Recollection

The morning is being kind to me. The mist has burned off the canal, but it is still cool with a subtle, small light breeze. Like a turtle, I have been basking occasionally in the sun as the early morning started out cold, especially in the shade and the added wind you get while riding on a bicycle. If the prothonotary brought me back to old plantations, it is Fairmount Park in Philadelphia I enter now. A yellow warbler with some markings is right in front of me. I finally see its spotted necklace draped across its throat. It is a Canada Warbler. They're also hard to see. They pass through here while headed north to lusher, deeper, cooler woods than these. The necklace sports some dangles—broken stripes are hanging down on a chest of yellow beneath a blue-gray back. A distinct, distinguished warbler, it has a pair of golden spectacles to set off its attire. I have not seen too many wherever I have been. That's why my first youthful find remains so vivid in my mind. I was deep within the urban woods, beside a waterfall. And bathing, feeding, playing was my Canada, holding me in thrall.

The Wealthy Phoebe

I soon am at Seneca Creek and the bridge at Riley's Lock. It is mine alone today. Claudia Wilds, who wrote the classic modern guide to birding in our area, says never go to Great Falls on weekends, there are too many folks about. There are even more these days with kayaks, picnics, dogs. But I go when I can. I chat and people-watch and miss a bird or two. It's why I take in all of nature now; we're part of a larger scene. But Claudia is absolutely right about where to find the birds and the advantages of quiet. There is an old sandstone lockhouse here where the aqueduct crosses the creek as it flows into the Potomac. It's near the lock and bridge. It is the stuff of postcards, paintings, photos—I've taken quite a few. But now it's simply what I think it ought to be—the elegant country home of a resident Eastern Phoebe. It poses on the bridge. It flies somewhere beneath it. It sits upon a fence. It calls "Phoebe, Phoebe!" with joyous springtime notes. I'm jealous of a little bird who has this large estate. It's been handed down through phoebe generations while carefully maintained for these sweet small birds by us hard-working human beings.

A New Eliot Porter

Near this Rockefeller of a phoebe, I see some Cedar Waxwings. They are dining on a sumptuous supply of berries. There are so many waxwings here, all feeding; I have five within my lens. They're posed, like a print from John James Audubon, colorful and caught in action, ready to frame and hang inside. The morning now is warming up; it's time to turn around. I stop and chat with birders and a fisherman I meet along the way. One birder has just graduated from college in English and pre-med. He, too, has found the dazzling Prothonotary Warbler that has already made my day. We watch and listen to "sweet, sweet, sweet, sweet" and marvel at our fortune. He tells me of a nest ahead on the small cliffs at Point of Rocks where he watched two Louisiana Waterthrushes go in and out of a grassy crevice in the rock. He shows his digital photo and then carefully describes the spot. When I move on, I look and look, but simply cannot find it, no matter how hard I try. Nature is more cunning than our best technology. The rocky nest remains sheltered, safe from prying eyes.

I see a couple birding; they seem to know what they are doing. It turns out she does medical policy and he's a conservation biologist who worked for a time with my friends at Defenders of Wildlife. Now he is planning how to prevent disaster from sea-level rise and global warming at Blackwater National Wildlife Refuge across the Chesapeake. This is where the eagles saved by Rachel Carson and by others soar above the marsh. But unless we change real quickly, or take some drastic measures, it will surely be engulfed by the rising waters in the bay. But today, in glorious springtime, it's best to enjoy the birds. My new companions have found a White-eyed Vireo, another bird that's mostly heard. We stand and stare at trees across the narrow strip of water. We hear the call, or see some movement that has us offer signals to each other. "Near two o'clock on the curving branch. He's moving up right now. No, now twelve o'clock, on the other side, where those two branches come together." We are hunting, spotting, chasing, like a Special Forces team. We want to see this bird that we have heard. It will not get away. "Step here in my line of sight." "Still moving up. Left of trunk. Behind the bare branch back in the leaves behind." Finally I get our quarry in my glasses. It is more striking than the red-eyed one, though it has a similar vireo eye ring. It's the yellow sides, white chest and throat and wing bars that make this bird stand out. I'm not sure I've ever seen the actual white iris in its eye. But, no matter, this one, eating bugs along the way, has finally made it to a sunny snag atop the tree for all of us to see. My new conservationist friends are on a roll; they tell me they've also seen a bizarre oriole, neither Baltimore nor Orchard.

And sure enough as we speak, the puzzler pulls into view. The Baltimore is orange. It's mate a duller orange-yellow. The Orchard Oriole is tile or brick, its mate a greenish yellow. Our bird is a bright and brilliant yellow with black on chest and chin. We talk, we look at books. We can't contain hold our glee. It looks like a Hooded Oriole, the one that lives out West! But, that simply cannot be. By now our medical student has caught up and joins our group to look. We confer excitedly. He spots our bird and announces without hesitation. "It's a young spring Orchard Oriole." He grabs his pack and reaches in to pull out one more birding guide. This one has photographs and extra views. There can be no mistake. He does not gloat. He's just so good at this. We wish him well in med school and know he will do fine. I secretly hope he'll keep taking photographs of birds and nature. We are on sacred ground out here along the C&O Canal. I tell him of those who have gone before—Peterson and Carson, Halle and Briggs, and Wilds and Burroughs, too. I may have just met a young Eliot Porter today. Porter was one of the premier and most popular bird and nature photographers of the twentieth century with lush and stirring pictures. He had been a professor at Harvard Medical School when he took time off on sabbatical. He started taking pictures out in nature and never returned to put on a white coat again.

May 27-29, 2012
Tropical Washington and the End of Spring

It has been hot and humid with thunderstorms for days now, following a period of cloudy, warm humid weather with occasional rain. The brisk rush of cool spring air each morning is now a memory. Bethesda is lush, green, almost tropical. There are day lilies and hydrangeas in full bloom, mostly blue from acid soil, but pink ones, too, and some mixed, in ways that defy all scientific logic. There are dragonflies I mistake for hummingbirds. The redbuds so enchanting only a little while ago are full of hanging, flattened string beans, catalpa beans squashed by some invisible hand. In gardens, orange butterfly weed has grown large, coreopsis stands erect and tall. But there are still luscious late spring features though summer really now is here. The sun and earth say three more weeks of spring; the calendars do, too. But in Washington in late spring, the word tropical will do. My giant specimen magnolia tree has started in to bloom. Its foot-wide white blossoms are glorious, their fragrance erotic. I can feel Faulkner's Mississippi, moonshine, and magnolias. This weekend a car pulls up and asks permission to cut a bloom or two for a pre-teen school report. Louisiana is his subject, the truly deep, Deep South. His mother has stopped by after admiring and inhaling this triumphant tree that has stood guard at our intersection for over seventy years. It calls up something in her childhood she cannot quite explain, but wants her son to know.

The birds are all nesting now or singing on their territory. Some feed young, who flutter as they beg another mouthful. I even have some kinder feelings, too rare, toward a grackle that feeds its youngster each day inside my yard. But on my neighborhood walks, a new sound rises above the usual feathered chorus. It is the loud, rapid, gargling warble of tiny House Wrens each couple of blocks singing off their heads. I spot a few with throats held high as they let out frequent yodels. Even unseen, their arias can make the hot streets heaven. I also have some resident catbirds now; they are a delightful puzzle. So quiet, even stealthy on the one hand, such miming, talking songsters on the other. The robins, too, are making merry; I cannot tell who's who. Some have found the mud and mulch that gathers in my garden. They fly straight off, but then I lose them. How many nests are now nearby, I simply do not know. But they will need them, I suspect, when I find a broken robin's egg in my yard. This long, unusually hot weekend marks for me the end of Washington in spring and the start of another long, hot summer.

1. Rachel Carson

"…taught to observe and study and love…" (p. xi)

(Photo by Shirley A. Briggs Rachel Carson Council)

2. Florence Merriam Bailey

"…birds through binoculars instead of shooting them…" (p. 3)

(Smith College 1886 yearbook. Notman Photographic Company, Smith College Archives)

3. Sharps Island Lighthouse

"…not too long before it is gone." (p. 10)

(Wiki Commons)

4. Trillium

"its blooming announced… true spring." (p. 29)

(Photo by author)

5. Tulip Poplar

"…horticultural homicide" (p. 31)

(Photo by author)

6. Captain John Smith

"a breastplate, a pointed sword…"
(p. 47)

(Courtesy Jamestown Rediscovery,
Preservation Virginia. Artwork Jamie May)

7. George Washington

"all leather and belts…" (p. 47)

(National Park Service)

8. Spring Beauties

"They peek out from the forest floor…" (p. 53)

(Photo by Tony Presley – HIKINGSOUTH.COM)

9. President Grover Cleveland

"sought refuge from the pressures of the White House"
(p. 55)

(Photo ©Bettmann/CORBIS)

Rail shooting on the Anacostia Marshes
Washing on. D.C. (page 18)

10. Shooters in Anacostia

"…many are shot for the market by gunners" (p. 61)

(Illustration from
Avifauna Columbiana)

11. Redbud Blossoms

"…a miniature pink lady's slipper shrunk down…"
(p. 65)

(Photo by author)

12. Golden Ragwort

"...flowers explode out of tiny, tight bead-like buds" (p. 67)

(Photo by author)

13. Daisy Fleabane

"...the size of a dime... symmetrical as a sundial." (p. 68)

(Photo by author)

14. Dutchman's Breeches

"…a tiny pair of white bloomers…drying on a line…" (p. 68)

(Photo by author)

15. Mourning Cloak

"…an old, white-bearded, Burroughs of a butterfly…" (p. 70)

(Photo by Fotalia)

16. John Burroughs

"…when he first arrived, Washington was a wilder place…" (p. 73)

(Wiki Commons)

17. Wood Duck Drake

"…a profile worthy of some ceremonial guard…" (p. 75)

(Photo by elvan74 - Fotolia)

18. Wood Duck Female

"…an understated beauty, a natural…" (p. 76)

(Photo by Wolfgang Kruck - Fotolia)

19. Early Cyclists in Rock Creek

"…men posing with their bikes…" (p. 76)

(Library of Congress, Historical Photos)

20. Pileated Woodpecker

"Dust and chips fly, a hole increases…" (p. 85)

(Photo by Kyle Bedell - Fotalia)

21. Bloodroot

"Each bloodroot flower is there for just a day or two." (p. 88)

(Photo by author)

22. Trout Lily

"Only a few inches high with drooping, curled-back petals…" (p. 88)

(Photo by author)

23. Veery

"…distinguished… by the dimness of the spots upon his breast." (p. 93)

(Photo ©Brian E. Small)

24. Red Admiral

"…bold red-orange stripes on their epaulets…" (p. 95)

(Photo by Doug Schnurr - Fotolia)

25. Orchard Oriole

"…just rich, deep color and a preference for parks." (p. 100)

(Photo by Dan Pancamo)

26. Magnolia Blossom

"Its foot-wide blossoms are glorious, their fragrance erotic." (p. 119)

(Photo by author)

27. Obama's Second Inauguration

"…a cross section of America…" (p. 124)

(Photo by author)

28. The Capitol on Inauguration Day

"…principled, patriotic pageantry." (p. 125)

(Photo by author)

29. February Climate March

"…young people stand around… without a hat…" (p. 136)

(Photo by author)

30. Song Sparrow

"…head thrown back, throat revealed beneath this wondrous warble." (p. 137)

(Wiki Commons)

31. Walk to Olmsted Island

"…a roaring section of the river has carved out its own gorge." (p. 141)

(Photo by author)

32. Olmsted Plaque

"…rich with weather and patina." (p. 142)

(Photo by author)

OLMSTED ISLAND
NAMED IN HONOR OF
FREDERICK LAW OLMSTED, JR.
1870 ——— 1957
ILLUSTRIOUS LANDSCAPE ARCHITECT AND ADVOCATE
OF THE PRESERVATION OF NATURAL SCENERY WHO
AS AN ORIGINAL MEMBER OF THE NATIONAL CAPITAL PARK
AND PLANNING COMMISSION FROM 1926 TO 1952 WAS
INSTRUMENTAL IN PRESERVING THE GREAT FALLS AND GORGE
OF THE POTOMAC FOR THE USE AND ENJOYMENT OF THE PEOPLE
PRESENTED BY THE
AMERICAN SOCIETY OF LANDSCAPE ARCHITECTS
1965

33. Cut-leaf Toothwort

"blossoms grow up from leaves deeply cut, with jagged notches…" (p. 168)

(Photo by author)

34. Turtles

"…happy bumps upon a log." (p. 175)

(Photo by author)

35. Unfinished Washington Monument

"…like a pencil that has been snapped off." (p. 179)

(Photo unknown)

Cover

Washington Monument, Spring, 2013, after earthquake damage.

(Photo by author)

36. Cherry Blossoms

"They emerge from
the bark and trunks
themselves…"
(p. 181)

(Photo by author)

37. Martin Luther
King

"…his folded arms seem
resolute and strong…"
(p. 182)

(Photo by author)

38. Barred Owl

"...the eyes that hold
me tethered..." (p. 186)

(Wiki Commons)

39. Rufous-sided Towhee

"...a trim and
tailored bird..." (p. 190)

(Photo by George A. Houseley, Jr.,
M.A., M.D.)

40. The Supreme Court

"...in full morning sun,
a scrim across its front."
(p. 196)

(Photo by author)

41. Dwarf Crested Iris

"…perfectly formed with jagged purple petals." (p. 202)

(Photo by author)

42. Goslings

"…four little, downy goslings, all yellow with an eye stripe." (p. 219)

(Photo by author)

43. Blackburnian Warbler

"…a sudden tiny burst of orange flame appears…" (p. 244)

(Photo © Charles Eiseman)

Chapter Three

Changing Spring

January 17, 2013
Signs of Hope?

Like the spring in Washington, I am eager to burst forth early this year. My little clump of snowdrops under the azalea out front has been in bloom for over a week. The large swath of snowdrops at the house near Suburban Hospital has since January 6 carpeted the pachysandra there as if snow has fallen. But there is none. A couple of decades ago when my daughter's appendix burst and she was rushed to Suburban on February 11, the snowdrops were just emerging. As I walk the neighborhood and roam to downtown meetings, I see forsythia in spots and the tips of flowers emerging everywhere. My lawn is muddy; there is no winter crunch beneath my feet. Robins are arriving, birds are calling, the mornings are filled with fog that burns off and brings the feel of Northern California. Temperatures are in the fifties and sixties. My winter overcoat hangs limp and lifeless in the closet. I have seen a lone, symbolic eagle soaring far above my home.

Yet I am more ambivalent than ever about these wonderful weeks of vernal winter weather that open up another year. I chat with neighbors about the lovely days at hand; I revel in the lack of ice and snow, the smells of early springtime, or perhaps of autumn, that are redolent in the air. But I must work to push down a deepening dread. Nature is my solace and my balm, my gateway to things eternal. My grandchildren, Catherine and Alex, who are five and three, already consult the Audubon bird app that's nestled in my Nook. They know and love goldfinches and butterflies and other beauties that surround us. They play with watery Audubon whistles that produce a gurgle of bird calls; they help me fill my feeders. They take note of deer that emerge from Rock Creek Park and wander by their house. They love the zoo, the beach, the things that I have taken for granted all my life. But all that is now at risk from global climate change. I read a study showing that Thoreau's careful notes on flowers in New England allow researchers to calculate that spring was nearly a month later in New England than it now arrives. How can one be a Transcendentalist in the face of tragic trends in temperature?

As might have been predicted, the shock of Superstorm Sandy that covered most of the eastern United States and devastated whole neighborhoods in New Jersey and New York is already wearing off. Attempts by congressional Republicans from elsewhere in the country to block federal disaster aid at the end of the 112th Congress enraged even conservative Long Island Republican congressmen like Peter King. King launched into a tirade against the stupidity and heartlessness of his fellow penny-pinchers that only a New Yorker could produce. Wall Street was closed, lower Manhattan and its subways flooded, parts of Queens looked like London during the blitz, or beautiful Beirut after it was bombed. Sandy's savage swath will put climate change in the news once more my environmentalist friends assure me. It will be at the top of newly re-elected President Obama's agenda this time around. Perhaps. That is what everyone said after Hurricane Katrina tore up the Gulf Coast, killed an estimated two thousand people, and left nearly a million Americans homeless in 2005.

And so I look for signs of hope, or something to sustain me, as I make my rounds in the natural suburban and urban settings that we have created throughout the United States. They are not the patches of wilderness that have somehow been saved since Captain John Smith and others first explored them. They are not the dwindling rural landscapes and towns that Thoreau saw in the mid-nineteenth century and thought so crowded. But they are better than the malarial swamps of the nineteenth-century recorded in Washington by Elliot Coues and others; they are not the pollution-filled skies that were the backdrop for Louis Halle's bike rides to the birds along the Potomac at the end of World War II. He and Rachel Carson and Roger Tory Peterson and other members of the Audubon Naturalist Society helped save the eagles and the Ospreys that virtually disappeared in the decades after the war. DDT and other pesticides were sprayed almost everywhere—as if we knew how to intervene and control the course of nature. The heirs of these environmentalists and others are still at work. But so is the human hubris and the push for profits that wrought havoc on ecosystems and people then and still are at work today. We are in a race against time to save every species now—including ourselves. I can no longer take simple, pure delight in nature as did others in the twentieth century and long before. I must choose how I see and feel about these things—an eagle or egret, a butterfly or blossom.

January 20, 2013
Inaugural Celebration?

Washington is abuzz about President Obama's second inauguration and its convergence with the birthday celebration of Martin Luther King, Jr. The weather is more typical of winter Washington—mild by New England and Midwestern standards, cold enough for wimpy Washingtonians to whine about a little. This year the politics seem more important than a year ago with its predictable, trivial, race horse coverage of the traditional early primaries in small, virtually all-white states. The news was the lack of traditional white snow backdrops for photo ops in New Hampshire. Now a splendid movie version of Lincoln's decision to introduce the Emancipation Proclamation has multiple Oscar nominations; there is much discussion of Obama's newly-discovered Lincolnesque qualities. I am headed to an inaugural brunch to host a reception for new senators and members who support diplomacy and non-proliferation of weapons over war, and then to dance and shout at the environmentalists' inaugural Green Ball. Caryn and I stand not ten feet from Vice President Joe Biden; he gives a rousing, short speech perfect for the environmentalists arrayed before him who have shed their backpacks and binoculars for fancy formal wear. But the massacre in Newtown, Connecticut of sixteen elementary school students at close range with a semi-automatic AR-15 assault weapon has properly provoked grief and anger from the public and the president. It is little wonder that concern for the climate is hard to focus on.

January 21, 2013
The Second Inaugural: John Burroughs and the Birds

President Obama and Vice President Biden are officially sworn in on Sunday in private ceremonies on January 20, the mandated inaugural day; the public swearing in and celebration is held on Monday. I have a ticket to be in a section of onlookers just below the ceremony and the seats for dignitaries. Again the weather is a Washingtonian mild, winter day. Temperatures reach about forty degrees. The Obamas exit their motorcade to walk down parts of Pennsylvania Avenue. But it feels cold as I wait and wait and wait at a security checkpoint before I can get onto the Capitol grounds. I am surrounded by a marvelously diverse crowd of ticket holders; we are a cross section of America and I chat ami-

cably with more African Americans than I meet in a year, with
Latinos, Asian Americans, with the young and old, obese and slim.
I even end up near friends from Connecticut whom I had tried to
find at the Green Ball, but could not. I try to amuse (and astound)
my fellow celebrants with inaugural trivia like the fact that the
longest inaugural address ever given was not by Bill Clinton, but
by William Henry Harrison. Old Tippecanoe spoke over eight
thousand words for nearly two hours on a very cold day back when
inaugurations were held in March and Washington was colder. He
caught pneumonia and died forty-one days later. But I do not share
my secret fears that Obama may, like Lincoln, die in office, too.
One eerie photo of his second inauguration (he was sworn in on
the east Capitol steps, we are on the west) shows John Wilkes
Booth in attendance on the balcony and stalking Lincoln from
above. But I squelch these thoughts and fight back tears, as I hear
Myrlie Evers, widow of the murdered civil rights leader, Medgar
Evers, speak, and a 240-voice choir from Brooklyn sings Julia Ward
Howe's stirring Union anthem, "The Battle Hymn of the Repub-
lic". President Obama echoes Jefferson and Lincoln and makes the
threat of global warming a highlight of his speech. His words ignite
and invigorate the huge crowd of some one million people.

My mood and motivation are elevated by this principled,
patriotic pageantry. There may yet be hope. My thoughts grow
lighter, easier. I muse that John Burroughs may have stood and
taken notes during Lincoln's second inauguration not far from
where I stand and walk. But somehow he still sought out nature
on that day; after Lincoln's historic speech, Burroughs headed out
to hike and look at birds. On March 4, Inauguration Day, he
notes, "After the second memorable inauguration of President
Lincoln, took my very first trip of the season. The afternoon was
very clear and warm,—real vernal sunshine at last, though the
wind roared like a lion over the woods. It seemed novel enough
to find within two miles of the White House a simple woodsman

chopping away as if no President was being inaugurated!... This day, for the first time, I heard the song of the Canada sparrow, a soft, sweet note, almost running into a warble."

John Burroughs was close friends with Walt Whitman and must have heard battle sounds and seen and smelled the wounded and the maimed who filled Washington in the spring of 1864. Victory for the United States was still not yet assured. By July, the rebel general Jubal Early and his troops were visible to Lincoln, who had to be pulled down amidst Confederate fire while monitoring battles from ramparts at Fort Stevens. Yet Burroughs wrote throughout this mayhem about veeries and verdant woods. Perhaps romantic environmentalists were not so naïve after all. Perhaps they learned to find solace, as well as celebration, in the spring.

February 4, 2013
Goodbye, Currier & Ives

I have been to a family birthday celebration in Mentor, Ohio, along Lake Erie, to be reminded of what winter is really all about. It is as lovely as a scene from Currier & Ives. In the evenings, full moonlight glistens on the breast of six to eight inches of powdery, new fallen snow. On the way here, red barns and dark old ones that still have MAIL POUCH TOBACCO painted on their sides stand beside silos along Route 44. The snowy, sedate scenes symbolize a long-past, soon-to-be forgotten America. Fir trees of all sorts show boughs laden with layers and layers of snow—shining and shaded—by some artist's hand. Chickadees and goldfinches hang from branches and from feeders. Brilliant red cardinals pose for their Hallmark moments, standing out against the greens and whites. But before long, the sub-freezing temperatures begin to rise. The morning we leave Ohio, there is a light and drifting rain. Grand stalactites of ice that hang from my sister-in-law's eaves begin to shrivel in the morning fog and drizzle. The snow is shrinking, turning into slush. We drive back to Washington in wind and rain and mist on slippery, not quite icy, roads. As we wind down through Pennsylvania and northern Maryland, the roadside snow thins, becomes a light cover, and starts to disappear. The green of prematurely early spring, though mottled, begins to reappear.

In Bethesda, the weather has been as confused as my consciousness. There is a wintry stretch of days just below freezing where everyone seems to have some strain of flu. Two small snowfalls of barely a couple of inches apiece put Washington in a tizzy. They drive me into my storehouse of a garage searching in the clutter for idle ice scrapers and snow brushes on arm-length handles. But the snow soon begins to melt. There is no need to shovel. No sleds, no snowmen, no scenes from Currier & Ives. Sunny days burn off morning fog, bring out scooters, basketballs, boys, and runners in short pants. January has been something of a replay of 2012. Daffodils are sprouting up, a few have visible buds weeks ahead of time. The Lenten roses in my yard have full mauve buds ready to burst wide open. There are flocks of robins moving everywhere. A Cooper's Hawk flies straight into my yard while I am at my study window. It wheels sharply as if to snatch its prey or simply to avoid collision with the glass. But it is as close as I have ever been to a hunting hawk in flight. My mind snaps a photo and holds the hawk in freeze frame, like a first-prize entry in *National Wildlife* or in *Audubon*. The wings and feathers are spread wide apart, turning, braking, full of tan and white and stripes. I gasp in awe and in surprise. I tell my wife who feels somewhat cheated that she has missed this sight. She is at home to pack and leave to give a speech in tiny, mountainous Andorra.

But before she goes, my spirit bird appears at our front window. I am not superstitious, nor is she, but how to account for the sudden appearance as we are together, talking of the wonders of nature and why we love it, of a Pileated Woodpecker six feet from where we stand? It is pounding, drilling, chiseling where it once appeared last year on the gnarled and split weeping cherry we planted by the window. But this bird seems bigger, stronger, more spectacular than the one I saw alone. Perhaps it is the very same bird grown into full adulthood, or its parent, or simply a different visitor. Who knows? We grab binoculars and stare as if holding this miraculous specimen within our hands. Small chunks of cherry wood fly off; small holes appear and then enlarge. Our pileated twists its head and bill; it probes. And then, just as suddenly, it is gone. We have not moved; we've barely breathed. We wonder at its disappearance. And then we see a walker and her dog stroll into view. Our transcendental time has ended.

February 6, 2013
Sputtering Toward Spring

The sun and temperatures are rising toward the mid-forties as I head out for my morning walk. I hear crows and then red bellies laughing in the trees. I stop to watch a comic Song Sparrow attempt again to let out a full-bodied "Hip, hip, hooray, boys! Spring is here again!!" The other day he managed only a series of strangled "hips" that sounded more like the chirps of a House Sparrow. The would-be songster shook and sputtered and hopped about, but no more than a few frantic sparrow sounds ever emerged. Today there is a series of actual "hips," but no gleeful, long "hoorays!!" I am reminded of Louis Halle, as I was last year, not far from here, when thanks to his observations in *Spring in Washington*, I first noticed a Song Sparrow trying to herald in the spring.

There are other signs as well. Many yards, including my own, have daffodils spiking noticeably above the bare ground; a number of them have pregnant buds bulging to be delivered, it seems, sometime in February. There are gray, wooly buds, like larger pussy willows, on the lovely deciduous magnolia that stands in a small traffic island on my walk. I watch one squirrel, and then another, munch happily on the first reddish buds of maple trees working up toward bloom. There are small yellow flowers in some gardens, the tops of crocuses and hyacinths are poking through the ground. But much is still and bare and brown. Too soon, even in these times, for spring to be declared. Spring is a perhaps hand, waiting to fully uncurl, unclench. But a slap of winter, a last clenched fist is still a possibility. And so I look carefully, hopefully, at times like these. I notice things more on the cusp of change, in the dying days of frail winter, than I do amidst a bower. I wonder why after all the robins that I have seen so far, there have been none around today. I pause to watch a Red-bellied Woodpecker work its way high up in a tree. And then, of course, a few scattered robins do show up, as if reading my mind's lament. I hear more of them ahead.

A Feast of Robins

I round a corner into full southern sunlight and the sights and sounds of robins everywhere. They are chuckling, chirping, flying in and out. Red breasts are a deep red-orange in the sun, slate backs and tails with white are flashing as they fly. The locus, or the lure, of all this robin racket is a single large holly bush, laden with berries, spotlighted by the sun, standing in front of a new, manicured mansion on the corner. No matter. I have never seen a robin feast like this before. There are dozens hanging, gobbling, flying in and out of this one small and sumptuous tree. Some seem to eat a single berry and then depart. But others take bigger second helpings. Then I watch one pluck and swallow six! Whether these robins are arriving as early signs of spring, or live throughout the year in balmy Bethesda, I can't be sure. But as I marvel at this display, I see one robin with a tiny hot pink band upon its leg.

Some ornithologist somewhere has banded this plump robin, presumably to find out where and why and how it spends the winter.

I will try to find out how to report my find. Scientists have depended on the observations, Christmas counts, and feeder records of amateurs like me for several generations. I don't see any other banded red breasts, even though they continue to land in this single holly, braking sharply like jets on an aircraft carrier. The word has spread both far and near. I fear this lovely ornamental holly will soon be stripped quite bare. There are red berries on the sidewalk, a sort of red, oval shadow of the holly's shape near the edge of lawn. I notice, too, that my robins are unconcerned by passersby walking their dogs this morning, or by noisy trucks, or airplanes, or even me as I creep ever closer to the clamor. The robins snap up berries whole in a single gulp. They do not hold them, chew them, or show signs of any sort of swallow. These ordinary holly berries, turned into banquet fare, just simply disappear. As I stand and watch, I notice other birds I'd missed before. Blue Jays call and fly about. There are nuthatches and chickadees even on the highly orna-mental paper birches that have been planted on this perfect, pam-pered lawn. Their brown patches of cloth-like bark flap like tiny flags in a steady morning breeze. Then I hear a jay cry out a warning call. I guiltily think it's me, or maybe some unseen dog and walker arriving once again. But a shadow passes overhead. I look up to see it is a Black Vulture sailing by. These carrion eaters do not prey on living birds like these. The robins, jays, and chickadees soon return to feast and frolic. It is a false alarm. But nature has its own pre-cautionary principle to avoid disaster. By the time even a sharp-eyed Blue Jay would decide whether the looming shadow is a vulture or a deadly hawk, any warning would be too late.

February 8, 2013
The Return of the Robins

The news is full of talk of a record blizzard bearing down on the Northeast. Planes and trains are cancelled in advance, emergencies declared. Two feet, three feet of snow, pushed by high winds, may swirl over the most densely settled part of the nation. But no talk of climate change and extreme weather events, of course, amidst the interruptions for alerts, the predictable chatter from worried, well-coiffed anchor men and women, and cheery predictions of disaster from the toothsome weather forecasters in Washington. Amidst such cheery, dreary news it is hard to apprehend that we are not likely to see much more than some overnight cool rain. I am worried about Caryn getting home from her speech to the Council of Europe's conference of higher education rectors and ministers in Andorra amidst the Pyrenees. She has to fly back through Newark, near New York City. All the chatter is of closings, cancellations there. It is time to clear my head and at least enjoy the warming trend that is now the new normal here in Bethesda.

Things are as before. Fairly quiet, bare, with the only signs of spring those that must be sought out and spotted. As I head into the cut-through, a long-closed off street gone green that I call Peter Rabbit Land, I am focused on a pair of dogs being walked on the narrow path before me. No chance of early rabbits or even birds right now I mutter to myself, when, once again, nature contradicts my grudging thoughts. It is like the other day a few blocks away. Even as the dogs are still in sight, I notice a couple of robins poking at the ground. A few more fly into view. I stop as the dogs depart, down past the rain garden at the end of the path. Come summer and early fall, it will be filled with huge Joe Pye weed, turtlehead, purple New England aster, goldenrod, and other good, weedy stuff. To the left is a long, low line, or hedge, of holly bushes, backed by roses. It is a gorgeous, impenetrable thicket where Peter, Flopsy, Mopsy, Cottontail, and the others hang out in real springtime and in summer.

Robins, as I look more closely, appear from everywhere. They are hopping and poking at nearby lawns, perched high above my head, clucking from inside a big old maple. And on a large holly, laden with tight clusters of berries at the end of the hedge, across from the rain garden, and Mr. McGregor's neat, wire-fenced gardens, there are robins. They dangle like ornaments, sit still for portraits, and swallow berries in huge numbers. They cover the small, bare dogwood across the street and one nearby. It is robin heaven—a single holly Holy Grail! I stay awhile and watch. No pink leg bands do I see. And how and why and when the robins come and go and have had their fill, I have no way of knowing. Time passes. I am in some sort of heaven, too.

Early Easter

When I end up at home, I do a few dishes and look at the feeders past my kitchen window with a pretty pastiche or potpourri of winter birds: juncos, white-throats, finches, chickadees, cardinals, burnished goldfinches, a nuthatch or two, and my own pair of Song Sparrows who have yet to utter a peep, let alone attempt a "hip, hip hooray, boys!" Then, what to my wondering eyes should appear, but Flopsy, or Mopsy, who has followed me here!

I take my rabbit to be some sort of sign of early spring, though it seems extremely early for the actual Easter Bunny to appear. But then I remember that Passover and Easter, celebrated with the changing annual appearances of the Paschal full moon, will be particularly early this year. I smile satisfied with this semi-scientific explanation that I will share with my grandchildren when next I read them *Tales of Peter Rabbit* and explain how and when the Easter Bunny can deliver eggs. (Like Santa Claus, he has many "helpers" like this one that may not be the actual, more magical Easter Bunny). I alleviate my guilt at such superstitious stuff by recalling that Beatrix Potter was a serious scientist as well as a painter and children's author, that Rachel Carson believed that the most essential trait to cultivate in children was a "sense of wonder." I smile again and turn back to my dishes.

February 9, 2013
Crocus Crowns

As I step out to check for mail, I see a half-flat tire on my Honda. Checking the others, I see that the once proud, pricey, and indestructible Michelins on our humble Honda that Caryn drives need to be, er, recycled. My afternoon walk becomes to and from the tire place on Old Georgetown Road, though I take my normal nature route most of the way to get there. As I walk back, I come to the same holly by Peter Rabbit's home. It is almost a burning bush, afire with late, slanting sun and flashing robins! There are so many berries on this bush that the ravenous robins still seem to have hardly reduced the rich, red clusters that I have previously thought of mainly as holiday decorations. I murmur a quick few words of astonishment, or maybe prayer, that this tiny corner of a suburban home can provide such providence.

As I head home, I stop, back up, and stare at a brownish sloping lawn. Four light blue crocuses have opened on this sunny side of the street. It is the earliest I have ever seen them. They are pointed like a prince's coronet, not full and cupped like the purple crowns soon to follow. Regal indeed! Has spring truly arrived? With our changing, variable climate it is hard to say. But I smile and think back to graduate school and how prospective students from the East and California found Northwestern balmy and beautiful; they had been lured to apply when they visited in May and saw crocuses, daffodils, and tulips all around. They had yet to see Lake Michigan frozen solid with ice outcroppings sculpted by the fearsome wind. It was along that lakeside in the late 1960s that I first saw masses of small, silvery, stinking fish—alewives—dead along the shore in summer. It was when I first read Barry Commoner's *Closing Circle* and began to think about ecology, as well as war.

I look again at my first crocuses. I am smiling, happy at the nearness of even an unnaturally early spring. I once again squelch down thoughts of climate change, catastrophe. But as I savor such tiny, royal beauties, Shakespeare's *Henry IV* slips unbidden inside my head: "Uneasy sits the head that wears a crown."

February 11, 2013
Sunset in Bethesda

My retired neighborhood acquaintance, Paul, from when I used to ride the Metrobus, is walking his old, unusually calm Welsh terrier, Duncan, on his normal rounds. Duncan simply lies down, relaxed, sprawled out like a cat, in the middle of the street. Paul asks me excitedly (that is, excitedly for a former Ph.D. researcher at the Congressional Research Service) if I have seen the Barred Owl that frequents our street less than a block from my house! Caryn and I had seen one in the autumn on an evening stroll and showed it, shared binoculars, with those who stopped and asked what we were looking at. It did not occur to us that a Barred Owl might actually reside or be a frequent visitor on Irvington Avenue. Paul tells me he usually sees it at dusk or twilight in a large tree behind the third house from the end of the block, a brick one on the western side.

When Caryn comes home from work, I tell her that we must look for this magnificent woodland bird. I am impatient and head out at about quarter of six. The sun will officially set at 5:49 p.m., (EST). We are armed with warm clothes, flashlights, binoculars, and hope. Together, experienced birders both, we scan the tree behind the neighbor's house, creep forward like burglars on the lawn next door for a better view. The tree is bare, the Barred Owl missing. But as we look up to the west, a large section of the sky can be seen between the houses; it is ablaze with bright, glowing streaks of deep, pinkish orange. We instinctively gasp, then noiselessly hold our breaths, as if afraid to scare away such divine display. We touch, stand close, lean into each other. Other sunsets rush through my mind when Caryn and I have shared such transcendental and romantic moments: lying on the rocks atop Cadillac Mountain on the shore of Maine; candlelight dinner at the end of the Cabot Trail in Nova Scotia; by a sea bulwark beneath a lighthouse beam in Brittany. Simply the hope of an owl has brought us here tonight, has transfigured our suburb, has transformed us once again.

February 17, 2013
Global Warming in the Cold

It is real winter once again in Washington, a frigid, blustery day like those recorded in mid-February by Louis Halle right after the war when he and Rachel Carson became friends, were still alive, and young. I put on layers beneath my warmest topcoat and pull a knit Defenders of Wildlife cap down around my ears. I am headed to the largest climate change rally ever to be held. As I come up out of the Smithsonian Metro station and walk on to the Mall, bursts of wind and roaring crowds strike me simultaneously. It was in the twenties in the morning; now past noon it reaches thirty-five. The sun battles with scattered clouds to see if this day will be labeled cloudy or sunny or simply in-between. Because temperatures have been in the forties and even fifties for quite some time, the ground is not yet frozen. There is no crunch beneath my shoes. I put my shoulder to the wind and head toward the American History Museum across the Mall where I may be somewhat shielded by the buildings. I smile and chat with some older demonstrators already headed home. Even an hour of such exposure has been too much for them.

I push on toward the sound of the crowd to the right of the Washington Monument ahead. The flags that surround it are stretched full, as if painted, pointing in the wind. I cross onto the Monument grounds, past banks of porta-potties, more flags whose flapping and slapping is audible now, even amidst the din of a demonstration. Some forty thousand people have assembled here.

There are printed posters, handmade signs, banners from churches and colleges—many of my American University students, on their own initiative, are somewhere here. The ground is surprisingly muddy. I am sorry I have not worn my boots. I make my way gingerly, but easily, through the milling throng. The crowd is in a mostly upbeat, somewhat festive mood despite the chill, despite decades of inaction on global climate change. There are families, strollers, babies swaddled in blankets, young people who can somehow stand around without a hat, armed only with a backpack and belief. All seem certain that their action is historic.

A year ago, twelve thousand surrounded the White House and urged President Obama to postpone the building of the Keystone XL pipeline. It is meant to carry oil squeezed out of tar sands in Canada all the way to the Gulf of Mexico where, ironically, most of it will be shipped overseas for sale. Obama listened, or so these folks believe. We all have been organized to come by environmental and religious groups—350.org, the Sierra Club, Natural Resources Defense Council, Interfaith Power and Light, and many, many more. The pipeline has not been truly stopped and so Obama must be urged again. The crowd hopes that perhaps, once and for all, after Katrina, and droughts, and forest fires, and floods, and Superstorm Sandy, and a record blizzard in New England, policymakers and the press and the president will grasp the meaning of our ability to change the entire planet's climate for the worse.

February 20-22, 2013
Similes of Spring

It has been mostly blustery cold, though not extremely so, as the sun draws us steadily toward March. I am teaching and writing, so walking less. Winter reigns, despite the buds and green. I make a stew and Caryn and I eat it with some wine by a roaring, romantic fire, heedless, at least for now, of CO_2 emissions, particulates, dioxin. The night is starry with Orion's belt, a painted, Art Nouveau half-moon, set off by one bright planet. In the morning, by my window, the Cooper's Hawk, shot from a crossbow, streaks past my window. Still no songbirds trapped in its talons. My guilt eases a bit since I have hung a new knit bag with nyger seed in full view of my kitchen. This act of generosity is really so I can better stand and watch the goldfinches that my grandson now loves as they are lured in for easy food.

I venture out to mail some bills and letters and hear my first full-throated, glorious Song Sparrow rendition of "Hip, hip hooray, boys! Spring is here again!" The striped songster must be one of the reticent, silent ones who hop around in my backyard in the oak leaves beneath the feeder. It is happily, dizzily perched atop the azalea by my driveway near the street where my huge crop of Shasta daisies will emerge in the latter days of spring. I watch the head thrown back, the throat revealed beneath this wondrous warble. It is more than the somewhat stronger sun and milder air that warms my heart and starts me in to whistle.

The next day is milder still, though fairly brisk and breezy. I pick up the New York Times and Washington Post from off the lawn. And there, undisturbed, using my azalea for its stage, is my suddenly spring-filled Song Sparrow shouting to the neighbors, "Hip hip, hooray, boys! Spring is here again!" I am filled with joy, pride, and a little competitive satisfaction that this bird likes me and my yard. It is my Song Sparrow, heralding in the spring. Last year, a Song Sparrow (perhaps this one or its sibling or descendant?) sang in springtime atop a finial on my neighbor's picket fence across the street. I am a bit embarrassed at my thoughts, but still smile and skip a bit, newspapers swinging from their plastic bags, as I head back into the house. This one is mine! I want to record this fact somehow, as if I own a bird refuge and a sign-in book beside the ranger's desk, "Seen: Feb. 22 and 23 near Musil gatehouse at entrance to park—first fully singing Song Sparrow!" But such things are normally not recorded. They are common enough after all. Later, as the day grows warmer, I see a pair of Song Sparrows from my window darting about and chasing back and forth. I think I detect come hither flicks of tail and wing, but again I can't be sure. I can't even tell male from female Song Sparrows. Am I reading too much into very early spring and these saucy sparrows seeking out each other?

A similar set of thoughts occupies me far too long as I watch a titmouse land inside the metal Sears 1960s awning that shades the sun porch outside my study. Pearl grey above and white below, a neat, small crest, and a huge dark eye, like that of a deer, lends this backyard bird its cuteness, its allure. It hops methodically, like a carpenter or architect, about its work, examining, measuring, probing each alternating, raised metal slat with its small corner, each one laid out in a row across the inner awning. This is where my House Finches used to nest before they were wiped out by some disease more than a decade ago, only now returning to their former numbers. I spent happy hours watching them build and daub their nests, seeing the incredibly wide, gaping, smiling beaks of baby finches waiting to be fed. Carolina Wrens check out my awning, too, though none have nested here. The awning has cobwebs and perhaps some tiny mites or bugs. Is this friendly titmouse searching carefully through each little corner for some food, or is this nesting behavior I want to see since it fits my simile of spring?

February 24, 2013
Early Signs of Spring at Great Falls

It reaches into the fifties today in the late afternoon on a bright, sunny day. There is talk of more snowstorms, blizzards on the Great Plains and in New England, but here in Maryland it is early spring. Contradictions abound. Outside, there are dads pulling red wagons with kids left over from *Dick and Jane*, sounds of bouncing balls, bird song in the background, like surround sound from the Dolby speakers in some big theater showing "Spring!" I am taking Caryn out to Dulles to head off into uncertain weather in Ohio and a trip to Louisville, in the style of modern airlines, through Detroit. As I return, I turn off at the last minute from River Road toward Great Falls by MacArthur Boulevard and the one-lane bridge, originally a Civil War-era aqueduct, built by Montgomery Meigs.

I pull up and chat at the park entry with Betsy, the friendly ranger, and ask if there are skunk cabbages that I can get to on foot. Since I have acted on impulse simply to get outdoors, I am without bicycle, binoculars, camera, proper hat, any nature gear at all. She tells me, as I had thought, that there are lots of them in the ravine you can peer into as you exit the park on the right-hand passenger's side. Last year, sometime in March or April I suppose, I caught a glimpse by car of low, large, broad-leaved plants alongside a tiny stream. I want to see them, one of the earliest signs of spring within any wet woods. They were duly noted by Louis Halle, my *Spring in Washington* mentor and guide, as he rode about in February almost sixty years ago.

Since I cannot park along the road, I set out on foot and head into the ravine some 100 yards from the ranger shack as you leave the Great Falls Park. There are oak leaves everywhere alongside a tiny stream or muddy rivulet that heads downhill toward the Potomac, the canal, and Betsy's ranger shack. Along the muddy, rich dark brown edges of this barely moving, meandering run-off water, I see my first tightly-curled, twisted cone of purplish green and black, with small stripes or black striations. It is a skunk cabbage pushing through the leaves. Another, half unfurled, stands nearby in the middle of this muddy, minute body of trickling water. And then another and another! I kneel down in my city shoes, like Richard Nixon in wingtips on his beach.

I am carried back to childhood on Long Island when I first saw skunk cabbage from a small boardwalk through some swampy woods at Tackapausha Nature Preserve, somewhere near Ocean-side or Massapequa. My Mom had brought me there to see and feel more nature—Red-winged Blackbirds dangling from cattails and these ancient, primeval-looking plants. It was the name that first got my attention—that a plant could be compared to a noto-riously stinky mammal. And the fact that later these purple and green, striped Carvel cones would have large leaves and a pungent, putrid smell. It is the sort of thing that captures a small boy's imagination; it has brought me here today. As I walk upstream, more cabbages appear, some near my feet. I walk care-fully now, all within a foot or two of the only mud and water here beneath the park entrance road; none of these skunks give off any smell at all. There is a fresh breeze, blue sky. Shades of sere and buff and brown with occasional bursts of green are restful to my eyes and to my soul.

Satisfied, I stroll back into the park past the big white 1889 canal-side tavern, across the small wooden bridge at Lock 20, and onto the slightly soft, moist, but not quite muddy towpath. There are people everywhere on this festive, fecund February day. Young couples, oldsters with walkers and wheelchairs, families with small kids chasing back and forth, small dogs on leashes, a Jack Russell sniffs around my shoes. Beneath us roars the river over rocks and rocky inlets, powerful, noisy, full of melted snow from far up river and the rains that have fallen here. On the other side, the canal is drained, all empty and forlorn. The canal barge, the Chester F. Mercer, sits beached like some old whale. I head onto the path that leads to Olmsted and Fall Islands and the classic view of the Great Falls. For years Caryn and I had hung in our house a large, reproduction nineteenth-century print of the falls in an antique frame we bought for a pittance from a dealer in a barn. Far above me circle a flock of unidentified, very white, sea gulls. Closer to me is a set of seven sailing Black Vultures, their white tips and short tails standing out in sunshine. These are part of that scary band that roosts by Riley's Lock, I at first suppose. But then I simply watch how at ease they are, how much fun they seem to have, as they soar above the tavern.

When unusual or spectacular birds or views are scarce, I notice things around me I haven't seen before. On the boardwalk, and then the narrow bridge, over a roaring section of the river that has carved out its own gorge, I feel a sense of awe up close to nature's power. Children run across in a sort of mock fear, or cling to the rail, or, if feeling brave, look down curiously as if they're at a movie. In a few more feet things grow still again. The land is marked by lichen covered granite, often split apart in boulders and in blocks. In the shelter of the rocks, thin dirt supports weedy stalks and other growth, some cedars and some pines. Not much to look at, some might say, unless the park signs did not call attention to the rules to stay on the boardwalk. We are in a special, fragile ecological zone—a dry floodplain forest. The first sign I see explains with helpful pictures that there are Midwestern Prairie grasses here like those the prairie schooners, covered wagons, saw. Big bluestem and little bluestem are prairie grasses that Native Americans who lived in the area used for grain. John Smith would have eaten some as he dined near here with his friendly local hosts. Now the bluestems are simply tall, grassy sticks with dangling bits of dried up flowers and grain. Further on there are wild oats, the kind that young men sow, a clichéd metaphor that takes on meaning here. They are scattered randomly about, tucked behind boulders, growing where they can find just a little soil to land on and seek shelter from the storms.

I cross another bridge, more thunderous water underneath and all around me. I, too, hang on the rail. I gaze out at a rocky valley and the real river in the distance. I have seen bluebirds here in somewhat warmer, actual days of spring. I picture them, a small group of hunched blue and white and rosy small birds, perched idly in a stunted pine beside the rushing, roiling water. I think, too, of old-time birders who have walked and hiked here long before today. Every author that I know has stood upon this spot. Rachel Carson, Roger Tory Peterson, Louis Halle, and real old timers like Florence Merriam Bailey, her brother Hart, and other early members of the DC Audubon Society, maybe even Teddy Roosevelt himself.

I stand at the rail in front of the large boulder around which the boardwalk is built at the end of the trail. I see other gawkers on the Virginia side perched on a wooden outlook also peering at the rapids. Usually in full spring, there are Great Blue Herons fishing here, oblivious to the dangers of the water and the warning signs nearby. There are none today. Perhaps blue herons are more sensible than we. There are, incredibly enough, two kayakers paddling madly in wetsuits, trying to get upstream toward the falls so that they can hurtle down the rapids and get the adrenaline rush we humans get from sports. Above them, circling patiently, is a pair of Turkey Vultures—larger, more familiar than their distant cousins, the black ones in the park. These buzzards rock back and forth on larger, feathered wings that make a V-shaped silhouette. The kayakers struggling against the mighty waters never see this pair of vultures; I hope they never do.

Each person who surveys this patch of wildness not far from Washington sees some different sight. Artistic, awesome, outdoors adventure, a special ecosystem that should be saved. My mind races through all these perceptions and personas and comes to rest upon a bluish-grey bronze historic plaque, rich with weather and patina. It is bolted into the central boulder that marks the spot where this scene was savored and set aside through the work of the noted American landscape architect, Frederick Law Olmsted, Jr. He is the designer of Rock Creek Park, Yosemite, Acadia and more. It says simply that Olmsted was the head of the Park Commission and that he saved Great Falls and its surrounding gorge.

Each time I see this plaque in different times of year, I want to grab the tourists and the hikers and the families here and shout, "Don't you see what it takes? What we owe? How we must do the same for future generations?" That's usually when I imagine myself as some sort of crank on a soap box in Hyde Park, with a beard as long as that of John Burroughs or John Muir. If I blurt out or shout at those arranged around the boardwalk, I would scare the living daylights out of every single child. That's when I smile at the image of one part of me that lurks inside. I pause, lift my camera or my binoculars, and simply admire the plunging falls.

The sun is lower now and it is getting cold. I walk back to my car and warm up, take some notes. As I drive slowly away, I glance down into my ravine and see small sprouting purplish buds beside a tiny stream. As I slow and look, of course, four white-tailed deer walk by. They are barely visible, mostly tails and slow motion as they pick up their feet carefully, gently, searching through the oak leaves, as I have done. I feel some small kinship I cannot name. I thank the smelly plants and memories that have brought me here. As I drive slowly along the Cabin John wooded parkway, a huge full moon looms low, just above the trees. It is the Lenten Moon, as round and large and rich with markings as a single silver dollar. Easter and Passover are indeed early this year. The Paschal Full Moon is still a lunar month away. But for me, at this moment, it is time to celebrate.

March 8, 2013
Nipped in the Bud

It has been normal winter weather in Washington for the past couple of weeks. Normal, that is, by the standards of the warmed-up past decade. Temperatures are mostly in the forties, with a couple of days around fifty degrees. The birds are calling, chasing, happy. Flowers keep pushing visibly upward, starting to bud. A few small yellow flowers can be seen. And the sun seems brighter. But it is often windy and feels chillier than I would like. I am busy teaching, finishing details on an academic book burdened with footnotes and photo credits. My nature walks and rides seem to recede with my winter work obsessions. There is no talk of climate change or warmer winters now. There are huge snowstorms in the Midwest; Washington is promised another Snowmageddon as in 2010, the year my daughter was married amidst two feet of snow and ice. But the storm passes to our north and dumps its snow in New England once again. The federal government and schools are called off in advance, of course. Bethesda only suffers slush with snowflakes that turn to water when they hit the ground. The gutters run as if it is a rainstorm, even as the air is filled with gorgeous flakes. The next day, a scattered, thin patchy cover of less than a half inch of snow here and there melts off. The temperatures are back in the forties and reach nearly fifty today.

I take my first full walk in brilliant sunshine in the early afternoon. The sky is cerulean with hardly any clouds. Colors are bright, shadows from saplings and small trees point sharply to the north- northeast like organic, living sundials. My own patch of land has its first real flowers, as four yellow crocuses in the southeast garden bed out front reflect the sun. There are small bunches of crocuses everywhere—the purple ones that fill the neighbor's lawn and heralded spring last year. Pale, wan, light lavender ones in older, shaded lawns as if they had been planted in Edwardian times. There are a few clean white ones that look like wildflowers—anemone or bloodroot—seeking adventure in some sod. Then I see the first real daffodils; I think they are narcissi, peeking out from overgrown corners of the older homes whose owners seem no longer to garden, but whose spirit lives on in these surging bursts of spring. The old gardening styles seem rarer now—the crocuses, narcissi, lilacs, and tulip blades, the survivors of a passing era. The newer, super homes that fill up all their lots have little room or patience for puttering, potting, or pampering plants outside.

My suspicions, or perhaps my mood, are confirmed as I come to a corner that resembles an urban construction site—the sort I recall peering at in Manhattan as a child—with huge holes and mounds of dirt and giant machines making monstrous sounds. Here on my walk I come to the corner where an original, early 1940s Bethesda house has stood empty, abandoned for quite some time. All the huge, mature shade trees lay scattered in large piles like boulders. Now the site is surrounded by a line of big, highway department-sized dump trucks filled with soil and rubble. The yard itself is a huge gaping hole surrounded by gigantic dunes of dirt. A big steam shovel (it really is a tracked front-end scraper) gnaws out the final edges of the cavernous construction site. My heart is swallowed by this sink hole. I think back to my boyhood on Long Island and how sickened I felt when the frames of new homes had replaced the fields immediately behind my home where I roamed freely with my buddies amidst Queen Anne's lace and goldenrod, small trees, and space as far as one could see, to the next town, Mineola.

I soon come to other giant homes that have replaced more modest, historic 1940s models with their yards and trees and occupants who seemed to like outdoors. One is all framed out with doors, windows, just waiting for some siding. It, too, has destroyed all the huge, mature yellow poplar or tulip trees that stood majestic here. I begin to feel like Michael J. Fox in *Back to the Future* where he watches suburban sprawl eat up farmland and a small town decline into a semi-urban slum. I come to a small cottage-style original Bethesda home with peaked roofs and leaded windows that looks like something from a story book with ivied walls and a carefully tended yard and flowers. Next to it, once nearly identical, is another charming cottage. But this one has a yard stripped bare to carry out construction as it is rapidly transformed into a mansion. There is an entire new second story and three big dormers. And these are matched by another section with dormers as big as the original house protruding from the rear. It is a nice architectural feat. The signs say the house will be energy efficient and the new sections are done in the older style. But the house is now more than double the size of its splendid, classic little neighbor. This block is where I find my hickory nuts and saw my flocking robins, where I take pride in the rain gardens designed by an environmentalist friend who now has moved away. How long before the whole block is pared and pruned of greenery, its square footage, energy, materials, doubled in the name of modernity, then sold as sustainable and green?

There is increasing noise as a helicopter circles overhead, more trucks roar by and are joined by the recycling trucks that are a day late because of the "holiday" from the snow that did not fall. Ahead there is an awful grinding noise as I come upon a few men taking down small trees and pruning larger poplars, feeding the branches into a chopper. There are even more branches piled up waiting to be destroyed. The wood is fresh and up this close I can smell it and see the tulip buds just starting to open with the advent of spring. I warn my students against clichés like "nipped in the bud." But it is not a cold snap, deep, freezing weather, that has killed these growths before their time. We have done them in. As usual, I try to shake off such gloomy, post-modern thoughts to get back to tranquil transcendentalism. But the few robins I see landing atop the trees as the giant trucks pull off, the tiny cro-cuses poking through the older lawns, the brilliant Kodak skies and colors, seem insufficient in the face of this march of madness.

As I turn toward home and near the corner where I live, I see a small carcass in the road. A squirrel, I think, and plan to stride quickly by. I have come to love squirrels. I feed them and enjoy their acrobatic antics, their hoarding of nuts, their chases as wild as cop shows. But there are lots of them around; they do play loose with fate. When one dies, though sad, it will not be sorely missed. But as I near my corner, I see the long ears, the back paws, the soft brown fur of Peter Rabbit, or someone from his family, stretched out, his head the part that has been shattered, squashed by some heedless, speeding, passing car. I feel helpless, angry, sickened; I pick up my pace. My mind tells me there is nothing I can do. Scenes from my boyhood once again appear involuntarily. We are playing in Rick Corson's backyard, a new one that has encroached just a bit on the fields behind. Down in the freshly-mowed grass lie the bits and parts of a baby rabbit - the stomach is what I recall—chopped to bits like the buds and branches of a poplar tree. Nipped in the bud. Killed before its time.

March 12, 2013
Persephone and the Rite of Spring

It has stayed fairly cold and gusty—something like Le Mistral in southern France. I see a freshly killed red fox near where I always keep an eye out for live ones. It has been hit by a car along the road to Little Falls. Between the cutting of trees and roadkill, I am beginning to wonder if I simply delude myself about the possibilities for nature in the urbanizing United States. As usual, I try to shake off such thoughts; they seem to me to do no good. But I am not in a mood to herald in the spring. But a couple of events on Capitol Hill to welcome in new environmentally-friendly legislators helps a bit to snap my mood. I feel as if I am not alone. The District is somewhat warmer and sunnier than my usual haunts. Now there are bunches of daffodils, even hyacinths, nodding in the breeze. At home the crocuses multiply and pop up overnight like an old-time Disney film with Bolero in the background. For several days now there have been daffodils in my yard, though still somewhat tightly furled. There is myrtle in bloom and onion grass and budding trees and flowers. Each day, spring pushes up from beneath the earth—or is it carried in by zephyrs? There is a tremendous force at work that is pushing all of nature into resurrection where all seemed mostly dead. For Christians, of course, it is a time of reflection and a wilderness-seeking, searching time called Lent. The pagan roots of all this springtime stuff are clear as the sun gets stronger and the days lengthen and are propelled even further on by daylight savings time. There are frequent showers and the continued growth of green things everywhere. It is a power that seems unstoppable, that gave rise somehow to the old Greek goddess Persephone who oversees both death and renewal of the spring.

March 16, 2013
Goodbye to Winter?

Spring hangs in the balance. I am eager this year to savor it. Ruby-throated Hummingbirds migrate north from Mexico. They reached Maryland about this time last year. I wash my feeders carefully and hang them in their old spots near where the red and purple and nectar-laden flowers in my yard will emerge—cardinal flower, red salvia, lantana, honeysuckle (though I fear I may have pulled too much out to save my sagging, rotting backyard fence). I hang a wren house according to intricate directions that come with a darling little house like those described by Rachel Carson in her earliest juvenile story. Putting out birdhouses was first pushed and promulgated by junior Audubon clubs in the early twentieth century. My current version, purchased at Strosnider's, looks like a well-done school wood shop project, or one crafted by a handier backyard, grown-up Boy Scout. I am ready for spring. But today is cool and damp, gray and a little grim, despite the daffodils and early budding cherry trees around the neighborhood. The buds are a deep raspberry and as they open turn slowly into pink.

I have just attended a fundraiser in a gorgeous, large home in Kenwood, the section of Bethesda no more than two miles from my standard red brick colonial home where, in a few weeks, those in the know will gather for the spectacular display of Yoshino cherry trees that line the winding, slightly hilly streets and cul-de-sacs behind the Kenwood Country Club. The main roads there are boulevarded with a storybook stream running through. It will be covered with Washingtonians, Japanese tourists with cameras, and affluent neighborhood children learning about entrepreneurship with their homemade lemonade stands.

But as I peer out my kitchen window into the gray of March, I want to defy Persephone, hold back the tide of birds and bushes and berries, the bacchanal that is truly spring. I watch carefully and fondly at the birds around and beneath the feeders in the back. It is a winter scene without the snow or charm. It is something different, something in between my memories of snow and blizzards on Long Island and New England, and even in Bethesda in the nineties. Currier & Ives are just collector's items.

There are chickadees, cardinals, nuthatches, Downy Woodpeckers—the wonderful year-round birds of winter. There are Mourning Doves sitting, puffed slightly against the cold. How do these beautiful, partly iridescent birds with such succulent chests survive at all? They are still hunted; they are delicate dishes for the Cooper's Hawks, owls, and other predators that prowl the suburbs. I have only seen their nests once, looking down from my wife's office window back in Philadelphia. And yet these pigeon-like, tasty birds seem almost ubiquitous these days, their whirring wings, their sleek, swept-back, and jet-fueled flight a common sight. Their mournful cooing, their clinging to phone wires everywhere is comfort to my urban soul.

But it is two small "brown birds" that take my heart. They are among the earliest finds of my adult birding phase, while still a neophyte. There, hopping backwards, mechanically and somewhat comically in the leaves and mulch, is a pair of White-throated Sparrows. They seem familiar, even famous, to me now with their striped black and white referee caps atop a sparrow's body. I still think of my earliest sightings and bird song lessons in New England and Canada in the 1970s. While nesting or brooding or whatever it is that the birds (and the bees) actually do, the male sings a long, sweet song of tuneful, separate notes, though slightly scooped. In my first bird book, the expensive one from Canada, the song is described proudly in nationalistic terms as "Oh, Sweet Canada, Canada, Canada!" Cross some invisible line (well, go through customs...) and the American bird books claim, with slightly less nationalistic words, but with a hint of New England pride, or old family snobbery, that the white-throat really sings, "Old Sam Peabody, Peabody, Peabody!!" I wonder what my striped-cap friends are really saying as they mark off some nesting territory. But here in Bethesda, they are silent. Soon to be gone. We celebrate the happy arrival of the robins, yet fail to mark the sweet sorrow of the parting White-throated Sparrow.

The same is true for that other "little brown bird" that got me started down a long and convoluted birder's path. A lone junco also looks for seed in plain view outside my window. At this range, even without binoculars, the Dark-eyed Junco (or as it used to be named—before meddlesome ornithologists merged two species— the Slate-colored Junco) is clearly a slatey, charcoal gray above and white below, with a cute white beak in front and a pair of white tail feathers that only show in flight. My junco works the same patch of ground as do the white-throats, but it walks as well as hops, and has none of the comic, backwards hops. Usually, in less suburban scenes, juncos travel in small flocks and make a distinctive, soft, low trilling sound. But here, they, too, are silent. Juncos still have deep, pleasant, even philosophical meaning for me. For all the years that Caryn and I camped and hiked or spent our suburban, almost country youths, we never saw a junco. They were always there, of course. We simply failed to notice. Before we were birders, birds came in large, visible categories - sea gulls, sparrows or "little brown birds" of varying sorts, sandpipers, no matter what the size or kind, and the colorful, common backyards one. Your robins, Blue Jays, cardinals.

How could we love or care about what we could not name, or know, or even see? A Canadian bird book and a pair of binoculars changed all that. But perhaps, more importantly, was our learning to sit and watch and listen and observe, to see that some birds live in different places, eat different things, sing different songs, are self-sufficient if we let them be, and come and go at times of their own choosing. No borders seem to bother birds, whether Canada or New England. It has been this ways for thousands of years. They live and survive and sing in nature as they find it.

No wonder I am touched by this little slate and creamy bird beneath my window. It will be gone so very soon. I don't know when or whether it will still be walking, hopping, finding safflower seed and nyger beneath my feeders. When I return from Louisiana, the land of alligators and anhingas, where I will soon be speaking, it will be full-blown spring in Washington. My junco and maybe white-throats will be gone. And, perhaps, I fear, the day will come when they will not return at all.

March 25, 2013
Backyard Birds in Snow

It has snowed overnight and Currier & Ives have become contemporary and cool again! Large flakes still fall steadily onto an inch or two of pure, puffy white coatings on every branch and bush, fencepost and finial that I see outside my window. It is slightly wet snow, perfect for snowmen and sleds if it accumulates just a little. But it is not that cold; the streets are clear, no schools or government called off. There are rivulets of water already starting in at curbside, rushing down my slight hill toward the storm drains down the block. But my wishes—or are they prayers?—have been answered. This late Washington snowfall in springtime has stopped the clock, slowed the pulse of the push past the equinox and into Easter.

At my feeders, it is a scene worthy of a Christmas card or an Audubon calendar. My backyard "winter" birds are rushing about, playing, eating, shaking their wings and stamping their feet like small children on a sledding hill. Every bird in the neighborhood has run or flown here with their tiny snowshoes and their sleds. There are chickadees hanging, nuthatches poking around upside down, titmice showing their cute, big-eyed profiles, Blue Jays swooping in for peanuts, pushing the unpopular grackles aside, Downy Woodpeckers pecking away at nuts and suet, Carolina Wrens—a pair of whom I hope will nest—getting seeds and nuts out of any feeder with their sharp, down-curved bills. The plump doves are on the ground bobbing and pecking for whatever pieces they can find. Every so often a bold, brash, and beautiful Red-bellied Woodpecker flies in and curls itself around the smaller nut feeder. My singing Song Sparrows skip their hip hoorays amidst the snow. Each morning they have been belting out their song from the big azalea down on the edge of my driveway by the street. But now, in real winter, they hang near the edges of the crowd, a tad bit shy it seems. But they search about with dignity, their slim, longish tails adding elegance to their striped waistcoats with a large brown button that holds it all in place. Even my English Sparrows (they are ubiquitous invasives brought in from Britain after all) look handsome in this bustling, happy winter scene.

My whitethroats and juncos will not leave today. Nor will the hummingbirds arrive. Goldfinches hang from my netted bag of nyger. They are burnished, subtle antique gold, dulled and made more valuable by time. Beneath the bag, two juncos feed with obvious delight. The small, black nyger seeds look big through my binoculars and seem designed to contrast with their ivory-colored bills or blend in with their slatey backs. As I watch, I think my juncos actually hop, skip, and jump, with an occasional sign of walking. They are stars of some old-time Olympic sport. They are champions because, perhaps, like Nordic teams from tiny northern countries with snow and ice and mountains, there are so few of them, so little competition in the miniature winter Olympics in the snow outside my window. The white-throats I notice still decidedly hop. Yes. There seems to be slightly more upward movement and that fancy backwards scratching hop they do. But they seem less comical, more self-assured in snow. Their colors seem a little brighter, more contrasting. I admire their white throats, a small white downward tie or bib that gives the look of a barrister, as well as their black and white striped caps. The small yellow patch behind their bill and eye (that those pesky ornithologists call the "lores") stands out today against the stark, white, freshly-fallen snow. The cardinals fly in and out or sit calmly, grandly, posing against green and white, their red mitres adding pageantry to my backyard Holy Week.

If my backyard view is now some old New England Christmas scene, I feel as if I am watching an Advent calendar operating in reverse. Each time I peer through a pane there is a different scene, a different bird counting the days until resurrected spring arrives. Or is it until they leave and head back north in search of Currier & Ives and Christmas? The birds, like my heart and soul, seem to migrate to those places where they can find peace, rest, food, and home. Perhaps they know there are surroundings, settings, simple things that can make them feel like champions amidst the melting snow.

March 26, 2013
Heavenly Day

The sun has decided it is spring. The quick, late snowfall has nearly vanished. It is in the forties by noon and moving higher. The sky is brilliant blue with classic cumulus clouds; only a few are somewhat dark. The contrast of colors is intense. As I head out to walk and check my yard and gardens and fill the feeders, a lone dwarf narcissus shimmers in the sun beneath a still bare azalea bush. I am transfixed by its tiny beauty, its orange cup, its tiny golden petals as if crafted and carefully placed down by a jeweler in a window. Standing silently and still, I look up and see a dove, patient and pearly grey, sitting serenely on the gable of my neighbor's house. For the secular and the spiritual, it is a sign of hope as ancient as the ark. There are daffodils nodding in agreement everywhere I look. Like me, they are emerging, slowly raising their heads up to the sky.

With the snow now sunk into the earth, the growth of green within the week that I was gone is glorious. Small shoots have doubled and tripled in size. I see the fresh start of columbine, lilies, tulips, even small, light green sedum leaves where there were none. It means the rabbits will soon be out in numbers, not just the sneaky, early Easter Bunny that I've already seen. I hear bird sounds everywhere—the laughing red-bellies, the scream of jays. I turn to see the jays and see that I have been fooled; my birding ears are badly out of shape. A pair of Cooper's Hawks race across the street toward the larger trees nearby. I replay their sounds inside my head, hearing now a deeper, fuller scream. As I search the trees to try to find them, a Turkey Vulture soars and rocks above. I wonder whether this sharp-eyed vulture somehow sees or senses that the hawks have made a kill.

As I walk, I greet old friends like the box elder near the cut through where I saw the Mourning Cloak last year. It is starting to bud out with reddish puffs of growth. It is an old, old tree for a suburban neighborhood, the only one of its kind that I have seen. Soon it will look somewhat like just one more red maple that are far more frequent here. But the leaves are smaller with shorter maple points that turn red and gold in fall. This grand old tree has been wounded by the PEPCO teams that have been ravaging the canopies throughout the curves and cul-de-sacs. One huge branch has come too close to power lines. What's left is a round, yellowish circle of a scar. But as the sap of spring surges through its limbs and gently feeds the buds, I relax a bit and simply look and feel and smile that spring and life cannot simply be held back.

More dwarf narcissi near the cut-through draw me toward a rivulet of run-off that gently flows into a storm drain. There are maybe ten of them, fairy-sized, no more than three inches standing tall. They gleam golden against the moss and tender plant growth that line the little stream of snow melt, this tiny patch of nature beneath suburban sun. They look a bit like their wilder cousins the trout lilies or adder's tongue that will spring up later by the moist places in the shady woods. Standing still again (how odd I must look staring lovingly at a drain), I hear the sounds of spring in bird song and from boys in shorts and short sleeves shooting baskets at a curbside hoop. There is a dog walker with some indeterminate small, black dog and a more glamorous collie on her leash. Dogs are few these days; larger, older breeds like collies fewer still. I have a theory I cannot prove, but the rise in rabbits that run free across the lawns, and through the gardens and the hedges that I see is linked somehow to the decline of the domestic dog. In my youth all sorts of dogs ran free - airedales, collies, setters, labradors, even springer spaniels like the ones on playing cards. There were no pooper scooper rules, no dog walkers charging fees. Big dogs of every kind would chase rabbits, squirrels, and other things and catch them just for sport.

I see robins now back listening to the lawns. The patchy somewhat greener sodden yards have made the world of worms and grubs fair game. Both my daughter and grandchildren excitedly reported just the other day that they had seen flocks of robins everywhere, that soon it would be spring. I hear robins chuckling, wrens and cardinals calling, and, of course, Song Sparrows singing on nearly every block. I watch one now across the street as it rears back and shouts its "Hip, hip, hip hooray!" But the tone and notes are slightly different than the one that sings at home for me. A singer and a radio guy, I know these vocals are distinct and different. Is it some regional accent? I detect a drawl that is not found the few blocks north of here where my Song Sparrows stay and sing. Are there individual voice qualities and patterns that other sparrows know? Do they say to themselves, "That must be Charlie chanting on the corner, I'd know him anywhere?" A Song Sparrow answers back. What are they saying, these distant relatives of ours? Is it romance, or pride, or bluff, or just the joy of singing in the sun?

I walk along savoring sights and songs, the smell of earth. My spirits lift. Perhaps I, too, am rising with the sun. At the house that I pass next, a long, full line of white daffodils are bending low, perhaps from snowfall, their foreheads to the ground. They seem deep in reverence, genuflecting gently, as the change of seasons passes by. They, too, will rise and face the heavens with returning spring. But prostrated, nearly prone, seems an appropriate posture for each of us to learn. I am musing on humility and gratitude as I come to the path that leads to Peter Rabbit Land. At the edge of the path, in the yard on the corner, is the poignant remnant of a snowman. Its face is fallen, its sticks protrude. It is wrapped in a purplish cloak or coat, now slipping to the ground. I think of Ozymandias, of human hubris, of the fleeting fate of human power. It is nearly April, the cruelest month, mixing memory and desire. It is Passover; it is Eastertime when, in a modern blur and blend of rites and rituals and remembrances, all things bloom anew.

Citizen Birds

My pace quickens. Forsythia buds seem to open into blossoms as I march toward sunlight from the shadows of the path. I turn south into full sunlight at the end of the lane where the hedges hide rabbits, where not long ago a flock of robins gulped greedily the holly berries that were waiting just for them. As I turn, I see the signs of building at the house that forms the tangled border of Peter Rabbit Land. My spirits, or my stomach, start to sink as I see, parked in mud, a front-end loader. It has ripped through the front rail fence, scarred the earth, prepared the way for an extension of the house where a couple of trees had already been chopped down. Near the fence, on a stake, is the now familiar building permit sign. It says a hearing will be held, as if a single project here has ever been deterred. This tiny, awful notice seems designed by bureaucrats or lawyers to meet some ordinance or law. Open to the public it says. I suddenly imagine birds and animals lining up to be let in, chattering and pecking at the window to see what we humans will decide. As I feel my anger rising, a Song Sparrow starts to call. It hops out of the hedges and up onto a wire. I cannot understand the songs of sparrows, no matter what the guide books say. I think he is an organizer, like the Audubon ladies of olden times, calling out to save the herons and egrets from their slaughter for the millenary trade, or the robins, Ospreys, eagles from deadly DDT. But perhaps I should also take heart from these survivors in the dwindling wild. He has picked a quite unnatural telephone wire from which to call his neighbors and bring them to a meeting. This organizer of a Song Sparrow seems quite at ease, even spunky or insouciant, on the soapbox we have made for him. The hedgerows and the hollering of Song Sparrows will still be there when the bigger house that will form the edge of Peter Rabbit Land has long since fallen down.

More Song Sparrows pass along the word and welcome spring as I continue on my way, my spirits, like daffodils, are lifting once again. I see things new and fresh again, especially after snowfall and a more snarling, windy winter. I see pale, pink camellia blossoms shining forth like luminescent lanterns from the deep greens in a painting by John Singer Sargent. Northern magnolias push tips of purple and raspberry through large, furry buds. I look closely at one to see how the seed pods unfurl and the blooms escape the final clutch of winter. As I move around just a few feet past some hollies into southern sunlight, there is a smaller, bent and tangled, bush-like magnolia beneath them that has struggled and grown crookedly to reach the sun. This dwarfed and crippled tree has found release at last and blossoms in its hard-won light. There are buds and opening buds and full-blown blossoms simply soaking up the sun. There are purple stains on white that turn paler, pinker, as they grow to fullest bloom. I want to call out, sing out, organize the neighbors to see this mangled, magnificent magnolia emerged now from the shadows, living full and free.

April 4, 2013
Spring on Hold

It has been blustery and cold far too long. The much-anticipated cherry blossoms at the Tidal Basin have been postponed twice, disappointing my relatives and restless Washingtonians. I rushed far too soon to get my hummingbird feeders out. I could have waited. There has been a light film of ice on the bird baths; the online maps that track the northward path of hummingbirds have slowed. The hummers seem stalled somewhere in North Carolina. I needn't have worried about missing my juncos and white-throats, either. They are still happily at home in the Canadian climate of my cold, barren backyard. The neighborhood seems in stasis, a frozen tableau of tardy spring. Each day seems practically the same. A few more maple tree buds, the lines and clumps of daffodils slightly longer, statelier. A few of the forsythia have blossomed fully. There are tiny dandelions here and there. But everything is on hold. I wear gloves to fill the feeders. The postman has his knit wool cap and gloves. It looks like early spring, but it is not. The skies are gray. There is a steady breeze that gets the weatherman chattering about "wind chill" factors, as if we lived somewhere in suburban Chicago. Only the birds seem to know that there is no holding back the sun, that warmth will surely swoop in sometime in April, even if the flowers hesitate. Wrens are paired up and poking around my rafters, inside my garage, singing with deafening vocal virtuosity for such a tiny bird. The grackles are here, sounding like rusty hinges throughout the trees, hogging things around the feeders and the baths, leaving black feathers in their wake. The Song Sparrows serenade on every block. They are now so reliable in their "hip hip hoorays" that I have taken to trying to learn their individual voices. This, I know, is slightly mad. There are no records I'm aware of distinguishing individual sparrows by their accents, their argot. But the words, the pacing, even the tonality, are subtly different in every case. I shall perhaps be fluent when at last true spring arrives. Though time seems stalled by temperature, the goldfinches reflect the realities of the sun, the season. All dull, antique, and burnished only days ago, I now see fully golden ones to match the daffodils. The sunlight has somehow gently polished them. They are new, no longer antique, and from a different era. They seem prouder, more confident, more visible than they ever did before.

But of the overall delay of spring, there can no longer be any doubt. The cherry blossoms are still a week away from their full and glorious bloom. Last year I know they peaked and drew their worshippers in March. This winter has been much colder and more prolonged than the record warmed-up one last year. So much for global warming! This March, average temperatures in Washington were thirteen degrees colder than they were last year. This is the second coldest March since 2000; the swing in temperature was the biggest since 1946-47. Last March we got to eighty-three degrees. This year's high was sixty-three. It shares a record with only five other years when we didn't reach a balmy seventy degrees in March. But that was back in 1891, 1906, 1915, 1931, and 1958. I learn this and more from the meteorologists at the *Washington Post's* "Capital Gang." But they simply ascribe it to a blocking pattern of air in the far north set off "by a powerful stratospheric warming event in January." Neighbors shiver as they pick the papers up off their lawns. People seem impatient to get to spring, to keep to a calendar of scheduled, predictable events. It is as if the cherry blossoms and other nature shows are mere performers, a troupe that has failed to show up in town on time, amateurs who have annoyed their anxious audience. But there is no talk, no buzz, that our wintry spring is somehow linked to global climate change, our propensity to burn up fossil fuels.

I search and find solace in obscure articles, websites, and scientific findings, though it makes me feel alone. The British paper *The Guardian*, among others, reports that climate scientists have linked massive snowstorms and bitter spring weather in Britain and in large parts of Europe and North America to the dramatic loss of Artic Sea ice caused by global warming. Ice in the Arctic Ocean fell to new lows this past fall. And right now the National Snow and Ice Data Centre (NSIDC) shows the ice cover is near the minimum ever recorded. That means there is 80% less Arctic ice than just thirty years ago when I was meeting Russians near the Arctic Circle, eating reindeer meat and drinking vodka as we tried to solve the problems of global radioactive waste. The open Arctic Ocean absorbs solar heat and warms the water which, in turn, warms the air and pushes on the currents, including the jet stream, that govern most of our weather in the Northern Hemisphere. OK. Tell the neighbors that they are freezing now in April because of the theories of some British researchers. Well, the US National Oceanic and Atmospheric Administration (NOAA) says the same thing in a recent paper. But the cherry blossoms do not lie. I am left muttering to myself. Why do you think spring would shift so rapidly? Have we offended Persephone? Is the Arctic ice all gone because things simply change, no further explanation needed? No wonder many Americans think that environmentalists and nature lovers are merely oddballs, cranks. I'll show them just how normal this kid from Garden City really is. As soon as things warm up a bit, I'll hop back on my bike in funny clothes and search for wildflowers in the woods. I'll wait at the window for my friends the hummingbirds who are somehow running late. And I'll choke back a tiny tear or two when my white-throats and juncos finally leave.

Chapter Four
Spring at Last

April 8, 2013
Spring Pops

Spring has popped open like the buttoned shirt of a well-fed man. It was around seventy yesterday; it has now topped eighty. Forsythias are in full, spiky bloom on every road and every block. The deciduous magnolias have burst their buds into glorious raspberry swirl. The weeping cherries of every size drape blossoms in thin folds of light pink. Bradford pears, a product of the eighties, are like giant candy tufts of white—on lawns, on road edges, in parks. Lawns look like Victorian living rooms with more draped blossoms of ivory and écru hanging from *Andromeda japonica* (I grew up calling them japonicas), that the nurseries now label, rather appealingly, Lily o' the Valley bushes. The small hillock of ivy on my way home has sprouted its annual display of over two hundred daffodils beneath the pine tree with the old hawk's nest. There are coral-colored quince on bushes here and there that were invisible just the other day. All is lime green and pink, pretty and preppy like the blouses, shirts, pants, and skirts in the sales tent at the Landon School azalea sale. Only late in the day do I notice that I have not seen a single one of my White-throated Sparrows or my juncos. I feel some guilt as with the passing of a relative without satisfactory goodbye. But I check the hanging of my hummingbird nesting material, reclean and refill their feeder bottles with ruby-colored nectar-like solution, and think about both the future and the past. Caryn and I stock up on some spring flowers at the plant store. I gingerly plant them, a small group of early spring, flowering native plants—hepatica, bloodroot, Virginia bluebells within our tiny woodland garden with the trillium, jack-in-the-pulpits, and false Solomon's seal. Life and springtime seem a bit uncertain these days. I hope to find my own small beauties in the spring, in case the wild ones disappear.

April 9, 2013
Spring Beauties in the Woods

I head to the C&O Canal and Great Falls for the first time this year when crowds are sparse and spring has finally come. It is supposed to reach into the eighties today. I fear I may be late for early flowers, even though the colder March has delayed most blooming things by two or three whole weeks. I want to see the wild hepatica, bloodroot, bluebells, anemone, or adder's tongue. In morning, it is still shy of seventy with brilliant blue skies. Scarcely a soul is to be seen. The skunk cabbages in the small ravine near the entrance are now fully unfurled with broad green leaves that look like a tiny plantation of tobacco. Even the ranger's shack is not yet open.

I glide into an early parking space beneath a pine for shade and haul my Trek from off its rack. As I do, something makes me glance upward toward the nearly cloudless sky. I stand at some form of attention, silent, still, automatically respectful. A pair of adult American Bald Eagles is circling in front of me, just past the parking lot and over the canal. One continues to circle and search for food. The other has moved off to somewhere else nearby. I have never seen an eagle in flight around Great Falls, its yellow beak, its talons, its contrasting black and white, lit up by morning sun. It is a few moments before I even think to lift the binoculars dangling from my neck up to my eyes. I want to shout and call to people so all can see the glories of our national bird that nearly went extinct. But I am alone. I wait and watch and wonder until this sign or symbol finally disappears. Typically, when seeking nourishment in nature, no outing can be planned out fully. I have come to travel slowly, softly, to look for small spring beauties on the ground. Instead, these eagles, these wild beauties of the spring have come to me. They reveal what was nearly lost and then was found. They remind me of resilience and the power, in humans and in eagles, of an untamed heart.

Another large, striking bird sails into view. It is a Great Blue Heron, flying with deep flaps of wing. Neck and bill and legs are all stretched out like some primeval creature. Great Blues in spring and summer line the canal sides here. They are a photographer's and, perhaps, a philosopher's delight. Their ancient, aged style, their cold, cold eye and steady stare, their spear-like bill, their luxuriant, lengthy, streaming feathers, their stealthy hunts are lessons in paleontology and in patience. Again I forget to move, to breathe. I am in awe that these avian messengers have somehow spotted me. I finally wheel across the wooden bridge over the lock to start out on the towpath. But something causes me to ride up onto the concrete overlook across from where there is an old, old eagle's nest. There has always been an aerie there atop a very large, old tree. It is almost invisible at this distance with just the naked eye. But searching and focusing as I do, I soon see the black and white of a bald eagle perched atop perhaps a ton of branches and of sticks. The heron, too, sails by again. These birds must have been easy prey in the days of the early twentieth century when they were shot, their gorgeous feathers taken to adorn some fashionable Washington woman's hat. It took the writing and organizing of Florence Merriam Bailey and other members of the DC Audubon Club who birded everywhere near here, and countless others like them, to end the senseless slaughter that seemed so normal at the time. I am standing, too, where Rachel Carson, and Roger Tory Peterson, and Edwin Way Teale, and Louis Halle, and other naturalists and writers of an earlier generation watched the decline from DDT of the eagles and the other birds and took action to prevent it.

My welcome back to spring in the woods continues as I finally head down the towpath on my bike. Once again, it is the slightly crazed Pileated Woodpecker that appears before me, swooping across my field of vision. It stays near me for some time, landing on nearby trees, always flashing large black and white wings and showing the large liberty cap upon its head. Then, as if to let me know that I am back in touch with some wilder side of the canal, or of my consciousness, it whoops an echoing cry that signals its visitation with me is done. It disappears as mysteriously as it had arrived. But this succession of signals or spirits or simply spectacular birds has yet to end. A large raptor floats into view above my head. It is a Red-tailed Hawk showing off the pinkish wash beneath the tail of its sunlit buteo body. It salutes me with something more like the dip of an airplane wing as it finally closes its wings, breaking its circling pattern along the canal above me, and flies off to begin its day of hunting.

I try to reflect for a moment what the significance of such majestic, soaring sights can mean when I have come to look for flowers. Perhaps it means that the rhythms of life are not yet fully broken, the seasons, though unsettled, yet intact. Where there is majestic beauty there is hope. And where there are eagle aeries, herons fishing, raptors raiding, and the pounding and whooping of giant woodpeckers, there are many forms of life that still survive and thrive. And the old trees and fish and scurrying small mammals, in turn, mean that the cycles of plant growth, of leaf rot, of bark and lichen and mosses still are out here as well. If only more people could slow down and see and feel and understand them.

My avian avatars have brought me to a standstill. All is quiet, peaceful. My apparitions have departed. Only now do I look down at the ground from where this life has sprung. Pushed up through the leaf litter of the forest floor on impossibly frail, tender stems stand tiny, mostly white, four-petalled flowers. They show miniscule pink streaks and stamens. A few are pink themselves. These spring beauties are scattered across woods near the towpath everywhere I look. Their beauty is somehow related to their fragility. They have sprung up amidst stronger, tougher plants. They are ephemeral, evanescent. I smile as I think how I have judged my trip here with perfect timing. Much later and other larger, showier plants, the miracles of migrating birds, of downy ducklings or gangly goslings, would far outshine them. Spring beauties need quiet, careful contemplation lest they be overlooked. There is no need to post "no picking" signs for these friends of forest fairies. They would collapse and die before they reached the car. They will never be shown in shops or shine forth from silver vases arranged to rouse the admiration of our esteemed, assembled guests.

I kneel upon the leaves and twigs and branches, peering, almost prostrate before these messengers of life and their wondrous ways of being. I tend to look at the longevity and stout sturdiness of trees. Most I see will outlive me by many generations; a few I've known go back to times before there was a Bible. I admire the agility, endurance, the colorful sights and singing of the birds. They span the earth, they cross our boundaries; they come and go at will. Trees symbolize for me both history and tradition. For birds, it is simply freedom. But what of the wildflowers, these wisps of beauty, soon to disappear? Perhaps it is just the simple joy of being, some Buddhist trait I lack. I flash upon a moment a few years back at an environmental leaders' retreat that featured meditation, silence, sacred texts. All stuff at which I am not good. But as I sat in silence or walked with tiny, measured steps, things began to open up to me, like wildflowers in the woods. I had often thought of Jesus's line, "Consider the lilies of the field, neither do they toil nor spin," as some odd aberration, a call to passivity, even sloth, not the stuff of social justice or of action, as when he overturned the tables of the money changers in the temple. But then and now, in the silence of the woods, these lines bring up images of lovely little lilies who are not anxious about adornment, or adoration, or anything productive. They simply are at peace.

At eye level, entranced by the evanescence of my beauties, I seem to see a different kind, though small and white and delicate as well. Mixed in among the spring beauties that carpet the floodplain by the canal is a white flower I somehow have never seen before. It stands taller, stronger, with somewhat larger petals on the top. My reveries and revelations are immediately interrupted. Small, white, early wildflowers of the woods—anemones, bloodroots, hepatica, Dutchman's breeches—all race through my mind, but are instantaneously rejected. These blossoms grow up from leaves that are deeply cut, with jagged notches down each edge. This arrangement makes a triplet of lobes, all long and thin, like nothing I remember. The leaves look like smaller versions of an amazing, very deeply-notched oak leaf—a pin oak, or better yet, some southern bell, but notched down deeper still. Arrayed in bunches near each other, these green, notched leaves seem like some field or hothouse full of marijuana reduced to miniature to evade detection or yield a stronger high.

I try nervously to remember each detail and then recall my notebook and my camera. I make notes, take pictures at different angles, different lights, to compare with guide books when I get home. I fear, as with other flowers, or early bird sightings long ago, that I will not find them or will remember or note the wrong details for my identification. I need not have feared (had the lilies of the field taught me so little?). These flowers are unique, though their name is ugly, unforgettable. Cut-leaf toothwort, it seems, is pretty common on the East Coast in wet woods. Yet somehow I have always missed them, never seen them. The name has nothing to do with the flower, but comes from toothy shapes found on their underground stems. Their rhizomes beneath the soil were once used for toothaches or chopped up as peppery additions to a salad. I am remarkably excited at this "discovery" of a simple plant that always has been here.

I ride on down the canal, noting pairs of Canada Geese not yet trailing little goslings. I see skunk cabbage that, again, I have never noticed here before on the right-hand bank of the canal. The broad leaves are visible, their deep green color revealing some previously unseen muddy rivulet of water, like cottonwoods marking a riparian area, an oasis, in the parched landscapes of Arizona. There are a few turtles basking now on logs and a butterfly or two. One flies by the corner of my eye. I think, I hope, it may be a Mourning Cloak, but the glimpse is too short to know much more than it is dark. I am somehow soon aware that I am in hunting, classifying, scientific mode. I try to just enjoy myself, an extremely large spring beauty wobbling contentedly upon the stem that is my bike. It is a glorious day in spring. I know it is a gift that I can ride and look and think and see the beauties of the earth. I have wrestled often whether to just go forth and sniff the air and look about and simply savor what I see and hear and feel. But as I have learned to look at little things and learn their names and see them intently while they are here, I think that simply walking, strolling, riding will not be as intense or rich as when I am aware. I often go in and out of modes of consciousness as I go about in nature, especially in spring. Right now I want to see the springtime woods as part of some broader scene—a grand painting perhaps, not small photos of separate, tiny things. I do not want to miss the bigger picture for the pixels. I want the panoply of nature, not just the pretty parts.

I slow my pace. I wobble on my bike. I breathe deep and long. I see what looks like one of the mile markers that appear at regular intervals along the C&O Canal. But this one says River Trail. Its arrow points to a winding path beside a stream that I, again, have never noticed. I alight and walk slowly down this gently winding trail toward the river, not too far away. It is a little shadier, wetter along the stream. Perhaps I'll see new flowers or something on the river. Spring beauties still spread out before me. There are my new friends, the cut-leaf toothworts smiling up at me as well. There are Dutchman's breeches with their feathery leaves and comic little white pantaloons in small bunches here and there. But I am not counting or describing. I am simply headed to the river through the woods along a stream on an early springtime day.

As if to thank me or greet me upon my reentry to the woods in an un-numerical state of mind, a Pileated Woodpecker swoops into view. It lands next to me in the nearest available tree. It repeats this welcoming gesture a few more times, making sure that I can see and thus appreciate the finer things of nature. Then it flies, lands somewhere unseen, emits its tell-tale whoops and leaves me smiling by the river. A pair of Bufflehead bob by, having missed the memo that it is spring along the Potomac. I wind my way back to the towpath, hearing soft stream sounds, smelling the springtime woods, still smiling.

A Blue Jay calls as I move along again. I stop and watch it, spectacular through binoculars against the dim background of the woods. Its blue is matched below by that of my first single wild phlox of the year, and then another, and another. For reasons I cannot fathom, they appear more and more as I reach mile 16 and beyond. Their blue is mixed, like the Blue Jay, with the contrasting whites of lovely, slotted white flowers on medium-sized stalks. These star chickweeds are nothing like the tiny, gnarly ones we battle in our lawns. They grow erect and proud, a proper companion for the phlox who grow, without our aid, in God's good ground, the only garden they will ever need. Every year I have looked, with mixed success, for trout lilies in the woods. Sometimes it is my timing that is off. Sometimes it's simply inattention.

But the deep, rich yellow of this small spring flower stands out like no other dainty denizen of the early springtime woods. Suddenly, I spot them no more than four hundred yards before the lockhouse at the top of the gently rising, bending towpath here that leads to Swain's Lock. This seems far too visible a venue to me for such showy flowers, however tiny, to be standing by the path. I wonder how many are crushed or picked or otherwise destroyed by the human traffic here. But here they are on pale green lanceolate leaves spotted with a muted, blackish brown. I can barely comprehend my luck in coming upon this clustered, cloistered group low amidst the leafy litter just a few feet from a short slope to the river.

A Zebra Swallowtail butterfly flits by as if to match the pale green lily leaves and show me that I have chosen well to come in April to the woods when no one else is here. This zebra is my first main butterfly of the year, not counting a couple of common whites. Soon there will be hordes of these small striped swallowtails, often leading my way and landing on the path ahead. This one flies ahead now and, nodding downward, it points me to a new miracle, a group of bloodroot in full bloom. There are ten of these mysterious single plants that emerge in a tight, green curl directly from the earth, like small, slim skunk cabbages, before they unfurl for just one day. Their single, stark white flower above a scalloped, still slightly curled-up leaf is large by wildflower reckoning, a brilliant star with eight strong petals around a golden center. This line-up of ten bloodroots is more than I have seen throughout a lifetime of birding in the woods. I am a living example of the blindness of a quest.

Rare Birds

It is no surprise that only a little bit further on, as I breathe deeply, surrendering to the soothing sere and buff and browns, dotted with emerging greens and white, and here and there a bit of pink, a cardinal flies, looming large in sunlight. In the woods, released from our suburban settings, a cardinal is a thing of beauty. It is a bird that on another continent I might travel hundreds of miles to see, to hear its springtime "teacher, teacher, teacher" calls, to see it fly, its brilliant red like Monet's poppies that light up an otherwise ordinary, unsung field in France. A pair of titmice works the trees in front of me. They, too, seem different here, away from feeders, free to hunt alongside streams as they were meant to do. I cannot count the titmice I have watched, but these seem new and fresh. I look at them as if they are the rarest birds that I have ever seen. Their calls, their crests, their great big eyes are things that I have loved. But now from underneath, I see anew the subtle wash of cinnamon beneath their wings. It, too, reveals an artist's touch, brushed on gently between the white and gray. It sets them off, these backyard birds, when they appear in empty woods, just sitting on a tree.

A bird of similar size, a single one, flies into view. I do not need binoculars to tell me which it is. It is another old friend come to let me know that it is back in town. It flicks its tail as it settles down, not far from human habitation. It is the phoebe, the bird of cabins, barns, and bridges where weary, urban vacationers seek refuge in the woods. This one flicks its tail some more, shows its whitish throat, but does not make a sound. I have already taught my grandchildren the phoebe sound (which they can imitate) and its picture from the Audubon app they love. They have not seen one in the wild just yet. But when they do, I hope they have the thrill of recognition as this tiny, tame flycatcher calls out its name, or flicks its friendly tail toward them.

Now that I am paused to look at this sudden infusion of birds, I spot a shape that looks different; a small bird moves above my head with a somewhat vireo appearance. I get it into the view of my binoculars and sure enough, what had been just another little brown bird, or really an olive-colored one, grows large, and now in color. A yellow throat and chest, a somewhat stout bill, a yellow eye ring that makes a pair of glasses, two bold, white wing bars, all come into focus. It is an early arrival of a Yellow-throated Vireo that will be somewhat common along the canal come May. The C&O is a prime spot for White-eyed and Yellow-throated Vireos, Great Crested Flycatchers, and other small birds that are otherwise hard to find, little noticed, but exquisite to observe.

But wildflowers soon recapture my attention as I come upon a patch of yellow flowers standing by the towpath. They are hard to miss. Like many wildflowers, they look like weeds. Indeed, if growing in some park or a well-tended lawn or garden, they would indeed be weeds. Allowed to grow free here, as native plants that light up the dubious, drab days of early spring, they are lovely, small beacons beckoning the heart toward warmth and spring. There are small, yellow, daisy or aster-like flowers in little clumps above relatively tall stalks with limited leaves. Near the flat composite flowers there are also tight clusters of small, tight, closed up buds that look like reddish brown, dull, coppery BBs. I stand and simply savor the small bouquets before me for a while before their name even slips into my mind. No wonder. These are golden ragwort, clearly a wildflower named before PR became a true profession. Near them are also three more yellow trout lilies, their petals curved far back; they have sprung up at my feet simply to prove that sometimes prayers are answered.

As I am in a thankful mood, a hawk decides to visit me as well. I quickly see its banded tail, its thick, straight wings. It is a Broad-tailed Hawk, the kind that I used to see every autumn by the hundreds in mid-September when I would hike up Hawk Mountain to watch their fall migration. Each year, in a few weeks some fifteen to twenty thousand of them pass across the ridges near Kempton, Pennsylvania. But a view like this is frankly much, much better. In greater Washington, the hawks come through the Blue Ridge in the fall. But here I can see the eye, the beak, the feathers the way they look inside a bird book. The broadwing circles, then settles into a tree across the canal to wait for some poor, unsuspecting prey. It is the watching and waiting that marks the creatures of the woods and water. If they are to live and thrive, not just survive, out here in what we call nature, they must wait. It does no good to run and rush about.

As my eyes turn toward the river that runs close near here, I see four black Double-crested Cormorants standing on a rock in the Potomac. They look priestly, still as the stone on which they stand, facing the sun with riverine reverence. I can see their orange throat patch, the long bills with hooks at the end to help them with their fishing, and tiny crests that now add a slightly comic touch, like the royal magicians in Dr. Seuss' *Bartholomew and the Oobleck*, who come shuffling up the stairs from the royal basement when summoned by the king to make some new, amazing thing fall down from the royal sky. Next to the cormorants facing obstinately in the opposite direction, facing to the breeze, as if in some form of disobedience, is a pair of common mergansers. I saw a pair up close near here last spring; I wonder if they are the same. I marvel at their crests, their long-toothed bills, their perfectly painted feathers. They will be gone soon as winter ducks depart the river. They, too, are still and waiting, at peace, perhaps resting or reminiscing, before it is time to truly fly.

A little further up the canal on the edge of a small rocky cliff sit, piled like dinner plates, a collection of twenty large painted turtles basking in the sun. If I could somehow transform the terms cold-blooded and reptilian into compliments, I would. Sleeping through the winter in the muddy bottoms of creeks and of canals, these ancient reptiles have short-circuited the seasons, smart enough to live out their lives in eternal spring and summer. To us humans they seem simply lazy, useless, sitting still like this. But they really are sustainable and run on solar power. Once warmed up they swim and play and eat. They are a joy to children who spot them first from between the paddles of their parents' kayaks and canoes. Come May there will be hundreds of them on top of logs and rocks along this stretch of the canal. I love to see them sitting, basking, useless, waiting, watching, maybe worshipping as well. They are absolutely motionless. Turtles are cold-blooded and reptilian—happy bumps upon a log.

I finally begin to move and wonder if I will get to see the banks of trout lilies that I discovered grow in profusion on the northern end of the cliffs beyond the turtles. The light, the soil, the sun may all be different than for the adder's tongues that I have already found in little bunches near the towpath. I scan the crags and cracks that form the ancient wall of stone that runs along the water on my right. There are small leaves and plants and dirt in many, many places. If they are here, they should be visible, I think, in just a little bit. I claim a growing feeling of excitement, anticipation, rather than anxiety. Like other things that live and grow out here in nature, my lilies will be waiting, watching, too. At first I simply see a blur, then streaks of yellow ahead along some sheltered strips of rock that have accumulated thin layers of soil and plants. With binoculars in hand, I see the first real trout lilies raise their heads. It is as I had hoped; they carpet the crags though not all have yet to bloom. There are dozens and dozens and dozens of them shining silently in the sun. They are oriented like the cult of cormorants I have just watched out in the water. My heart leaps like a hart in Old Testament appreciation though I, too, stand absolutely still. I realize that I am oriented like the mergansers on the river rock who, like me, may have been considering the lilies.

A Palm Warbler

I finally move along toward mile marker 19 when some motion catches my eye. I pause to find out what kind of small brown bird this time has revealed itself by moving. I haven't heard the sound of chickadees or titmice, and the ringing song of a Carolina Wren was further back behind. This small bird is moving in some branches, neither low or up real high. Its pace is measured; it almost strolls along a branch. I focus in and furrow my brow a bit in puzzlement and wonder. It is a warbler that I have captured in my sights. It has an eye stripe and a reddish cap like you might see on a chipping sparrow. It bobs its tail. There can be no mistake. For the first time in many years since a spring break in the South, I am looking at a Palm Warbler hunting bugs right here beside my bike. When the kids were small, Caryn and I brought them to the Okefenokee Swamp and Harris Neck National Wildlife refuge where we camped out in what had been an old plantation where live oaks festooned with Spanish moss and parula warblers lined the way to fields and swamps. It was there we saw Palm Warblers, Wood Storks, Prothonotary Warblers, and springtime blooms that followed us and opened up as we drove north. We were following in the steps of Edwin Way Teale, the great naturalist writer and friend of Rachel Carson's. His classic, *North With the Spring* has inspired us ever since. His trip covered twelve hundred miles and many, many birds and flowers. He ended just outside Washington, near Monticello. But now I double check my sighting in a guide. The Palm Warbler has an olive rump and lovely yellow below the wagging tail. The throat is also yellow but with some streaking; the back is brownish like some ordinary sparrow. The Palm Warbler is an early arrival in the northward wave of warblers that will have birders out here in numbers in just a few short weeks. It hunts with tiny little flights all around me unconcerned for quite a while. Then it walks, or seems to hop a bit, along each branch searching for its food. I think about and thank for just a moment the premier Washington bird instructor, Florence Merriam Bailey, from a hundred years ago. Without her, I never would have seen this early harbinger of spring. She started off the sport of birding, the wild idea of watching through binoculars, rather than shooting birds like this. Her *Birds through an Opera Glass* came out in 1889 when Grover Cleveland was President and fished near here just a couple of miles ahead.

As I head back home, I see a Belted Kingfisher sitting up ahead. Each time I see one, it rushes ahead to some presumably safer spot alongside the canal. But this one waits as if to welcome me back to springtime on the trail. It is a magnificent bird found along streams that looks to neophytes a bit like backyard Blue Jays. A crested head, with a longer bill to catch and swallow fish, it's blue and white, with a prominent black band upon its chest below a throat of white. It is the very bird that caused Florence Merriam Bailey to become an organizer at Smith College for the early Audubon society and work to stop the slaughter of such splendid creatures. Women's hats did not merely feature the feathers of egrets or herons for the fashion of the day. They often were decorated with entire birds around the brim, hummingbirds included. While at Smith in 1886, Florence was horrified to hear a classmate exclaim, "I saw the most beautiful hat in the city last weekend. It had thirteen blue birds on it, each with a white collar and a curious topnotch. Thirteen - I counted them!" I continue to admire the kingfisher through my binoculars, but wondering for the first time where and how they were collected for nineteenth-century hats. Perhaps even here along the canal? Such thoughts drove Florence Merriam Bailey to write and teach since she shared the belief with other women nature writers of the time that once young boys learn to love the birds, they no longer will want to "murder" them.

As I am thinking of Florence Merriam Bailey and of saving birds, perhaps in appreciation, my kingfisher, who has been sitting, suddenly dives into the canal to get a fish. I cannot see if he is successful since he flies to the other side and then proceeds down the canal a bit, whether to enjoy his snack or because he has come up empty billed, I do not know. As I proceed to ride again, the kingfisher loops forward each time that I get close. It is a fitting escort for end of day in springtime along the C&O Canal. But one final greeting and surprise awaits me. I am looking at the water and not at flowers as the kingfisher leads me home. I see ahead a little duck-like bird in the middle of the canal. As I get closer and look at it, it turns into one of the cutest birds around, a tiny diving one called a Pied-billed Grebe. It is not much more than duckling size and has a short, stout bill on an odd-shaped head atop a mostly brownish body. This one has a few streaks of white along its head and throat. The male in summer has a black ring on its bill and a slash of black that slants along its throat. I usually see my Pied-billed Grebes along the Potomac in the winter or on ponds and small lakes in summer. I have never seen one here before. When pied-billeds have their babies, they carry their tiny precious cargo way up on their backs. But that will be later in the year, if I have such luck at all. But now in one last show-off gesture that is clearly aimed at me, the Pied-bill Grebe, which usually dives beneath the water, simply slowly sinks beneath the surface like a submarine at sea. I have read that they can do this, but I have never seen this sight before. It is a signal of some sort of things to come. Of what, I can't be sure.

April 10, 2013
Cherry Blossoms

Sometimes it takes out-of-town tourists to refresh the sense and sensibilities of those of us who live in Washington and too often take some things for granted. My close friend Stephen, who ran a peace group and a radio program with me, is in town with his wife and another couple from when we all lived in Philadelphia. Stephen, who studied at the same seminary as Martin Luther

King, is now a Unitarian Universalist minister and writer. He is describing how he felt at the new King memorial along the Tidal Basin. He is deeply moved as he shares the sense of the great civil rights and anti-war leader that comes over you as Dr. King emerges from the granite in the park. I have not made time, or maybe bothered, to go there yet. I rationalize internally that I have perhaps been deterred by media controversies over the Chinese artist's rendition, or the shortened, somewhat misleading, version of one of King's quotes that is chiseled now in stone. A few days ago it was also, I now recall, the forty-fifth anniversary of his assassination in Memphis, Tennessee. My daughter and her husband had been there recently and extolled the civil rights museum that now surrounds the Lorraine Motel where King was shot; I had gone to pay respects in earlier years when there wasn't much there to see, except for haunting recollections.

With the delay in blooming because of the colder winter and colder spring this year, I decide to go to see the cherry blossoms that my relatives at Easter had hoped to visit. Caryn and I get up early and take the Metro to Smithsonian to beat the crowds and see the Tidal Basin, its cherry trees, and monuments in early springtime light. A month ago when I stepped onto the Mall, I nearly froze in wintry winds. Now it is quite pleasant. The Washington Monument has scaffolding half way up its height to repair the cracks and damage from the earthquake that shook things loose in Washington in August of 2011. I am reminded of old photos of the Monument looking like a pencil that has been snapped off. But it simply stood unfinished for decades from 1848 to 1884. The pinnacles of the Washington National Cathedral were also damaged in the quake of 2011. They, too, still have scaffolding on them. And at the Smithsonian Castle behind me on the right some decorative parts of the exterior were also damaged. Even in the Smithsonian Museum of Natural History across the Mall, some fifty bottles with specimens inside were rattled off their shelves.

As we approach the Tidal Basin, once swampy, disease-ridden bottom land, Washingtonians and tourists of every kind pick up their pace a bit and start to stream onto the sidewalks and the grounds. There are moms with strollers, folks with dogs, some elderly with canes and walkers, various languages being spoken, and cameras everywhere. The Yoshino cherry trees are at full blossom thanks to a couple of days of sudden warmth. Those who had to come on the weekend that has just ended saw only partly-opened buds. The blossoms hang down from the trees and frame the views of the Jefferson Memorial shimmering in the early sun. There are ducks and geese floating and flying through the photos. I look for mergansers or other ducks that were seen here by Louis Halle two generations ago when the neo-classical marble dome of the Jefferson that calls up Monticello was just a few years old. I realize now, incredibly, that the Memorial that seems iconic, historic, along with cherry blossoms, was also just a decade old when I first came here as a boy. We can thank the persistence of a couple of women, including President William Howard Taft's wife, Nellie, for the fact that we have cherry blossoms here at all.

Caryn and I admire the blossoms that are best seen very close. Everywhere we look there are people snapping pictures, posing, peeking, poking their eyes and noses inside of blossoms. The birds that seem most at home within this beautiful bower are the clownish starlings who are making multiple sounds in the branches up above. And some are actually nesting in the holes and splits and other cracks and crevices that dot these old, old trees. I watch a mother starling disappear inside a cherry hole to tend to her new nest. In the brightening light of morning, the springtime starlings are quite colorful, all speckled with iridescent highlights of black and purple and green. These ubiquitous birds are invasive, too, part of the plan of Shakespeare aficionados to give us British birds. But they have driven out generations of gentle native birds like the bluebirds who now need boxes put up in country fields. They have ruined many statues, buildings, parapets with their droppings by the ton. But here today in a park that marks peace and friendship with a sometimes enemy, I decide to enjoy the comedy of starlings, their persistence, and their spunk.

Looking closely at the cherry trees, I also am humbled by the hardiness and steadfastness of those that have stood a hundred years. They are gnarled and notched and broken, pruned and sometimes amputated so there is not much left but stump and glorious pink white blossoms that refuse to give up on life. They emerge from the bark and trunks themselves, amidst old moss and sawdust. They reach for light on slender branches that somehow grow out from their massive, mangled trunks below. I find myself smiling, almost grinning, as I observe the life of trees and of those who have come to be bewitched by their stubborn boughs of beauty. In the oldest part of this long, long line of trees there stands a small and simple monument of stone, a gift from the Japanese. It looks a bit like a Celtic cross in some old Irish graveyard. Americans come up to gaze at it. They grow silent, almost reverent. No one need be reminded of our two nations' troubled past—of Pearl Harbor or Hiroshima. There are war memorials not far from here, far larger, monumental. But this single stone is needed to remind us that people can create friendship and peace as well as war.

Dr. King in Springtime

I stroll on through blossoms and bent trees, feeling serenity and silence amongst the swirl of people and tiny, torn paper bits of pink that line my way. There is a break in the circle of cherry trees that surrounds the Tidal Basin. I refocus my attention to people drifting in that direction, to what is drawing them toward a different view, a different vision. The statue is much more massive, more monumental than I thought. I must look up to gaze at Dr. King. It is an appropriate way to admire this man who has touched for the better so many lives including my own. I had not really expected to like this memorial to Martin Luther King. But now his folded arms seem resolute and strong, not posed or patriarchal. His somber, almost stern, stone-chiseled face shows gravitas, not merely granite. But it is the setting that enthralls me amongst the cherry blossoms. The statue that emerges from the great block of stone is the center of a small, semi-circular park that is backed by low granite walls. There are cherry trees and benches and small bits of lawn and trees. The site blends in with the symbols of life and beauty that are the lure to those of us who are here today. The low, curving walls are filled with quotations from Dr. King, they echo, in a peaceful way, the Vietnam War wall not far from here. "It is not enough to say we must not wage war. It is necessary to love peace and sacrifice for it. We must concentrate not merely on the negative expulsion of war, but on the positive affirmation of peace." I feel myself being moved by more than beauty, more than blossoms, though these things are all connected. I am standing in a memorial in our nation's capital that will be seen by countless Americans who come here. It is dedicated to a vision of peace and to a Nobel Peace Prize winner. Only the Theodore Roosevelt Memorial that is literally off the beaten path in the center of Roosevelt Island can compare. So much of monumental Washington is made up of those who led and fought in wars, however valiantly. Now at least there is an unambiguous testament to a peacemaker and "a drum major for justice" that all who venture here to seek some sort of refuge from our violent world will see.

The FDR Memorial

I blend back onto the path that surrounds the pink reflecting water. In just a little while I am aside the FDR Memorial. It seems permanent now, though many still call it new. The cherry trees march into it as do I and others to rest and to pay homage to another fallen leader. The waterfalls over huge blocks of stone are man-made like much of our modern outdoor environment. But the statues here, the quotes, the trees all blend together as if we should draw no distinction between our love of nature and its beauty and our best leaders who have given their lives to protecting people as well as preserving the natural environment in which we live.

My favorite quote in massive stone that sits inside this refuge is simple, quite straightforward from a man who led a global fight for freedom. It says simply, boldly, "I hate war." Eleanor Roosevelt is here, too. She dedicated her life to the UN Charter and preventing war and working for human rights. I look back at the King Memorial and the circle of cherry trees that symbolize spring, new life and peace. I listen to some Mallards giving low, clucking quacks. I watch them fly. I slowly blend back into the flow of Washingtonians and tourists who move, almost as one, around the Tidal Basin beneath the blossoms. There is springtime in my steps.

April 11, 2013
Farewells in Spring

Though still cool, it is truly sunny. But my thoughts and feelings still vacillate like this chilly, unsettled season. It is a time I associate with death. My wife took solace in the beauties of a grand, old stand of weeping cherries at the Baldwin School, not far from Bryn Mawr Hospital outside Philadelphia where her father died at the end of March. My own Dad died just two days before his birthday on April 9, my mother at the end of April, an uncle on Easter Day. And, of course, King, and Lincoln, and FDR all died in April. All are symbolized for me by Walt Whitman's elegiac poem, written in Washington, "Lilacs in the Courtyard

Blooming." And so, each April, I turn to look at life that pushes up through the soil and soars on wings outspread, each tilted toward the sun. The Carolina Wrens are picking around the awning of my porch as I head back out to the canal. As I roll toward the tavern at Great Falls, a heron greets me with its deep flaps, its legs dangling as it sails above my head. I stop in at the museum and shop that isn't always open and chat with volunteers who are gathered by the counter. One strong young woman is clad in nineteenth-century dress. She seems amazingly well informed until I learn that she is indeed a park ranger who does many things here at Great Falls, including riding the barges and telling tales of olden times. We chat about the history of the canal along with a long-time volunteer who clearly knows the flora and fauna of the park. They both know the Pileated Woodpecker that hangs around the tavern and the lock that I watched in this spot last spring. I thought it was a special sign, but they just say he's "showy." Same for my sighting of a Barred Owl just sitting alongside the canal in daytime, not very far from here. His territory is well known, but he often is "real hard to see" and "blends right in to the tree" he chooses to perch upon within the first half-mile as the canal runs north and west. I grab some checklists and brochures to help me make tough calls of birds I see only fleetingly or flowers I don't yet know. Then I'm off into the sunlight in search of signs of springtime, that if no longer eternal, at least will give me peace.

Flower Arrangements

As I move along there are still huge spreads of spring beauties, but the Virginia blue bells, the showiest native springtime plants that grow beside the towpath, have now leapt up and bloomed. There are clumps of them, arranged as if by a florist, with taller plants in the middle and shorter ones grouped around.

Most of the dangling blossoms are a light, slightly lavender blue, but others, before they open, hang underneath and add pink fringes to the plants before they fully open. Most are about three-quarters of the full foot to foot and a half they'll reach. A few are even smaller, about the size of the new six inch ones that I have planted in my backyard woodland lot. As my pace slows to look at flowers, I feel my heart leap again as I come upon more trout lilies that I must have missed the other day, no more than a third of a mile from the Great Falls Tavern. I take some pictures and admire their miniature magnificence, their rich yellow dangling single blossom of curled back petals over spotted blades. Magnified like this, they make a sumptuous, sylvan centerpiece.

The Look of an Owl

As if to let me know that I am indeed in touch with some sort of spirit bird, a Pileated Woodpecker suddenly and silently appears. There is no ringing call, no resonant pounding on a trunk. This red-capped super bird simply sails into view. It welcomes me back and then is gone. As seems to happen whenever I stop to look and listen, an apparition comes to me. Again from nowhere visible, a Barred Owl silently leaps onto a low branch no more than fifteen feet away from somewhere off the ground. This must be the owl I saw near here last year, the one the rangers say is "hard to see." It not only has moved to show itself, it proceeds to peer at me, to inspect me quite intently. I do not breathe, I do not move, I send out tender feelings. I am afraid to raise my binoculars or make a single move or sound. But, finally, I begin to slowly, slowly move my hands like an incredibly slow loris in the nocturnal house inside the National Zoo. The only motion on my owl is a steady, slight flapping of feathers just below his face. They flutter silently as if he's breathing hard. All else is motionless as if carefully carved in wood. The body is somewhat heart-shaped; it slopes down from powerful broad shoulders like those of someone who swims the butterfly. The face has disks, the head a cowl. But it is the eyes that hold me tethered to this feathered predator. Like John Donne's ecstatic lovers, our gazes, our eyes, are completely intertwined. Seen up close and through my glasses, his black eyes stand out like onyx marbles. They protrude, are rounded, are all seeing, all knowing, deep and wise. We commune like this for quite some time until I barely shift my gaze. In this brief moment in which I haven't even moved, my owl has vanished, as silently, mysteriously as when he first appeared.

When I begin to breathe again, I move at last further along the canal. I soon come upon and stop some distance away to watch a Great Blue Heron standing on the water's edge. It spears the water and comes up without a fish, but with something slender that dangles in its beak. It isn't a snake, which herons like to eat, but some sort of vegetation. I expect this master hunter to spit it out or let it fall, but it snaps off the end and swallows it. This heron's salad seems strange to me; it is the stuff of geese and ducks. Who knew that this primeval descendant of some pterodactyl now has the omnivore's dilemma? Not so the little insect-eating phoebe that I now see sitting on a branch across the canal, the first one of the season. I bless this friendly little flycatcher who likes to live near humans. If I could market phoebes instead of bug spray and electronic backyard zappers, the world would be a better place.

As I get near Swain's Lock, I see three more starry bloodroots. Though tiny and ephemeral, they are visible from quite a bit away. Near them are the beginnings of the May apples, or mandrakes, that have popped up like tiny green umbrellas that you find in Mai Tais or other tourist drinks in some pseudo-Polynesian restaurant. In just three weeks they will have opened wide to provide some shade for fairies. And underneath, as if on cue, the small white blossoms that form the apple will be dangling like an ornament marking May Day. Some motion causes me to look up now toward the trees behind the water. A Broad-winged Hawk does several turns to also welcome me. But this welcome sighting is soon matched by one that is less cheery. I see a junco up ahead that is gathering grit from off the dirt and gravel towpath. I have not seen one at my home for several days now it seems. This may be my last of the season before spring migration takes my favorite winter bird back north for cooler mating grounds. I sigh and smile almost all at once as the season seems to shift before me. But my sentimental thoughts are soon pushed out by the screaming of some crows. I snap to full attention wondering what has stirred up these raucous birds. I see them circle, cawing now, toward the tree where I last saw the Broad-winged Hawk fly in and settle. Of the group that has now surrounded the broad-winged's tree, two dive in for an attack, perhaps to defend their nest. The hawk flies out and heads for the river with all the crows in hot pursuit. They are smart and social birds, these crows who can communicate and fight in packs. The lone hawk keeps hightailing it until it is completely out of sight and the crows fall silent and relent.

Another Spousal Introduction

In the newfound, sudden stillness I see a pair of little birds before me. It is my Palm Warbler who has brought along his wife. They poke and hop and walk along the branches as a pair, almost in unison, like some long-time married couple checking out antiques and bric-a-brac on vacation at a fair. A bit like juncos, they, too, have white outer stripes upon their tails. They are a delightful little couple; I watch them happily shop for bugs with two small sycamores for a store. Not far from here, upon the ground I see some Dutchman's breeches. This little group has three rows of tiny V-shaped pantaloons like chevrons stitched upon a sergeant's sleeve. Across the Potomac is another martial figure that seems as small as are these little woodland flowers. It is our nation's symbol, of war and peace, depending on how it sits. This bald eagle is perched in a peaceful pose near its long-time nest that can be seen before the trees leaf out across from mile 18. From here the eagle looks, with just bare eyes, like a tiny blob of black. A crow, perhaps, who has come to rest upon a huge, white, patchy sycamore that is bathed in sunlight on the shore.

Hunting with Binoculars

My gaze and thoughts are interrupted by a giant leap and splash of some monster fish on my side of the river. The noise is audible and ancient, the same that John Smith heard. I don't know if this is bass or carp or shad, but I am impressed that any fish can make such sounds and sights and still survive this long. As I look out over the Potomac, two Wood Ducks streak by; I think of hunters now. These gentle, gorgeous ducks of small streams with woods nearby seem so vulnerable and fragile. I cannot imagine who would ever shoot at them or why. I try to keep in mind that all species have their predators, that duck stamps paid by hunters help preserve the dwindling wetland refuges where most ducks and geese are found. But these things of beauty can be carved from wood or photographed or looked at through a glass. I think one more time of Florence Merriam Bailey who has brought me out here with binoculars instead of shotgun blasts.

As I am musing on survival, adaptation, and our changing views of nature, a veteran of all these things drifts slowly into view. An early butterfly lands in a bush near me. It is a venerable Mourning Cloak, a true butterfly survivor. It is one of the few that stays the winter seeking shelter underneath logs or sticks or bark. This one has managed to escape a host of predators; it is nipped and torn along its edge. It is still a thing of beauty, though scarred and tattered from its lengthy life. It shows its mahogany wings with inlays of old, old ivory on the rim. The yellow edges of its youth have faded now to something far less visible, yet far more valuable. Its legs and antennae are long and graceful, if slightly bent by age. My Mourning Cloak sits still, though quite alert as it, too, stares at me. It seems to ponder just who I am and why I have appeared. Then, satisfied at last, it, too, just disappears.

As I head back, I hear the phoebe call. I hear frogs grunting from the lagoon near milepost 20 while a snake swims up to see me. Now the pileated calls out to me, two or three times from in the woods. The light is dimming as I finally wheel out of the park. Even the ranger station has closed its windows. In the road stands a single small, quite unassuming bird. It is a junco come to bid me farewell before it starts its journey north.

April 12, 2013
A Backyard First

My juncos seem to have at last departed, though the White-throated Sparrows linger on, hopping about backwards in the leaf litter beyond the kitchen window. I am watching them somewhat amused and thankful when something entirely else hops into view. My mind tries to verbalize "a robin," but it doesn't seem quite right. Soon I focus my mind on this "not a robin" bird to see what it could be. I am observing white flashes along the tail in almost constant motion as my mind rejects a giant, colored junco and begins to say a towhee! It is a funny thing, this mental world of expectation and exaltation. I am looking at a Rufous-sided Towhee (now named, dully, the Eastern Towhee) one of my all-time favorite birds. But my mind keeps rejecting this lovely notion since it simply cannot be. I have lived here in Bethesda for over a quarter century since we first arrived from Philadelphia. I have watched the birds and kept decent track for all the years before. I have never seen a towhee in my yard or neighborhood or even on my rambles. This striking specimen must be quite astray or simply passing through.

The towhee is a bird of the edge of wood and forest floors, not suburban lawns. It is an upscale bird, a rich man's robin that, like Brown Thrashers, needs a decent wooded area to find enough to eat. A towhee is not zoned for houses on quarter-acre lots, no matter what their value in assessment. I am looking at a handsome male with black head and beak and back with contrasting, formal white below. But both sides and shoulders are filled, as in its name, with a matte-finish brick or subtle orange- reddish tones that brighten up with light. The tail is longer than a robin's and flicks each time it moves. That is when the white edges show and flash both off and on. There are a few white spots or patches on the wings that add some contrast to the ebony that is etched above the rufous. It is, all and all, a trim and tailored bird that, though common in the zip codes where deer and thrashers live, is pretty hard to see. It scratches at the oak leaves like a giant white-throat. It walks and hops and pokes around. By my feeders in the back, it seems to be enjoying safflower seeds that draw the cardinals in. My heart soars as I watch this bird of woodland floors parade around my garden. I do not know why it is here or how long it will stay. But for now I am transported to a simpler, wooded time.

April 13-16, 2013
Towhee Buntings, Chewinks, or Marsh Robins?

It has been mostly rainy, cloudy. I am much indoors, fascinated by the pair of towhees that have taken up life inside my yard. The female is as lovely as her striking mate, but, as with most birds, of a subtler style and hue. The patterns are the same, but black is substituted by a soft, light, earthy brown. It makes the rufous sides stand out, especially the shoulders, when seen from the front as in a formal portrait. I wonder if such birds will really nest and stay. I am entirely obsessed; I look for them each morning. I count the days that they appear. I read up on their habits. I am amazed that Rufous-sided Towhees, or their ancestors, were once common in DC.

In the first definitive book on the birds of the Washington area, *Avifauna Columbiana*, by the noted ornithologist and physician, Elliott Coues, first published in 1862 and then revised in 1883, the Rufous-sided Towhee is called the towhee bunting or, its local Washington name, the marsh robin. Coues says the marsh robin is "Chiefly a spring and autumn migrant. A few breed with us, but none remain during the winter. It is abundant from April 25 to May 10, when most individuals pass north, and in the fall from the first to the third week of October...it haunts at all times the thickest undergrowth along streams, the recesses of laurel brakes, and likes sequestered spots, just such as the cardinal loves. Much of its time is spent upon the ground scratching among fallen leaves."

Even by 1898, when Florence Merriam Bailey is writing in *Birds of Washington and Vicinity* and leading birding classes in the district, Washington still is filled and surrounded by wooded countryside where towhees, or chewinks, can be easily found. "Passing along a country road, bordered by woods where the undergrowth is thick, you are likely to see the chewink flitting about in the bushes, showing his white tail feathers as he flies, and you may hear the musical questioning call which has given him his name—*chewink?* He will also be found in any woodsy, bushy place where last year's leaves are not cleared away." Bailey says, "the Chewink is very handsome in his tri-colored suit of black, white, and chestnut-red, and his rich voice has a metallic quality which would put him among the brasses in a full orchestra... His most common song has been translated 'Come with me,' the last word trilled on his highest note."

The towhee, whose song I learned as "Drink Your Tea!," even appears on President Theodore Roosevelt's list of birds prepared for the second edition of *Birds of Washington and Vicinity*. It includes those that he has seen at the White House and while he was in Washington. Although the towhee is not listed as on the White House grounds, they were then open to the public and far more wooded, a good place—according to Florence Merriam Bailey—for birders to go. TR lists among the species such woodland residents as Screech and Saw-Whet Owls, Yellow-billed Cuckoos, Red-headed Woodpeckers, and nesting Wood Thrushes. Now the White House grounds are closed and closely guarded except for massive public events like the Easter egg hunt on the South Lawn where some 30,000 people stand in security lines before piling in for photo ops and chaos on the grounds. There are trees around the White House, which is encircled primarily by lawns and fences for security. The trees are controlled, contrived, well-labeled specimens planted in small outdoor rituals by modern presidents and their wives.

April 17, 2013
Return to Rock Creek

With a colder, wetter late winter and early spring, I head off to Rock Creek Park to see how it compares to last year's heat and drought. It is still early for bird migration, though robins do abound. The garlic mustard has just appeared but is not yet in full bloom. The ground is moister; there are tiny rivulets and streams. The spring beauties seem more numerous, yet that is hard to tell. I see some nice specimens of my new friend the cut-leaf toothwort, and other small, white flowers. But it is wide patches of trout lilies spread behind boulders and alongside rotting logs at creek side that capture my imagination. I try to figure out exactly where and how they grow. Their peak seems to have passed in the middle of April, so all I see is their spotted blade-like leaves. From the sun and shadows, mosses, lichens, and other signs that are used as compasses in the woods, I find these adder's tongues grow in

moister areas on the north or northwestern side where there is
sheltered, partial shade behind the fallen logs and branches that
are left, wild and uncleared, to rot in Rock Creek Park. Many are
near the path. I wonder if they have been picked or trampled by
dogs, walkers, joggers, or baby strollers that come here in surprising numbers in the middle of the woods. I am not sure if I will see
the little blossoms that I love until I find a patch of lilies within
a tiny fortress that nature has built behind a mighty oak amidst the
rotting logs and mossy green. Small boulders, or more properly,
large stones create a miniature wall that offers defense and shelter
from marauders of all kinds. It is here at last that I see the final
dying, drying survivors of once proud flowers dangling brown and
yellow. I salute these final hold outs who have rescued me instead
of the other way around.

Then I hear a racket in the woods along the creek from not
too far away. It is the sound of voices, of pre-teen boys at play.
There are six of them who have ditched their bicycles, shoes, and
helmets to frolic on the rocks that give the creek its name. They
jump and call and seem to be deciding who will be the king of the
rock. They seem heedless of the nature that surrounds them and
at first I hate the noise. But I slowly turn ambivalent and finally
cheer them on. Such after- school, untrammeled hours are awfully
rare these days. Even less so time spent in woods jumping shoeless
in a stream. They may squash a wildflower or scare a duck or two,
but their sense of wonder, as Rachel Carson called it, is being
formed right here. As a boy I played like this in fields behind my
house before the post-war boom. I saw box turtles, rabbits, birds,
and hidden treasures that I now can still recall. I still feel good in
some weedy field with Queen Anne's lace and goldenrod and
chicory and pearly everlasting. Something like this must have
moved Florence Merriam Bailey here in Washington when she
wrote of weedy fields. "In looking for birds that prefer dry fields
and thickets there is a delightful old juniper field to visit just west

of Chevy Chase Circle. Here Thrashers shout out their approval of life, shy Chewinks scratch up the dead leaves under cover of the evergreens, clownish Chats pour out their rapid volleys - loud whistles and mocking laughter - from the thicket, and sweet-voiced Prairie Warblers mount the juniper tops and with leisurely serenity run up their rich scale."

The weedy field and junipers are all long gone now around the Chevy Chase Circle. There are old churches from the first couple of decades of the twentieth century, an aging bus terminal from the late '40s, and lots and lots of cars. My grandchildren went to preschool at the nursery in the basement of the Baptist church where Florence probably found her chewinks and heard her lovely warblers. Chevy Chase is, by modern standards, a sedate and elegant place with stately homes and country clubs and gardens that are beautiful in springtime. But even in the best of zip codes in our modern time, one must look very carefully to find some carefree nature.

April 21, 2013
Earth Day Sunday

It is a glorious spring day in Washington. Sunny, cool, warm enough to be comfortable outside, but not yet too hot to move around or play. The pair of towhees is still in my backyard, raising my spirits and the value of my property. The feel of Easter is in the flowers, in the air. I give an Earth Day Sunday sermon at the Westmoreland Congregational United Church of Christ. There are thousands of such events around the nation, as many as there are Starbucks or McDonalds! I want to celebrate the goodness of nature, of what we faith-based environmentalists call God's creation. But I am ambivalent and worried as I often am. Loving nature often leaves out people who are struggling or suffering. Focusing on social justice, poverty, or human rights alone can similarly ignore the perils of a dying planet. I choose two "green" commandments on which I have seen liberal and conservative Christians, people of many faiths, or none at all, finally agree. First, God is love. God loves the world, not just people, and everything made is good. The other is, "In as much as you have done it to the least of these, you have done it to me." It is what has brought liberal Baptists like Bill Moyers and Al Gore together with the very conservative heads of the Southern Baptist Convention to finally agree on climate change and the poor. Amen. May it be so.

I go to my daughter's house just inside the District line to hang out after church. We are playing with the grandchildren who have shed their Sunday best when we spy a Carolina Wren. I finally see it head into the wrought-iron flower basket filled with flowers, dirt, and sphagnum moss that hangs right near the kitchen. Our wren has a caterpillar in its mouth and slips between two well-wrought iron bars. This procedure is repeated many, many times. When things are still, we creep up close, bend heads down, and peer between the bars. Just an inch or two inside are two tiny, yet outsized, gaping mouths that open wide and quiver. We lead each grandchild slowly, quietly, up to this sacred spot. They are delighted, amused, and awestruck all at once. There is no need for sermons; the love for these small beings, for children, as for wrens, seems suddenly enough.

April 22, 2013
The Crow's Nest

It is Earth Day. I am writing, working, preparing for my environmental politics class, but pause to stroll in the neighborhood. It is cold as it has been in much of April this time around. But a quick succession of blooming dogwoods, Kwanzan cherry trees, and redbuds has transformed Bethesda into some kind of bower. As I head back inside, I hear the Fish Crow with its nasal, softer, almost mournful "car." I have seen it in the birdbath and grabbing food within my yard. I had not paid it much attention until just now as I turned slowly back to look. The sound is coming from atop a neighbor's tall, thin southern magnolia tree, just fifty yards away. I lift binoculars to see if a dark patch is it. I see instead a pile of sticks jammed in between some limbs. It is different than the squirrel nests, all piles of leaves that abound in all our trees. I would have thought it a hawk's nest if I had not seen my crow. I am staring at a crow's nest, a maritime cliché if there ever was one. I fight back thoughts and images of pirates, ships, and two years before the mast. I have loved the lonely sound of a Fish Crow somewhere across the street for years now since the raucous, cartoonish American Crows were decimated by West Nile virus. I feel relieved and somehow honored that these smaller, gentler crows have made a home nearby. It may not be an eagle, but it gives my suburban strolls a little touch of wild.

April 25, 2013
Capitol Views, Now and Then

After more unseasonably cold weather, I head downtown for meetings on a somewhat warmer, though cool and breezy, sunny day. I am right near the Capitol so I head over to its grounds. The Supreme Court is in full morning sun, a scrim across its front. They are doing major renovations. The net out on the front is like a stage set with a picture of the columns and the pediments so tourists may know what lies inside. But it is hard to imagine that these grounds once held the Old Capitol Prison where Lincoln assassination conspirators Dr. Samuel Mudd and Mary Surratt were held, as well as runaway, freed, and contraband slaves during the Civil War. It is from a spot like this in the 1840s that slaves were chained and sold. Solomon Northup, a free black man from upstate New York who was kidnapped and sold into slavery in Washington in 1841, wrote in his book, *Twelve Years a Slave*, about spring in the capital when he was still free and could watch the pomp of President William Henry Harrison's March 4 inauguration.

While free, Northup strolled the Capitol grounds as I do nearly one hundred seventy-five years later. But after he is kidnapped and in chains in a slave pen, he is bitter at the irony of his proximity to the Capitol: "The building to which the yard was attached, was two stories high, fronting on one of the public streets of Washington. Its outside presented only the appearance of a quiet private residence. A stranger looking at it, would never have dreamed of its execrable uses. Strange as it may seem, within plain sight of this same house, looking down from its commanding height upon it, was the Capitol. The voices of patriotic representatives boasting of freedom and equality, and the rattling of the poor slave's chains...." Northup's view is from the Williams slave pen on the Mall, ironically less than a block from today's Smithsonian National Museum of African American History and Culture. Called the Yellow House or Williams Slave Pen (at about 800 Independence Avenue SW, now the site of the headquarters of the Federal Aviation Administration), it was the most notorious slave pen in the capital. A modest, well-maintained, two-story yellow home concealed a very large basement in which slaves were chained to walls in windowless rooms, while a thirty-square-feet yard surrounded by a 12-foot high brick wall provided space for the training and selling of slaves. Later, as he is being taken to slavery in the Deep South, Northup is led through Georgetown to the Potomac onto a boat where he sails past Washington's tomb at Mt. Vernon on the river. He longs for freedom like the birds and nature that he sees and then records:

> After sunrise in the morning we were called up on deck to breakfast. Burch took our hand-cuffs off, and we sat down to table. He asked Eliza if she would take a dram.

She declined, thanking him politely. During the meal we were all silent—not a word passed between us. A mulatto woman who served at table seemed to take an interest in our behalf—told us to cheer up, and not to be so cast down. Breakfast over, the hand-cuffs were restored, and Burch ordered us out on the stern deck. We sat down together on some boxes, still saying nothing in Burch's presence. Occasionally a passenger would walk out to where we were, look at us for a while, then silently return. It was a very pleasant morning. The fields along the river were covered with verdure, far in advance of what I had been accustomed to see at that season of the year. The sun shone out warmly; the birds were singing in the trees. The happy birds—I envied them. I wished for wings like them, that I might cleave the air to where my birdlings waited.

After the Civil War, Washington underwent a number of beautification plans so that the misery and pestilent sites near the Mall, the unfinished Washington Monument, and the malarial swamp land where the Tidal Basin and monuments sit had all been eliminated. The Capitol grounds that Solomon Northup had strolled upon as a free black man and then observed as a drugged and kidnapped American being sold into slavery were given today's park-like appearance by Frederick Law Olmsted, Sr., whose son designed and saved the Great Falls area. The lawns that surround the Capitol today are an arboretum whose edges are graced by large, historic specimens which date from the beginning of the twentieth century. I stop first beneath a huge old tree I do not recognize with giant limbs and large cavities. It is labeled "English Elm" and one of the high up cavities houses a sleeping squirrel who is sprawled over the rim like a bather at the beach. Near it is another gigantic specimen, this one a "Hybrid Oak." The signage tells me that it dates from April 30, 1912, almost exactly a century ago, in honor of Sen. Jacob Gallinger of New Hampshire, president *pro tem* of the Senate in 1912-13.

I stroll, like Solomon Northup, trying to simply enjoy the grounds, the park-like feel, the stately trees and views of the Capitol with its statue Freedom. There are large, old trees of many sorts—gingko, tulip, bartram and bur oak, bald cypress, horse chestnut, and even a white pine, now grown large, planted in 1975 by the Idaho Federation of Women's Clubs. I stop and snap pictures of the springtime views of the Capitol and its dome where I have walked; the dome was the thing that stood out the most for John Burroughs when he walked here throughout the Civil War. I look at a Civil War exhibit at the Library of Congress, the least known, best gem of monumental, historic Washington. I want to understand, to feel, what it must have been like for Burroughs and Whitman and Lincoln and Elliott Coues and all those who tried to enjoy Washington in springtime amidst horrific war. I leave after a ritual bow to Thomas Jefferson's leather books which I have seen and wished I could touch and read many times before. I stop beneath the tree at the southeast corner of the library that has always given me shade and respite in the heat of summer. I glance down at the memorial marker of the four librarians who lost their lives in World War I and think of how much I should enjoy each free moment that I can of books and peace and nature.

April 26, 2013
Native Plants in Washington

I head out to hear a lecture on native plants and biodiversity recommended by a landscape architect friend. I go to Brookside Gardens, a combination garden, conservatory, and woods with a small lake and ponds in Kensington, Montgomery County, Maryland. I hope to learn and, of course, to find a simple way to see some birds and wildflowers and maybe early butterflies. The lecturer is upbeat, expert, funny, relaxed, engaging. His PowerPoint photos are astonishingly good. Caterpillars, butterflies, birds, flowers—all shimmer in minute detail on the large screen in the education room. The lesson is simple. We need every species, not just some, to be saved if our "ecosystem services"—clean air and water, the source of human health and livelihood—are to survive. There are nice islands of wildlife and wild spaces, amidst our growing human sprawl, but they are increasingly disconnected. The end result will be failure for a number of species and less well-being for us humans, unless we act to connect up such spaces with large corridors of native plants, including throughout suburbia and our lovely over-manicured backyards. He is especially good at explaining why certain bugs and birds and plants have all evolved together. Some caterpillars which are the source of food for many, many birds will eat only certain kinds of leaves for which they have a yen. The birds, in turn, eat bugs, drop seeds, and do other useful things. When we plant non-native plants, like the white flowering Bradford Pears that have been in bloom the past few weeks and are popular with nurseries and homeowners who don't like messy trees, we are cutting off the food supply for caterpillars and chickadees who simply pass them by.

As I head outside into the gardens and toward the little lake and ponds and patches of woods that surround the Brookside visitors' center, I spot a bird in a nearby tree. It pops behind some leaves, then slowly peeks its head out, still well camouflaged, to see what it can see. This furtive bird is none other than a catbird that I fear will not come this year to my slightly cleaned up yard. Thrilled to see this first one of the spring, I stand and watch him as closely as I can, even taking photos to capture the occasion. Such a sighting feels as fresh to me as some new lifetime bird that I have trekked and tracked for many miles to see. Another common bird on the edge of the woods also feels like a fresh find, a welcome sight, in this odd, cold, wet spring, like one I saw some forty years ago. I have heard its call before I see it; it sounds like a hoarser, less happy robin. It is the Red-eyed Vireo. I still cannot believe it has been described as the most common woodland bird in the Northeast. But vireos stay high up in the trees and don't move around a lot. Their voices are thrown a bit so the sound is hard to place. On top of that, they are somewhat dull. Their great big deal, their identifying mark, is the fact they have an eye line. The rest is creamy, dull, with some greenish wash on top, and a cap you don't often get to see. But they eat up bugs and sing a lot, even though like lesser robins. They are no one's favorite bird. But if our expert speaker is correct, they need these woods and we need them no matter what their markings.

I turn back toward the lawns that surround a flower garden. Here real robins are having fun, showing off and listening, as they do, with head cocked sideways, before they stab a worm. They cluck and flutter and sing oh so "cheerily!" No wonder everybody loves them and were frightened, or mad as hornets, when they began to die from DDT. Near this rockin' robin on the lawn in brilliant sunshine is a Red-winged Blackbird wandering around and feeding on the ground. I have loved these birds since I was a child. But I associate them with cattails and swampy, marshy places. This may be the closest, easiest look I have ever had of a bright, male Red-winged Blackbird. The red, bordered with strong yellow on an otherwise black body, is scintillating vermillion in the sun. As it walks right up to me in an optically-enhanced appearance, it "burr, burrees!" and opens up and spreads its radiant, shimmering shoulders. They are facets on a stained-glass window with lighted reds and yellows in the cathedral of the sun.

I head to the woodland walk nearby as if toward some medieval copse. My mind and spirit have been transported to another time and place. I enter on a boardwalk that winds through a strip of woods with dirt and mud and wildflowers along the edges at my feet. Red-bellied Woodpeckers call and chuckle in the distance, bewitched to live in this enchanted forest. A sparrow makes a short, low flight into a nearby bush or shrub. It has a little rufous cap, a Chipping Sparrow that I have not seen in years! I am back down to earth a bit as I look at wildflowers that are well labeled. There are showy trillium, the size of trumpets. There are little spread-out spikes of white and fuzzy blossoms called foam flowers that some old-time wag has named to make us smile.

Across from these is a sight that stops me. I stand silent, still. I am a judge in a major flower show, the entry is before me. In shadowed sun with sharp, contrasting colors is a single crested iris sitting on the edge of the scalloped circle of a rich and rotted stump. It is low and wide, a former sycamore, or ancient oak perhaps. It is filled with humus, a deep and dark mahogany. There are touches of moss and slanting sun just beneath the iris. It is small and proud and perfectly formed with jagged purple petals. It is the placement of this elegant, single stunning iris, this setting, that will win the best in show.

There are other flashes of color along this small woodland stroll. Wood poppies here and there dab in a touch of yellow along with golden ragwort, my neighbor from Bethesda, whose composite heads are rays of sunshine in the darkest paths we walk. Such small golden gifts have slowed my pace. I walk relaxed, unhurried; I barely move at all. I am on a boardwalk labyrinth in tune with wonders large and small.

April 27, 2013
The Canal on Foot

I want to keep an eye on the canal and not miss any breaking springtime news. Caryn's bicycle needs repair so we head out the old-fashioned birder's way—on foot from Pennyfield Lock. It is a different feel along the canal on foot. Before full migration, I can't expect too many unfamiliar, fancy birds. But I can slowly savor each small find and observation. Since I have come to expect a welcome to the woods by some new startling creature each time I visit, I am subtly disappointed as we quietly trudge along. I try to look at flowers, but want to see some birds. This needy approach will surely do no good; it's the sort of conscious-ness that leads to zoos and theme parks and TV. I shake off some sense that other weekend warriors should not be here at all. We have walked by kayak classes and been passed by cyclists shouting, "On your left!!" or ringing jarring bells. Finally, I smile when I realize that I am usually one of the kamikazes who has just whirred by. I look at sky, at woods, at rocks, and water and start in to relax.

Perhaps waiting for me to deserve a view, we suddenly get a visit. A Mallard drake drops down from the sky, out of who knows where, plummets, turns, brakes, and skids to a splashy stop nearby. He proceeds to emit a low, soft quacking that sounds much softer than we humans when we pretend to be a duck. Its emerald head is iridescent in the sunlight; its cinnamon sides are richly painted. Each time I see this classic, common duck, I wonder if I acknowl-edge its beauty, instead of its commonness, enough.

As we walk, we stop and chat with birders who share what they have seen—Wood Ducks, Louisiana Waterthrush, a Solitary Sandpiper or two. The birders along the C&O, like most I meet, are older, pleasant, soft-spoken, somewhat rumpled folk with large hats, funny vests, binoculars, and gear. They look comfortable in life and with themselves and the quiet scenes they find out here. "Blue-gray Gnatcatcher up ahead and some orioles further on." Some know the trail real well and seem to live nearby. Others are just happy see what they can see on an early springtime day.

As we walk ahead, we see some swallows darting in and out by a mud-banked feeder stream that runs into a culvert beneath an old stone bridge. The light is shaded, dappled; it is hard to say what kind these are. Tree Swallows have a shiny blue back and are often seen in sun. Purple Martins are not likely here, but then one never knows. They don't have the long, deeply notched tails of richly-colored Barn Swallows. They could be cliffs or bank; we'll need a better look. We clamber down the bank and sit down for a while. They soon return. There are two of them, deep brown above with white below, even in some light. When they sit still upon a branch, we can look into their small, black lively eyes. One is clearly younger and hanging out with Mom. We rummage through our field guide and wonder if they are Rough-winged Swallows that are indeed common in parts of the canal. There is no band across the chest, but we can see that what we have is a female and a juvenile. They fly back and forth, catch some bugs, and then disappear inside the culvert. This time they are joined by another bird—a phoebe who must live in there as well. If we were younger, more surefooted, and if it were warmer, we might try to slide into the water and take a closer look at their homes inside this tunnel. But we are content to watch them fly and eat and catch the swarming gnats that already are a bother. These are among my favorite birds—the graceful swallows and the friendly phoebe. They are well-developed bug-eating machines, sustainable and fun.

Blue-winged Teal and Wood Ducks

We walk along and find white phlox that look exotic amidst some classic blue. There are turtles basking on small logs in the lagoon. I see shape and color atop a nesting box. I think I see some blue. Brought in range by binoculars, a Tree Swallow is perched proudly on this potential home. It is as bright as a reflector, a beacon over shallow water, mud. Pausing to admire this patch of color amidst the browns, we see a trio of larger ducks paddling slowly where the water meets the muck. Two of them have white crescents on their head, not much else to see. It is a family of Blue-winged Teal! We have never seen them here before. They are quiet and move slowly. We watch them for a while. They are a very light brown on the sides with an all-black bill in front. There is a white patch toward the back, but no blue speculum along the wing that we can see from here. Then, not too far away from them, we see a pair of Wood Ducks as our birder friends had said we would. The Wood Ducks are smaller; they are slowly swimming side by side. The drake shows off his royal plumage, while his more muted mate moves easily with understated pride. Nibbling as they move, all five ducks look quite contented. They look glad to be alive.

It is in this moment that the pileated enters onto the stage. I see him in profile, moving up a single, dead, branchless tree that has been drowned by the lagoon. He shows his profile, then starts to drum. The sound is quite incredible. It resounds and booms and echoes. After each set of sounds, this woodpecker of the deep woods moves up a little higher, like a flag being hoisted in the morning on a mast. First the part that still has bark, and then the bare and smoother top. The booming keeps a rhythm until he reaches the highest, thinnest topmast and takes a look around. His reveille is over; he flaps and sails away. His undulating flight, as if at sea, shows black and white until he fades away, perhaps to signal other searchers.

As we return along the trail, we see a small, gray, flitting bird ahead. It stops; we zoom in to watch its wagging tail. In sunlight and very close to us in Technicolor, a Blue-gray Gnatcatcher comes into focus, another promised, welcome sight. The bird is sitting still for once; its eye ring is quite prominent. There are white stripes on the long and ever-moving tail. Our visitor looks like a miniature mockingbird that has been dyed a subtle blue. We cheer for this little bird who lives on the nasty little gnats that plague us on the trail. And for all his flying cousins who are feasting, though not fast enough, to keep the bugs at bay.

The Hope of Tadpoles

Nearby in some water sitting on a stump are two different Wood Ducks, posed in partial profile, looking carefully carved, as if on sale by some local craftsman. The helmet, chin straps, and colors of the male, and the soft, hushed hues, and smaller, subtler helmet of the female are extraordinary sights. Such ducks are captivating, worth caring for and capturing in art. They are indeed a prize; we keep our eyes upon them.

Finally, we must leave. A magic time is over. We tiptoe by some muddy tractor tracks where we have parked the car. Some large vehicle, maybe pulling kayaks, has left a parking space that is filled with ridged, big puddles that I avoided when we came. I look down in the warmer, shallow sunny side out of habit, nothing else. The tire tracks are full of life that wiggles, swims, and squirms. Tiny tadpoles are everywhere humans fear to tread. Now I look down more consciously at the tractor hole right beside our car and, sure enough, one more colony of tadpoles wiggles into view. These are tiny new ones, perhaps a few days old, no wider than a pencil. They are dark with little flagellate tails that propel their outsized heads. Soon there will be frogs around, at least a few, after the birds have had their fill. Caryn grabs some sticks and small branches that are in the brush nearby and creates a little battlement to deter the parking cars. It is probably a futile, existential gesture of biophilia. The fate of these myriad little creatures, laid down with hope, is, at best, uncertain.

April 28, 2013
The Return of the Catbird

A catbird has arrived sneaking and skulking about my yard beneath the plantings and azaleas that dominate the front. It is the first one of the springtime despite my fear they might not return at all. I have been a little guilty that I might have cleared my yard too much of its tangled honeysuckle weighing down an aging fence. Catbirds may be among the least appreciated of all the springtime wonders of suburbia and of cities. Their mimicked songs add rich rhythms to the soundtrack that we hear. The mewing sounds they make astonish little children who find it hard to credit that a bird can sound just like a cat. Their formal gray and black-capped elegance is the Mourning Cloak of birds. And, though stealthy, their typical closeness to the ground makes them easier for folks both young and old to see. They have nested near my yard many times before; we shall have to wait and see. This one has just arrived as the neighborhood is leafing out. It is full of springtime beauty with azaleas, dogwoods, fading cherries that have piled their petals on the ground. Here and there, left over from olden days, are lilacs blooming by some fence or corner where no gardener tends or picks them anymore. Ancient, hanging, rope-like vines of wisteria can still occasionally be seen—off wires, over fences, on top of wooden pergolas, or on some old-time porte-cochère.

April 30, 2013
Rabbits

Another day of cool rain like Oregon, a fine mist mixed with streaks of springtime sun. I take a shorter walk, mail some bills, and loop back toward my house. It is rabbit time in late afternoon; most neighbors' grass is long and wet, unmowed. Toward Peter Rabbit Land, I see a curious and brave young rabbit who must have had at least a walk-on role for Beatrix Potter. I watch him from behind his cotton tail and take notice of the nice chestnut patch below his nape and ears. He rears up a bit to peer above the first brick step that leads up to the neighbor's fine brick stoop. He hops up one step and then the gesture is repeated. He peers up and over the last brick step as if to say, "Is anybody home?" Then he jumps up onto the stoop and waits patiently at the door. It is unmistakable now. He is visiting and looking for a friend to come outside and play. Since he cannot ring the bell or knock, he simply sits and sits. I begin to suspect that after all he is trying to find a way to get at the petunias by the rail. But they are out of reach and there is lots of other food around. No, he is looking for some human friend—a little girl, or boy, perhaps—who lives inside this house. At last he turns away, looking somewhat disappointed. He hops back down, with one look back, then skips off through some nearby bushes.

At the very next house I see a pair of rabbits who are sporting on the lawn. One runs at the other, facing straight head on, until his playmate jumps straight up over him and then turns around so they are staring at each other once again. This game goes on for quite a while as each one takes a turn at rushing at the other who then hurdles over his buddy pretty far up in the air. I have never seen rabbits act like this before, playing leapfrog on a lawn. Are they kids at play, rough rivals guarding turf, or a couple courting through the racy ritual of dance? A third, larger rabbit then shows up as I am taking notes. The first two smaller ones then dash off together, bounding onto the next neighbor's lawn. With what looks like Mom around, I tone down my thoughts and decide they are kids at play. Flopsy and Mopsy, or their relatives, are still alive today.

May 1, 2013
Hunting Huntley Meadows

The Voice of the Audubon Naturalist, the recorded and on-line list of bird sightings in the greater Washington area, has lured me here to Huntley Meadows. It is the few simple words, "a female Hooded Merganser with eleven chicks," that has brought me to an open, muddy marsh. It is still very cool, yet sunny for the opening day of May. I struggle with the irony that I have whizzed around the Beltway and driven through several miles of ugly sprawl to commune out here with nature. I have been on twelve-lane highways that need high walls to block out the sounds and smells and sights of autos streaming by. The quaintly named Richmond Highway, that is actually Route 1, then offers a mélange of gas stations and gastronomy that can be carried off and eaten as you drive. I make a right-hand turn to find my mergansers at the corner of Sunoco and Exxon/Mobil. Not far away from traffic lights and Taco Bells, I finally see some woods. I turn left down an entrance road that has been put here by some time machine. It is quiet, wooded, winding just a little bit. I roll down all my windows to sniff the air and let the old-time ambience soak in.

I park and walk a little way along a wooded path with spring beauties underneath the trees and bird song in the canopy. I pass several friendly, smiling people as I near the visitor's center. I scan the sightings listed there of recent days, no mergansers can be seen. The helpful volunteer who greets me now says the merganser and chicks were seen a week ago it seems. No one has reported any sightings since, she ruefully reports. I should have learned by now not to hunt or chase my sightings like some Labrador in the bay. Such narrow, snapshot views of nature are bound to disappoint. But soon an older, wiser naturalist in uniform with binoculars around her neck steps up and tells me that she has seen the merganser. It was on Sunday, just a few days ago, though her brood has been reduced to only three surviving ducklings.

I am grateful for this news and heartened for my search. We chat awhile about predators out here—snapping turtles, owls, hawks, and other things that would like to eat a duckling. I move along down the woodland path to the boardwalk through the marsh. I don't see much with an initial scan. I stand instead and listen. There are some warbler sounds and Red-winged Blackbirds calling out from the marsh, their proper home to me. There are some honking noises from Canada Geese and the low thrump of a frog. I am comfortable out here in this sheltered, somewhat artificial piece of paradise. I begin to open up. I feel the breeze, I soak up the sun. My mind slows down. I am suddenly at ease. Off to my right, across the swampy pond, I sense, then see, some movement toward the back beneath the trees. It is a duck with ducklings, that much I know! There may be only three or four of the little ones sticking close to Mom out here. I raise my glasses in anticipation to get a better look. It is a little brood of Wood Ducks that soon come into focus. I watch them swim about as my slight sense of disappointment fades. These are the first ducklings of my spring; I have yet to see them along the C&O Canal as I usually do in May. There can be no finer sight than fluffy little Wood Ducks swimming, scudding, scattering like living toys at play along their watery way.

Now I see a huge, reedy nest in front of me that I had simply overlooked. There is a Canada Goose curled up cozily in the sun on a tiny island no more than thirty yards away. I see Canada Geese each time I go to walk or bike along the C&O Canal. But I never get to see a nest like this with a brooding hen waiting patiently for her goslings to arrive. I have taken geese too much for granted. It is one bird that has thrived amidst the growth of lawns and golf courses, of human-altered scenes. Many of those we see are no longer truly wild. We grumble at their numbers and their spoor in places where we want to walk or play. But it is we who have changed the landscape, not these gorgeous geese, whose haunting honks and flying Vs still call us back to visions of a time when everything was wild.

Just then a muskrat rambles out from underneath the boardwalk. I could reach down and stroke its fur if it were a pet and I were so inclined. I point it out to a mother and her toddler who are ambling right behind. The mom is over-thankful while her baby girl squeals in wordless wonder and delight. Is such biophilia instinctive or is it learned at mommy's knee? All I know right now is that a furry little animal has made these fellow humans' day—and mine. As if on cue, a pair of Barn Swallows now swoop overhead, a show of small Blue Angels without the mighty roar. These are the birds who really do have swallow tails, long and forked, like Winston Churchill urging victory, or a student urging peace. Even without binoculars, I can see their multi-colors—a bluish, purplish black on top with brick red underneath and at the throat, a patch of white behind. As these swallows wheel and dart above me, I finally catch and follow them in my binoculars' field of vision. I am dizzy with delight at this aerial display. They are catching and eating bugs right now, their colors all ablaze. They are, indeed, some sort of angels, protecting, watching out for toddlers down below.

I walk along this opening edge of Huntley Meadows that really is a beaver dam. There are gnawed down trees with ends as sharp as pencils. Piles of sticks and mud hold back shallow pools of water. One group of large, furry, cute, and flat-tailed rodents has created all this life I see, has even brought me here today. What I would give to have some ponds and pools like this in my backyard in Bethesda! I'd take more bugs and gnats, and even more mosquitoes, if it brought along the swallows, frogs, and warblers that eat them every day. As I am thinking warblers, I hear some sounds far off. It takes some time to penetrate that there must be yellowthroats nearby. The bird books say their song goes, "witchety, witchety!" That's fairly close, but the real yellowthroat song is less verbal, sweeter, less distinct. I want to see their smiling, small masked faces, their beauteous, flashing yellow. But these are somewhat far off, perhaps among the trees that line the shallow, muddy marshes that I am walking through. I wait and listen as best I can to find them like a bat by some form of echolocation. I wait and wait until I see some movement in the trees. I zero in and there is one. He is now out in the open. He throws his head back just a bit and calls to me that he is the first one of the season. I am fascinated by his burglar's mask, as I am by those upon raccoons. There is another yellowthroat that seems to answer him from somewhere to my rear. I slowly turn and look some more where I think the sweet witchety song emerges. Again I wait and scan and hope to see some golden feathers. At last the other one moves into view. It is closer and I can see some olive back and a slim band of white above the famous mask and yellow throat that gives this charming swamp-side bird its name.

Sparkles in the Water

I scan now across the larger pool in front of me. I see Spotted Sandpipers, turtles, geese, then something in the back. There are subtle little flashes on the water. They are moving in a line. I focus in on the farthest spot from here that a bird could possibly be. I try to ignore the orange plastic, netted fences and front-end loaders at the edge of the woods that intrude into my view. I concentrate and look again just at the sparkles in the water. There is another duck with ducklings, perhaps five or six of them. It's then I see the pointed bill, the swept-back block of pale, reddish-brown umber feathers on the head, the small, stout build, that make this distant duck a female Hooded Merganser!

The ducklings are in a short, tight cluster, too far away to count. I am excited nonetheless. It is hard to see Hooded Mergansers at all. The books call them uncommon. I will never forget the sight of the first one, a male, I saw in winter in a pond along the Jersey Shore with ice glistening in the sun on the large white patch that marks its head. I may see one or two a year if I am lucky. But here is an entire clutch of them nesting just off Route 1 and its suburban sprawl. As I walk through the woods around the edge and toward the back of the watery mud flats in the middle, the little family of ducks that I have come to see works slowly, steadily in my direction. I take a little side path down to the muddy water's edge. My mergansers are now in view as if swimming in my yard.

The puffy little ducklings are very hard to count. They are bunched together behind their mom and stick with her real close. They overlap, then separate a bit, and then close up their ranks. I finally settle after many counts that there must be nine of them. The snapping turtles and the hawks have not decimated all the siblings. At first I thought that all the mergansers were gone, then mostly eaten by some raptor or other rapacious beast out here. But this is a good-sized brood and who knows if they really started with eleven? As I am watching, counting them, the mother plunges her head into the water and comes up with a small and struggling silver fish. Ah! Maternal caring right before me is what I think at first. But mom snaps and chews upon this fish until it is entirely gone. How she feeds her young I do not know. But I relent from shock and just assume she needs her own reserves of energy to tend this busy little vulnerable flock before she gives them food.

Green-winged Teal and a Snipe Hunt

Near the mergansers I now see a little group of ducks all dabbling in the mud. They are small and low and seem mostly brown until I see a vertical stripe of white upon the side. And then a head with a large loop of green against some ruddy brown. I have come upon a group of Green-winged Teal who are fairly common in a muddy marsh like this. Then next to them I see a small bird that doesn't seem to fit probing at the mud. It looks something like a woodcock or a snipe with a bill that seems as long as its body which is striped on mostly brown. I have only seen a couple of snipe in a lifetime of traveling. An experienced birder who is standing near, but has never been at Huntley, gently opines that perhaps it could be a Wilson's Snipe, though he does not know if they live here. I have never heard of such a bird. I am confused and then excited. Perhaps I am adding a lifer to my somewhat stagnant life list of North American birds that I have seen. I take notes carefully of all

I see, but it is the checklist that convinces me. The only bird that is ever seen at Huntley Meadows that fits my bird's description is here in springtime. It is the Wilson's Snipe! I read a little later that this species was created in 2003 when ornithologists, who track such things, decided it was no longer just a subspecies of that funny bird, the snipe, that I last saw in the Tinicum Marsh by the Philadelphia airport some forty years ago.

Near this new find is a familiar bird whose name is not appearing now upon my mental screen. I keep thinking Semi-palmated Plover or some such thing that I see around the shore. I also think it could be that bird, whose name escapes me, that nests in playgrounds, parking lots and gravel drives at old-time roadside motels. It fakes an injury with broken wing and runs away, acting like Quasimodo to draw attention away from nest and eggs or chicks who are out on open ground. But the mind is a funny thing. It will not name a bird I think should not be here. But then as I imagine it on just such a gravel driveway at the print shop across the road from my wife's sister in Ohio, I hear it cry out with broken wing, "Kill-deer, Kill-deer!!" Of course, it is a Killdeer I suddenly remember. It is better known to me on land than here in muddy water.

Entranced by birds, I now look down into the shallow edges of the water at my feet to see what else there is to see. Sure enough there are lots of tadpoles here. This bunch is larger than the ones I just saw in the ruts near Pennyfield Lock. They are twice as big, perhaps a quarter inch, and rounder, moving faster. Those that survive out here will soon be frogs so I can return, perhaps, with my grandchildren; they will be more excited by frogs and turtles than staring at a snipe.

In a final send-off some Tree Swallows now salute me over-head. They are white beneath with blunted black-tipped tails. But it is the iridescent blue on top that makes these birds so special. They are delta-winged and darting as they gobble up the insects, too. They dip their wings at me and then streak off somewhere in the distance. The show here now is over. I slowly, reluctantly, head for home.

But I recall that the helpful ranger that I met had wished that more folks left sightings, records, memories in the visitor center's ledger. I see her now with a group of school kids all in tow. They are looking down for turtles and for frogs. I tell her that, miracle of miracles, the mother merganser and her ducklings, at least nine of them, are still safely living here. I write down all I've seen when I get back to the ledger. There are no mergansers reported on the page, but everyone else has noted Wilson's Snipe. Before I leave the center, I tour around and see a nature classroom whose great big mounted beaver and a history of Huntley Meadows shown in panels quickly lures me in.

Huntley is All That Is Left

The Doeg Indians had lived right here in settlements along the Potomac for thousands of years. Then the first European visitor to come was Captain John Smith himself. He feasted and found favor with the Doeg in the spring of 1608. But by 1651, Virginia settlers and the legislature claimed the land, and the Doeg were soon gone. In the mid-eighteenth century, George Mason, the drafter of the Virginia Bill of Rights, acquired lands around here and Hunting Creek and built his plantation, Gunston Hall, on Mason's Neck just seven miles away. Mason's grandson's built mansions overlooking the river here, one of which was used by Federal forces as a smallpox hospital and then burned to the ground. The remaining one, Huntley, is still nearby, maintained as a Fairfax County Park. The surrounding land later became farms and then dairy farms to supply the growing city of Washington. In the 1920s, the entrepreneur Henry Wodehouse wanted to create a major airfield to house an airfield for trans-Atlantic flights by dirigibles which he imagined, wrongly, as the future of air travel. The military used the Huntley area during World War II and after for anti-aircraft batteries and such. Then came housing and development except for 1,261 acres of Huntley Meadows which was saved in 1975 by the Federal Legacy of Parks program which sold the land for just one dollar to Fairfax County exclusively for park use. The overhead photos of Huntley Meadows today reveal a tiny spot of wetlands, wildlife, and biodiversity in the midst of urban growth. The photo reminds me of the lecture I just heard at Brookside Gardens on the limitations of isolated bits and pieces of land like this, no matter how full of life they seem.

The front-end loaders and construction that I saw while searching for my mergansers are part of a wetlands restoration plan for Huntley Meadows. In the 1970s and '80s, the central wetlands of the park that was technically a hemi, or emergent, marsh was highly productive and diverse. A hemi is half open water and half vegetation. It had been created by the beaver dam in a low flood-plain area that had been a forested wetland for years. The hemi created by the beavers soon attracted uncommon species like bitterns, rails and grebes as well as reptiles and amphibians. But the marsh has been steadily filling up with silt and with debris from surrounding suburban neighborhoods, as well as invasive species like rice-cut grass and the cattails used as landing pads by my beloved Red-winged Blackbirds.

This patch of wildness amidst the sprawl will need constant rejuvenation now. The water flow must be controlled with earthen berms and pipes and gates to adjust the flow. There will be more pools and deeper ones to allow for otters, the darling critters we mainly see in zoos. And, of course, a place for more diving ducks like Hooded Merganser mothers and their broods. My grandchildren may bring their kids out here someday to feel, commune with nature. But it will all be for naught if we don't learn to reduce, control, and remove the ugly, fossil fuel-driven sprawl that waits outside the park.

Chapter Five

Spring Migration

May 4, 2013
The Sound of Spring

I call ahead to the Tavern at Great Falls to ask the rangers how spring migration is moving along. I am shocked to hear that despite the cold, many warblers, at least a wave of early ones, have already been through. I can only ride and bird and write on certain days and have planned to crane my neck and ears to see and hear these tiny miracles of life, the colorful flashes of wings among the leaves that signify that the peak of springtime has arrived. I sense some failure, a little bit of gloom, in my having mistimed watching nature. But Kelly, the upbeat ranger, assures me that there is plenty to be seen. Have I seen the Rufous Screech Owl she inquires? Another lifer opportunity! I do perk up a bit. But what in the world is a *Rufous* Screech Owl and why have I not heard of it? Is this another case of my newly elevated Wilson's Snipe, where ornithologists have counted feathers I cannot even see? Or like the time Caryn and I drove into a blizzard at Montauk Point on the furthest tip of Long Island during gasoline restrictions under Jimmy Carter and were rewarded with a lifer in the form of an ordinary sea gull. It had just been elevated from a subspecies of Herring Gull to the suddenly superb new Thayer's Gull! My new ranger friend explains without any condescension that a Rufous Screech Owl is simply a different, reddish color phase of the otherwise quite brown, though darling, Eastern Screech Owl. I have not seen a screech owl for many, many years. We used to hunt for them on a stream in Ridley Creek State Park outside Philadelphia with a tape recorder and a flashlight in the otherwise spooky dark. Caryn can do an amazing screech owl call which I feebly and humorously try to imitate in falsetto. No need, the ranger says; the owl is right outside the tavern sitting in plain view.

I get an early start and roll up to the tavern, the lock, and the canal long before the rangers. It is cold, but mostly clear, and somewhere in the lower forties. I head straight for the big old sycamore that stands beside the tavern and spy a round hole in the end of a stump high up, just right to hold an owl. I focus in, but it is barren. No signs of rufous there. I feel my spirits falling as I search around the tree. When I am done and empty-handed, I look across the lock and spot the other big old sycamore where I have seen a flock of cedar waxwings and my "showy" pileated. It, too, is bare. It is beautiful in the morning light, but lifeless, barren too. The whole park seems empty, swept clean of life and sound. No skinks, no butterflies, no flowers, nothing. Just a long, cold trail and an empty, shuttered tavern. I try to rally myself a bit. At least I'll get some exercise. Then I can go back and work. I start out on the towpath at a slow, dejected pace. I am somewhat shocked at my own crestfallen mood, my reaction to unmet expectations. I have fallen prey, it seems, to some of the worst aspects of birding as a sport, not too far off from trophy hunting.

A Great Blue Heron, an old friend, flaps by overhead as if to try to cheer me up with a card or candy, or a calming conversation. I nod, I notice, I think I feel just the corners of a smile. A flicker tries next. I don't see them much when I am here. I hear them calling, or see their round, drilled nest holes, or confuse their whoop a moment with the more dramatic pileated. This one has been feeding on the ground and then flies up in a tree. I can see its white rump flashing as it flies with undulations to the closest perch nearby. Now I watch its profile, with its black mustache, a landlord in some high school melodrama. I am about to really smile, but the flicker is upstaged by the entrance of a pileated. It makes some chuckling noises, then lands, then makes its loudest whoops. It is then I see just ahead a pair of Canada Geese in a slow, stately march across the towpath toward the water to my right. In between their upright postures are four little, downy goslings, all yellow with an eye stripe. They look about the same as baby ducks, though maybe twice the size of the merganser and Wood Duck chicks I saw the other day. All six geese are nibbling now at the grass and plants beside the towpath, oblivious of me. Another cherished common bird now streaks into the water and splashes to a halt. Perhaps it is the Mallard of the other day who dropped like Icarus from the sky.

On a quiet morning it is sounds that touch the heart. Blue Jays call everywhere. I don't know what it's about. But the raucous cries are like madeleines, stirring memories of my youth. The jays are joined by Red-bellied Woodpeckers that are always hard to see. They shout, Barack, Barack! Campaigning in the woods. Then these instruments are joined by the booming of a drum. The drumming is resounding, resonant; it must be a hollow tree that a percussionist pileated has set upon to play. This fine, small orchestra is soon joined by a pan-like flute nearby. It is my first Wood Thrush of this spring; it nearly makes me cry. The notes are gentle, rolling, and softly fade away. Then they come again from in the woods as if to say, "Come play". Another sound now enters. The canal is suddenly the setting for Prokofiev's *Peter and the Wolf*. The entrance now is of the call of nearby honking geese. It starts with some guttural, short, almost growling sound, as if done in Van Gogh's Dutch. The geese out here don't simply honk. They start within the throat and then croak the sound a bit. The end result is something more like grr-awnk than honk. I try to say it several times aloud with some actual amusement. I am Peter without the wolf.

It is gosling time on the C&O. I love it every year. Although there are no wolves around out here, I have seen two goslings carried off by foxes. I count each brood and wonder which gosling will get snapped up or pulled beneath the water by a hungry snapping turtle or snatched from off the water's surface by a prowling hawk or owl. They are tender things, these goslings; but well-guarded by their parents who walk and swim beside them and hiss at those of us who come too close. In front of me now is a pair of geese with another four goslings in between. They walk and scurry about a bit as if trying out for comic roles in one of nature's Charlie Chaplin movies. I bike by at a walking pace as far away as I can be. I send out all the friendly Franciscan vibes that I can muster; I would sign the cross if it would help. This pair seems comfortable with me as a brief companion. They look up at me and do not hiss. I take it as a sign.

Now that I am moving very slowly and looking at the ground, some flowers appear that I must have just rushed by. I am near a small stream to my left where both blue and white phlox are in mixed bunches on the banks. As I move along, the phlox increase and are joined by golden ragwort. Their blue and gold stretch out before me in small bouquets as my mind and soul unwind. I stop amidst the flowers and gaze up toward the sky. A sound and sun both lead me to a single, lovely bird. I first see brick red beneath and then a black head and the sharp, curved beak of an Orchard Oriole. An Orchard Oriole is always a welcome sight for me though far too uncommon. It is a kind of underdog to the Baltimore mascot of the baseball team that is blazoned on caps and banners throughout the region. I even like the Orchard's name which the ornithologists have yet to ruin. The Baltimore is called the "Northern" now, as if its rooted, real identity has been swallowed up by our megapolis that's marked by widening, unmitigated urban sprawl. Orchards once were easier to find in small households and farmsteads everywhere back when bluebirds were quite common. Bluebird boxes and sighting Orchard Orioles are a small attempt, however, feeble, to hold back the surging, sprawling tide. For Florence Merriam Bailey or John Burroughs, Orchard Orioles and bluebirds were easy enough to see. In President Theodore Roosevelt's time, he recorded both bluebirds and Orchard Orioles nesting within the White House grounds.

Standing now by a rushing, rocky, gurgling inlet of the Potomac, I am transfixed by sight and sound. The oriole is joined by titmice intoning, cardinals flashing, and a female Common Merganser basking on a fallen tree as if she is a turtle. My cold bare woods have come to life, or maybe it is only me. Large motions and some sounds to my right call my attention to the other side of the canal. Four big does bound off, their white tails bobbing through the greens and browns. I pause then to see if I can see down in the water where some circles and bubbles have appeared. A fish, a frog, a snake, or turtle? What has made this circle? I focus in my binoculars underwater as if I'm wearing goggles. But I don't see a fish right now. What life force has moved these gentle waters is but one of many mysteries.

I am moving slowly, gently now. The woods are full of life. I see two small birds off to my left and scan to try and find them. I am puzzled once again because I see a wren that does not fit most patterns. It is small with stubby tail, but is not a House Wren, or a Winter. It has an eye line like our more common Carolina Wrens; but at a glance it looks and moves like some other, different species. Next to this small, strange bird, its mother soon arrives. She is a full-grown Carolina Wren. It is mom and her brand new fledgling that I see! I have Carolina Wrens around my yard and they have nested inside my neighbor's garage. I have just seen hungry babies in the iron flower box in my daughter's yard in Chevy Chase, DC. But fledgling wrens, which leave the nest after perhaps a dozen days, are something I have rarely seen. I watch them move about in the brush close to the river. They are after bugs and the little one is somewhat all a-quiver. I want to shout and call to folks, "Look what I have found!" But the woods are empty still except for the small, orchestral sounds and sights that now are clear to me.

As I have been riding, I have heard some warbler sounds. But they are faint and too high up for me to search out all alone. I prefer to listen, as if I'm blind, to imagine what I see. A ringing *threep!* now stimulates my cortex, some sort of flycatcher is what I'll see. My verbal self says "great-crested" before I can trace the sound. I stand and listen, slowly scanning, circling the tree from whence such threeps arise. Again, it is a yellow breast that I see first and then the blue-grey-crested head. I watch this colorful, loud bird that without some practice, or binoculars, would be pretty hard to see. Though small (it is only big in the little world of flycatchers), it opens up and blasts out loud an incredibly large, rasping sound that can be heard by anyone around. Then suddenly, without warning, it jumps off its branch and nabs a bug with a swift and deadly mid-air move. I see no knee bend, or tilt of head, or other warm-up, warning movements. Just a sudden leap into the air, a laser-guided strike.

A Buzzard Beauty

A thing of beauty is a joy forever, but would Keats have meant a vulture? In the background of my rasping flycatcher sits majestically some buzzard. It is close at hand and in my sights, so it looks as huge and mighty as an eagle. It is posed upon a large log that has fallen to make an ideal artist's stand. The wing tips are white, the tail is short, the head is black. It is not a Turkey Vulture. Soaking up the sun, the rays upon its back, is a Black Vulture resting, warming up, its giant wings spread wide in full repose. There are shades of color on its back that I have never seen amidst the shining ebony. Subtle browns and coppers and charcoal gray glint against the black. Its feathered wing-tips are spread out, each one with six long, shimmering, separated feathers that reflect the steady sunlight to our rear. It was buzzards that Mary Austin celebrated when writing of scavengers out in the western desert. This woodland vulture near me deserves my new respect. It cleans up after all the predators out here who leave behind remains to rot. But because it lives off such fetid, horrid stuff, soars high above the dead, we revile vultures of all kinds. I stand and briefly try to worship along with this grand and glorious bird. I spread my arms in kinship and glance upward toward the sky.

Along the river where I stand, five cormorants are in a circle in the water. Another one flies by so low its wings are nearly scooping up the river. It is a sweet sight, but I hear sweeter sounds a few trees up ahead. There are two clear, rounded notes that are followed by three more. It is a Baltimore Oriole that is singing in the sun, a bird that everyone adores. I think that such prejudice is not fair to the vulture I just admired. But as I watch this oriole sing forth above the moving river, its flaming color draws me in. Its orange blaze of captured sunlight is dazzling to watch. Its head and wings are black with streaks of white and wing bars. This all contrasts with glowing orange, the richest shade that I have ever seen. This new arrival here on the C&O Canal enchants me like no other. I do not want to leave this thing of beauty; I want to stay forever.

Birders Bond

A fellow birder wanders up, the first I've seen today. We talk of orioles and warblers in migration. It soon is clear that this tall, gray curly-haired, gentle man knows the birds of Maryland. He's been to Hughes Hollow and Patuxent and other sites not frequented by tourists. My hopes for migrants are a bit revived as he talks of the latecomers yet to arrive like the buzzy blackpolls that usually show up toward Memorial Day. And he is somewhat skeptical that the early waves have all passed through, especially given all the recent cold, autumnal weather. This leads to talk of global climate change and the local changes we are seeing. He is a meteorologist who works at NASA Goddard and researches climate change. His real specialty is in astrophysics and the motion of particulates high up in the atmosphere. We talk of how to convey to others what has got real climatologists worried sick about the future of the planet. I thank him for his work. But we soon turn back to talk of cameras and birds. Time enough, but not out here, to figure out the future and what is needed to avert a slow-moving, serious disaster.

As happens when one stops by woods while wearing battered clothing with binoculars, a woman dressed in running gear stops and asks what I am seeing. I show her where the oriole is and hand her my glasses for a look. She is delighted and we chat a bit about how in recent years she has begun to discover birds. She runs, then walks, and stops far more now that age is setting in. Her friends all kid her and warn that if you jog with Susan, you must be prepared to stop for birds. Then I head back for home and try to simply bike. Little groups of goslings cheer me on as flowers line my way. Before too long, I am back at Lock 20 and the old, historic tavern. It is nearing noon with people streaming in. The rangers and the volunteers are now inside on duty. I look for Kelly, but she's not there. I want to give my Rufous Screech Owl one more try. I ask a bargeman in full costume if he knows where the owl that Kelly mentioned might be in a nearby sycamore. I tell him that I have searched, but come up empty-handed. He smiles and says you were close, but it's in the one directly across the lock from our sycamore here on the corner. He pushes wide the door and says, "Come on. I'll show exactly where it is." He points to a row of four sycamores to the left of the one across the way that I examined. It takes a little while for me to get the third one from the left or right and which branch is the one he means. And then I see a hole about the size of an old mule collar. It is at the end on a big, left-branching stump about two-thirds up the tree. Sitting in it, sleeping, is a screech owl plain as day. I thank my guide profusely; he will never know how grateful he has made me. I wade through the growing groups of people and go across the lock. I raise my binoculars almost nervously. I am really very close. The old oval hole has framed this bird as if it is a portrait. Its face is wide with two small tufted ears. Its eyes are simply slanted shut above a small and hooked black beak. Its color is more varied than rufous is alone. The burnt sienna red is blended with some tawny tones, a chestnut triangle in the middle. The chest is streaked with darker red with a white blaze down the middle. I cannot see his talons; they are covered by the hole. But I am seeing most of him about eight to ten inches all in all. I stare and stare and cannot believe my good fortune on this day. As often is the case I want to shout out loud. The visitors all around me are having fun with people, friends, bikes, strollers, children, dogs. If I were to stand up on the lock and announce what is overhead, they might think me weird. They might even look and show mild interest but be bored or disappointed. I just look and look, examining each feather. At times this rufous owl, with its wide triangular, reddish head, looks somewhat like a fox. At others it is simply a colorful creature, however small, a predator from the wild. It shares its life, its space, its beauty, with us humans at its feet. But I stand puzzling why so few of us will know that he is here at all. I try to etch his features in my mind. I take a distant photograph or two. I feel renewed, restored, refreshed with just a morning's ride upon an old canal. I walk my bike toward the parking lot when I see a familiar face at the corner of the tavern just walking into view. It is the runner, walker, sometimes birder, Susan, in shorts and nylon-numbered top. I call out and say, "Would you like to see something that I've found? It's right here in a tree". It's a Screech Owl sitting in a sycamore. Come on. I'll show you where it is. Like Jeff, the bargeman, did for me, I lead her to the line of sight. Up there to the left, about three-quarters up the tree. She sees it with her eyes. I hand her my binoculars. She is happy, moved, and glad. "I have never seen an owl before. I have always wanted to!" She is beaming, watching as the owl wakes up a bit and slowly moves its head. Its open eyes look down at us. It seems to notice, welcome us. It then nods off, relaxed, to sleep again in sun. Susan is still quite gleeful. She tells me how I have made her day. I do not know why a small red owl has filled her heart with joy. I barely understand myself why this feathered apparition has done the same for me. Susan trots off toward her car. I turn and watch the owl. It is bathed in sunlight, its brownish brick red standing out for anyone to see. As I am saying my farewells another bird sails, then soars into my view. It catches sunlight, too, and circles over water. I see the white head and tail of our most majestic bird. I am sent off, saluted, by an American Bald Eagle.

May 7, 2013
You Don't Need a Weatherman

There is sullen, sodden rain, with heavy downpours. It is in the fifties in May when the normal daytime temperature is in the seventies. I am beginning to resent the cold, wet, unseasonable weather and the loss of sunny, springtime rambles. Everything is hunkered down. I see a squirrel huddled under an azalea whose blossoms are forlorn, downcast. Branches on these and other bushes nearly touch the ground, battered and weighted down as they were by snow after the unusually heavy blizzards a few years ago that became known as Snowmageddon. All of this is exacerbated for me by the cloying, clowning style of the local TV weatherman who reports how cold April has been as if it were a victory by the Redskins or a reduction in the unemployment rate. He shows two line graphs in color. The top is this year, 2013, which is colder than normal; the one below is 2012, last year's "winter that wasn't" and the unusually warm spring. The lines are, on average, over ten degrees apart. This is an incredible spread and major shift. Our weather is not different; it is totally disrupted. Hot and droughty, then cold and wet. Does he not wonder why?

May 8-10, 2013
Spring Redux

Caryn and I drive to Duke for a board that she now serves on for engaging Duke students with social issues. I have been looking forward to rolling back the spring a week or so and the beautiful drive that, once free of Washington, is all pine woods and sweet gums that in the fall will be hung with jewels of gold and garnet. On other trips, I have seen a Barred Owl perched on the pines and I like the feel of urban life slipping away as we move south toward Durham. But surprisingly heavy rain is still the norm in this unsettled season. First, gathering storm clouds looming dangerous and dark on the horizon. Then pelting rain that strains the wipers and slows down even strong and steady, speeding SUVs. We unload at the Washington Duke Inn, the manicured and muffled mansion-style hotel on campus where we are as pampered as sultans for our short sojourn. The next morning, the skies have cleared, though it is cool and partly cloudy in the morning. I walk to the Al Buehler trail, a woodland ring of perhaps three miles that also serves for cycling and for jogging. It is fairly quiet so I can hear the thwack of golf balls at the nearby driving range. Then forest sounds and smells begin to win me over, start to lift the clouds of climate change concern.

I see some butterflies and wildflowers as I begin to unwind along the trail. I am in the understory of a mature pine and oak forest with tall trees that soar up branchless toward the sun and sky. There are thick old tulip poplars and some sweet gums and magnolias mixed in here and there. The floor is a mix of loam and humus, pine needles and oak leaves, and the rich, relaxing aromas of slightly tangy, spicy air. I see some Solomon's seal in bloom and little foam flowers that I have just discovered. I quickly come upon some signs that explain that a newly recreated swamp awaits me up ahead. As I am reading about the efforts by various federal agencies and Duke to reclaim and improve some wetlands here that filter drinking water, I hear a thin high warbler sound and look straight up to see. My neck is craned, my shoulders ache, my binoculars bounce around. I used to be much better at this sport; it seems I'm off my game. But then I spot a bit of yellow high up in the trees. It is a Magnolia Warbler that's been escaping me as it works its way up north with spring. The broad black streaking on its yellow breast and great patches of white upon its tail and wings make this small bird a standout. Add a small black mask, a white eye line and grayish cap, a yellow rump, and there is your magnolia.

I walk along and rescue a turtle; we must be nearing water. I turn down a little boardwalk that leads me to a small, but steady stream. I see two Solitary Sandpipers near the mud as if I'm back along the C&O Canal. I am greeted by a phoebe and then a parula warbler! My spring migration has begun. The stream and trail lead to a pond that is surrounded by some trees and fields. From here I literally have a field day as I spot a Red-shouldered Hawk out on a snag, some Rough-tailed Swallows, Wood Ducks, and then Mallards with their ducklings all lined up. Best of all, there is a group of Eastern Bluebirds that remind me, as do the magnolia trees and warblers, that I'm really in the South. But I'll soon head north along with spring like Edwin Way Teale and Rachel Carson and others long before me.

May 13, 2013
Hughes Hollow

From Bethesda, I drive far out the River Road, past mansions, to Hughes Hollow, an area for deer and duck and goose and turkey hunters. It features fields, impoundment ponds with dikes, swampy woods, gravel and dirt roads, and trails alongside all of these. It is a favorite of Washington birders, along with the locks of the C&O Canal. Claudia Wilds's directions and sightings from forty years ago are still quite useful since this part along the Potomac remains fairly undeveloped.

It is early and cold, the kind of weather made more for shot-guns than binoculars. But the sun is coming up, the grass along my trail is dewy, and all seems right with the world. As if to prove the point, an Indigo Bunting sings lustily from a perch, then flies boldly and full of blue across my path. A pair of Canada Geese streak by, low and beautiful, against the morning sky. They call aloud without a care. It is spring hunting season here for turkeys, not for geese. A deer looks up at me down the rutted road and simply stares and waits. The deer have received an amnesty as well. A large, dark silent bird silently and lightly flaps and flies across a nearby field. A hawk? An owl? The look is too brief for me to tell.

I hear more indigos ahead, their notes trailing off into inde-cipherable babble. I see them eating something off a sunlit chokecherry tree now in blossom. Soon there will be small, pellet-sized hard green fruits that will turn into purple berries that many birds love to eat. As a boy in the fields behind my house, we used the green "peas" to carry out small wars with plastic pea shooters that we got at the five and dime. As I am thinking about the role of a supposedly weedy tree like a chokecherry, my first Green Heron of the spring sails overhead. It is dark and shorter, stouter than the elegant blue heron. Stiff short wing beats carry it away.

The Green Heron is headed toward some water that seems farther up ahead. The only water near me now is a puddle in a muddy field left behind by all our rain. As if by special sensor or by sonar, a single Solitary Sandpiper has found the only water in this field. It is busy probing this tiny, muddy microcosm that will soon enough be gone. Up close, the solitary is elegantly dressed with sharp white polka dots on its back of almost-black dark brown. Its longish bill has a slightly snooty upwards curve and it wears a monocle from the cover of the *New Yorker*. It bobs its pointed tail with tailored bars of black and white and slowly walks about, examining the mud and water quite precisely, as if on parade.

A cardinal appears alongside the field looking redder and more wild out here, a tanager without the black, contrasting wings. In the far-off distance, I pick up muted sounds of barking, baying dogs. Their echoes call up scenes of hunting dogs, not small suburban pooches. My mind goes all Faulknerian for just a fleeting moment. But, of course, I remember that I am in Maryland, not Mississippi. I am more likely to see a Barred Owl than a bear. But I feel myself slowly shedding the consciousness, the clamor, the controversy that comes with city life.

I head toward an impoundment that is filled with water plants and woods along its edges. As I walk in, I hear the shorter, rougher robin's call of a nearby Red-eyed Vireo. I track it down and get to watch it snatch and eat a caterpillar. Now I am greeted by a larger group of honking Canada Geese, but the main attraction is the noise of Red-winged Blackbirds, dangling from cattails and sitting out on tiny shrubby trees. I watch them closely with their vermillion shoulders puffed up slightly against the chilly morning breeze. I see one fly out over water and start to chase a hawk. I hear its shrill, shrieking cry as it heads off for the woods. A Red-tailed Hawk has been driven off by a bird one-tenth its size. I hear two hawks, then see them flying in agitated circles over the trees that line the water. They make their exit out of sight as a Great Egret, grand and white, takes off and glides across the water. I hear a catbird singing and then am surrounded by flashing Tree Swallows, showing deep metallic blue. A Great Blue Heron flies above me. It gives out a prehistoric gronking noise, then bends its wings to land.

All is still and peaceful now in this sunny, swampy place. I only hear the sound of Red-winged Blackbirds singing "brr-burree" or, as it sounds to me when different birds and colors are around, a cheerful "potpourri!!" The Tree Swallows fly right by me as if I am a tree and not a person. They are busily grabbing insects as they race and glide and dive. I cheer them on as they eat with endless relish. Then one flutters by me very close and circles back again. Only then do I notice I am standing directly in front of a freshly-made nesting box; it shows no signs of wear. I hold my breath and do not move, a statue now, not just a tree. After a few short and fluttering passes, I watch a shiny blue and white swallow disappear inside the box. It stays a while though I can hear no peeping nor see any signs of gaping mouths. I edge away and try to stroll off nonchalantly. I don't wish to frighten any baby birds or parents by skipping with joy at what I have just witnessed.

A short, sweet call can now be heard in the trees as I stroll by. I swing my glasses up to see before my mind can even think a name or wonder what kind of bird I'll find. The Orchard Oriole is sitting, calling in plain sight. I see it all at once. There are small trees and fields nearby, but too wild to be an orchard. Its brick red breast is most apparent, but the entire bird seems posed and picture perfect. It is a male, dressed in its best breeding plumage, with jet black tail and chest and head that makes it look so elegant.

As if in competition for best-dressed bird of the day, more Tree Swallows in evening dress swoop by, a pair of goldfinches appears, and Indigo Buntings fly in and out of an even larger chokeberry that's nearby. Then across the way I see the undulating flight of a slightly larger, bluish bird that lands out on a snag.

It is a female Eastern Bluebird with a soft wash of red on its chest of white and a pale, blue back that has been added, lightly, with a brush. It is this single, final entry, in watercolor, that wins my heart and prize. I gaze and stare and hope it does not leave. I don't get to see enough of these gentle, lovely birds. I will hold this one in my mind; it seems painted here for me.

I then see a pair of bluebirds, the female and the male. I try to capture them in my heart and not dwell too long on how common they once were; how we now try to help them with nesting boxes, mealworms, and the rest. We blame the sparrows and the starlings and other urban birds we brought. But it is our own human nesting boxes, with air conditioning and pools, that have grown so much and been spread around, that have driven bluebirds out. I don't want to go back to plantations and falsely happy days. But surely there can be some better compromise so we all can see some springtime days like these. An Indigo Bunting chimes in now and brings me back to nature. It is singing from an autumn olive bush, the one that is invasive. But there are bugs and berries and blossoms all around, a faintly floral air. I soon hear loud, ringing "threeps!" I am fully back with my noisy friends the Great Crested Flycatchers who look a bit like titmice painted yellow. As if to mark the magical morning that is really here, a Green Heron flies across my path; its legs are dipped in orange.

It's then I hear "sweet, sweet, sweet" a set of rising, gliding, gentle notes. It is a Yellow Warbler somewhere here in brushy trees beside the water; I have not seen one close for quite a while. I stop to trace the sound. I look and look and stop, then pace around for views. I cannot find this brilliant bird among the pale light greens in front. I have reluctantly decided to move along and simply savor this spring morning when I see a small bird move about from the corner of my eye. I swing to it excitedly and find an old friend, the Eastern Kingbird. It is sitting on a branch and busy chasing bugs. It sits and waits quite patiently as if enjoying sun and songbirds singing. Then out it flies and grabs a meal and returns to sit some more. There are lessons here I tell myself and sit still to watch this fable. I also note the tail that's dipped in white, the slightly crested, somewhat pointed head. My neck and shoulders loosen up a little bit. I start to breathe more slowly, deeply, to get some floral air. A smile is lightly turning up my mouth when a flash of yellow pops into my view. It is the Yellow Warbler come down to see me and show off a little bit. It is one of the sweetest, prettiest birds, a canary without cage. Its yellow breast is streaked with pale red stripes. Its back is light yellow blending into palest olive green. The head is dull green and yellow contrasting with black bill and eye. It opens up and sings for me and for our friend, the kingbird. The sweet rising notes are haunting now, a gift that's freely given.

I walk back down the dike and head toward where I've parked. Another low Green Heron flies across and shows its bright red-orange feet. Another little patch of yellow then lights up a nearby tree. I look and see the robber's mask and hear the "witchety, witchety" call almost simultaneously. It is a Common Yellowthroat, or just yellowthroat, as I prefer. The books describe it as an abundant bird of moist shrubby areas. But most folks don't know the call and don't hang out in swamps. Even then a yellowthroat is not all that easily seen. This one is right in my face. I can see the white border on the mask. It sings and sings and I am truly happy now. It must be time to ring the curtain down on this delightful scene.

But there is still an encore to be had from this troupe of nature's actors. More threeps announce the entrance from backstage of another pair of boldly costumed Great Crested Flycatchers. They are walking, hopping, flying all about a thick and gnarled old limb. It is split in places and has a hole at the end that could almost hold an owl. I see one flycatcher poking, peeking in. I cannot tell if this bird is seeking bugs or feeding somebody inside.

But it surely looks as if I may have found a nest. The setting is much like the one I saw along the C&O Canal where a pair was hanging out around a big old broken limb that looked a lot like this. I watch them go round about and eat and poke and walk out to the end. I don't see any baby birds, or hear another sound. But I am pretty sure that these threepers have proudly let me visit them at their cozy, woodland home. Florence Merriam Bailey, who taught Washingtonians and the world the proper way to bird, loved this small, showy species found in wooded, rocky hillsides, though she usually watched them at the National Zoo when it was new, or at the Soldiers' Home, some forty years after Lincoln. "This fly-catcher's nest is in a hole, not like a Woodpecker's, but in a natural cavity, and most often in a hollow limb. The nest is interesting from the bird's habit of using cast-off snakeskin in its construction, presumably with the intention of frightening away intruders."

The show seems over now and I am pleased, so I head out toward the exits and my car. But as I walk to the tiny, graveled parking lot, a female bluebird drops right down at my feet! I am practically in a theme park. If I knew how, I should probably send a tweet. The bluer, handsome husband now lands beside me, too. These quintessentially happy birds are getting dust or grit or some such stuff from right beside my car! But for me, this pair of blue-birds is another sign. They are wishing me Godspeed, farewell.

I should head home, but I decide to make one more stop at the road to Sycamore Landing. It leads down to a pond and then meets up with the towpath and canal. I drive very slowly with the windows open and lean out a bit to smell and hear the spring. I pause at a rushing stream that flows beneath a one-lane bridge. I stop and scan the water and the lush greens that now surround it. I look up and down the stream to simply feel the view. As I am doing this, a small, dark bird hops onto the galvanized metal railing that is curled up close in front of me. If birds could really talk, it would say, "Welcome, sir, to my bridge and home. You will like it in my woods!" The bird that is thinking this then starts to bob its tail. It is a friendly phoebe who seems grateful for what we build. I do not need binoculars, this phoebe is so near. I marvel at how it adapts to us and shows so little fear. I nod and thank my little woodland welcomer and slowly pull away.

I come close to the pond where the gates say no more vehicles after here. I walk ahead and hear and see a pair of catbirds in the brush. Their lively, imitative, triplet songs are really quite nice and cheery. I watch and listen, glad that they are here to liven up the woods. Then I hear them mewing like a cat and I really start to grin. I think about my grandchildren and amuse myself by imagining telling them a bedtime story I'll make up about the loud, grey bird who thought he was a cat!

I watch a Red-bellied Woodpecker hang upside down from a bent tree trunk and peck near some old pileated hole. Red-bellies are far less often seen in woods than at a backyard feeder. Pecking at this old dead tree, it seems somehow wilder, more accomplished. I look across the pond and watch a Great Egret take off and fly right in my direction. It is big, white, and sleek with black legs stretched dangling out behind. This is the very bird, with others just as handsome, that was nearly shot into extinction until, at last, the Migratory Bird Act was signed in 1918. The legislation had been pursued and pushed by Theodore Roosevelt, probably our greatest conservationist president. But TR was also urged on by other Washington birders and writers like Florence Merriam Bailey, Lucy Maynard, and John Burroughs. I am glad they birded here.

As the Great Egret settles down at the edge of the pond, I see about two dozen huge old painted turtles piled upon each other on a log. These cold-blooded reptiles must bask in warmth or they will die. Their communal love fest and togetherness is not a product of love or ideology. They form this reptilian rugby scrum merely to survive. It is very quaint and touching, these turtles huddled close.

Yet it is so obviously driven by evolution and adaptation to the natural world around them that one cannot help but wonder what forces act upon us humans despite our fancy consciousness and brains. Each spring we humans migrate from Nova Scotia or Ohio to sunny southern climes. I seek out sunshine, bird song, and spring breezes; I want winter to be gone. We celebrate the season with rituals of many kinds, with spring breaks and spring vacation, with religious holy days and holidays, of shopping, and of sports. For some it is the first pitch thrown on opening day, for others it is warblers and wildflowers that now can be observed. How much of this is what we need, how much is what we want? We have evolved and seek the sun like turtles or a tanager. It has been ten thousand years. If all this changes rapidly, can we adapt so soon?

The Blue and Gray

I walk on to the towpath in a reflective state of mind. This place has seen destruction, economic hardship, bloodshed, not just Eastern Bluebirds and Virginia blue bells, or Blue-gray Gnat Catchers chasing bugs. The blue and gray were both right here a century and a half ago. I am walking now where J.E.B. Stuart rode on a night in 1863. While Coues and Burroughs were recording birds, rebel cavalry slipped across the river from Virginia to the Union side in Maryland. This place was then called Rowsey's Ford where the water is rocky, truly shallow. Some clop of horseshoes, some glint of swords were all that could be seen or heard. Unless, of course, a Barred Owl called out like a Union sentry, demanding, "Who? Who? Who? Who?!" There is a little noticed historic marker where I have just been birding. It reads, "This crossing was used by Confederate General J.E.B. Stuart on the night of June 27, 1863, to enter Maryland on his ride around the Union Army during the Gettysburg campaign." It was during this period that Lincoln issued the Emancipation Proclamation to take effect at the start of 1863 unless the Southern secessionists surrendered. They did not. He then lobbied for the Thirteenth Amendment, including in Maryland, in order to free American slaves. It was at the cottage at the Soldier's Home, another birding hot spot, where much of this occurred. It is hard to disentangle such a history of bloodshed and men like Stuart's defense of slavery from the bird song overhead. And so I stare at the rows of buttercups that fill the fields around Locks 22 and 23. Perhaps they are a version of the poppies that symbolize the blood at Flanders Field in France. I shake off the shades of soldiers and slaves and breathe deeply once again. I hear the smooth rich notes of an oriole and look up to see. There is a pair of Baltimores singing in full color in the sun. The orange of the male, the one of baseball caps, is brilliant, startling, stunning. If only we could find a contemporary symbol like this with which we all could live.

I stop and chat with two birders on the towpath now, the first that I have seen all morning. We talk of what is near and what we've seen as birders like to do. The younger of the women is new to birding since her children are now mostly grown. Her older friend is really good. She is a singer and a teacher and can tell each song apart. They say that there are prothonotaries right nearby. They each have heard their songs and seen them not so very long ago. I review the song on a hand-held app that the younger woman holds. It is a series of rising notes, a little like a Yellow Warbler, but stronger, with richer tones. As I am listening and refreshing my recollection of the prothonotary song, I spy a small duck in the pond behind. It is black and white and my mind signals, Bufflehead? It is late in the season for a Bufflehead, though I have a hat and thin gloves on and Sharon, the novice birder and reemerging mom, has a wool cap pulled down toward her ears. Mardy, the experienced birder and a woman more near my age, is made of sturdier stuff. No hat, no shivers. Meanwhile, I am glancing at the small duck on the pond behind them. The spot is smaller, the plumage less black, but this is indeed a female Bufflehead. This little winter diving duck is a favorite of mine. I say to my new birding companions, "Look behind you, a Bufflehead"! Mardy reviews the plumage and field marks aloud, unconsciously, though nicely, checking out my call. She seems pleased with this unusual find, while Sharon has been looking carefully and pronounces happily, "It's a lifer for me!!" This is a special moment for all birders, though not the stuff of chest bumps or champagne. Birders, like their clothes, tend toward more umber, understated emotions.

We chat for quite a while about winter ducks and wanderings on shores and lakes. The conversation drifts, like ice floe, slowly, steadily to global climate change, nature books, invasive species, friends involved in environmental groups, and other nature lore. I explain that I am walking and writing in the footsteps of Rachel Carson and Louis Halle and others who have birded along the canal and throughout greater Washington. Mardy suddenly recalls that Louis Halle's *Spring in Washington* is a book she has read and loved and still has somewhere on her shelf. I mention how he had seen lots of Buffleheads in late winter and early spring at Roaches' Run, but now there are very few. On the other hand, Mardy and I console ourselves that when he birded there by the airport, the air was filled with black soot and grime from the coal-fired locomotives steaming by. The prothonotaries, meanwhile, have all moved on. There is silence. Their only songs are left on Sharon's hand-held app. I love the golden glimpses of prothonotaries, but hearing them is balm enough for me. I am even happier to get recent information since my new friends are more active, steady birders than am I. They have just seen a big day of warblers in Rock Creek Park and share details, delights, locations now with me. Then they are headed off to look for Bobolinks and meadowlarks sighted at Lily Pond Park. Sharon is building up her life list and will surely have a lovely time. I think silently about the large reductions in numbers in Bobolinks and other field birds as development slowly eats their turf. But it is just such discoveries, counts, locations, detailed information that has helped track changes in our surroundings and warned non-naturalists about long-range trends that otherwise are too difficult to note.

I see in my mind's eye my first Bobolinks and meadowlarks and what a thrill it was. Eastern Meadowlarks are more numerous and easier to see in fields and farmlands once you break free of the bustle and the beltways and slow your pace a bit. They sport a golden sweater with a black V-neck; they show off white stripes when they fly and then drop down again to disappear amidst the amber waves of grain. Sharon had not really heard of Bobolinks and so is eager to see one. I tell her how I had wanted to see one for years before I ever did. I had been introduced to Emily Dickinson's poetry as a boy by my grandfather whose grandmother had gone to Mt. Holyoke when Dickinson was there. Later I memorized her poetry to early rock and roll tunes (the meter is the same) and loved the brilliant, staccato lines of her appreciation for the beauty and religious transcendence found in the rich universe of backyard Amherst. As a young man I rushed to see the great actress Julie Harris bring Dickinson alive in her one-woman show that revealed how imaginatively rich, how full, Dickinson's supposed lonely and reclusive life truly was. I quote Emily by singing briefly to the astonishment and amusement of my new birding buddies. "Some keep the Sabbath going to church. I keep it staying at home. With a bobolink for a chorister and an orchard for a dome." It is the end of Dickinson's short poem that I particularly like. "So instead of getting to heaven at last, I'm going all along."

May 14, 2013
Rock Creek in Migration

It is again a very cool morning for the middle of May, but a sunny one with only scattered clouds. I park at the Nature Center in Rock Creek Park and slowly walk about. There is already a birder or two craning at the trees, but there are workers with machinery nearby and the birds are hard to hear. I sense some high, thin warbler notes way up in the canopy along the nature boardwalk behind the center. But nothing I can identify or locate. I move across the parking lot and down toward the horse barns. I am drawn by bird song down near there. Before too long, I spy a little bird moving rapidly from branch to branch. I catch it in my sights and squeeze gently into focus. The colors pop into bright contrast. A yellow cap and yellow on its shoulders. The face is nicely contrasting with a slim, black patch amidst a blue-grey head and upper back. This sets off a jet-black chest and white beneath the belly. The bright male has white wing bars and yellow where the back joins to its tail. The black tail itself has showy white patches that sit on either side. What was once a little brown bird is now awash in clarity and color. It is a Myrtle Warbler (the name has been changed to Yellow-rumped Warbler, but that's much too literal and prosaic for me), common in eastern woods, but beautiful to look at carefully and savor, since they only come in spring. I see several now, including the browner, duller female who has the yellow cap and rump, but is otherwise mostly brown and striped.

The Ovenbird

I am listening carefully now like a robin after worms. I hear a Red-bellied Woodpecker and some titmice and a call that's sort of like a Carolina Wren. I look around until I see a bird that's close and in the lower branches. My heart beats a few beats faster, but my verbal brain is running close to empty. Not a thrush, not a warbler, not a Louisiana Waterthrush. It is a darling bird with a great big eye ring that fills it face with a mixture of insouciance and wide-eyed innocence. It has an orange cap which runs my mental search to orange-crowned warblers and things I haven't seen for quite a while. Its chest is heavily lined with dark dots that form linear streaks that made me think of thrushes. The back is olive green and there are some black stripes above and below the friendly, wide-opened eye. I remember that I've brought my book and jammed it in a pocket. There is no one near, but I am a touch embarrassed that I have to check a guide and can't call up this familiar, long-lost friend. I am trying to appear nonchalant as I check the pages, even just a little furtive. There it is near the waterthrush. It is a kind of warbler. I have come upon an Oven-bird, one singing in plain sight. It is a bird that walks on forest bottoms and builds its domed, Dutch oven-styled nest right on the ground. The book tells me that Ovenbirds are common in deciduous woods. But that is not my experience since, like vireos, I find them hard to see. I've only seen a few of them in many years of spring migration birding. And one of them I found in my back-yard some years ago. It was lying still and perfect, looking as if embalmed and prettied up for burial. It had been killed and left there by somebody's household cat.

This Ovenbird may soon be headed north to live where Robert Frost wrote about its familiar call that in the midst of summer in New England marks the end of something. The leaves are old, the pear and cherry blossoms all rained down, the summer flowers in the woods rate a one in ten compared to spring. The call of the Ovenbird raises the question, what to make "of a diminished thing?" But for now, I want to forget Robert Frost and far New England and revel in this lovely, living bird in Washington in spring.

Warblers on the Ridge

I drive a little down from the Nature Center and the horse barns and maintenance center to a place that is called the "ridge."

It is a high point in Rock Creek Park where migrating warblers are found congregating in the treetops. I pull up between small indentations in the road that are marked as places to park or mini-parking fields 17 and 19. There are cars and bikes and birders here. I see one dressed for work who is headed for his car. From behind I recognize my friend Ken, a big-time energy lawyer and big-time birder, who has served with me on several environmental boards. We chat a bit. He offers clues of what he's seen and where. He's already done and headed off to his firm. I feel a little guilty, though not much, that I have gotten up pretty early for me, but not for top-notch birders. Ken tells me happily that he thought he might see me here. He has already seen my new friend, Sharon, who has told him we have met. As at a gym, or a golf club for some others, I suppose, we nature lovers get to know each other and show up somewhat predictably with the seasons and the birds. Whether this is biophilia or some deep, primeval stirring, or just a social network that is outdoors and free, I really can't be sure. I bid Ken farewell and start my search and sidle up near those who seem to know what they are watching. There are yellow-rumps and even a Cape May. I hear several people say they have heard or seen a Blackburnian Warbler, a spectacular find on any day. I watch with one fellow I have just met. I mention the rumors of blackburnians. He is eager to spot one. We talk of ones we have seen and how magnificent they are. But as we chat, we see and track down together the rumored, nice magnolia. It's somewhat like a male myrtle, with a yellow rump, but all bright yellow with dark streaks below a darker back. It has a big patch of white upon its wings, not just two smart stripes that sometimes can be hard to see. It has large white patches across its tail. They form a striking band much higher up, and wider, bolder than the smaller ones you see on either side at the end of a myrtle's tail. The magnolia has a slate-blue head with a thin mask of black that is set off by a nice white sort of eyebrow. I soak in this burst of color, its movement high up in the trees. A Magnolia Warbler is worth the watching, waiting, worth the hope that I may see one, however fleetingly, each springtime before it is only a memory once again.

As I marvel at my magnolia, perhaps flown in from Duke and Durham, a movement much lower, closer takes my eye. On a small tree right before me on the lawn between the roadside and the woods, a little flycatcher has just plucked a little tidbit from out the morning air. It is a cute, small bird that returns to an outer snag to show itself to me. It sits very still so I can get a portrait as if I'm Audubon or Wilson or Roger Tory Peterson. I watch this small gray-green bird catch several bugs that mistakenly fly by its little lair. It is the kind of small predation that is actually fun to watch. But underneath I worry just a little that I will not be able to name this bird. It is one of several species of *empidonax* fly-catchers. That means it is cute and small and very hard to tell apart from its other bug-catching, stupefying cousins. This one is not a yellow-bellied and seems larger than the least. It has a white throat, but so does the Willow Flycatcher and the similar Alder Flycatcher. They tend to be more northern, however, and this is not the right terrain. I watch some more and simply try to enjoy the aerial hunting prowess and successes of this little woodland warrior. If I were working on my life list, I could not really make a call. I'd need to hear the sounds that this *empidonax* makes. Bird song is like a finger print. It's why those recordings are now on bird apps, why some bird guides show sonograms, and why the old-time writers made up varied verbal concoctions to capture the uniqueness of each voice. Again I sneak a peek at a source, the Rock Creek birding checklist. There only two kinds of flycatch-ers ever seen here. One is the Least Flycatcher and this is not it. The other is the acadian which is common and nests within the park. Thank goodness for all those rangers, real birders, even ornithologists! I calmly count it as acadian; I make some notes and watch it now, but strictly for the fun.

Here Comes the Sun

As often happens when I am finally in tune with nature, no longer counting finds, a burst of color flashes somewhere far above my head. I lift my binoculars nearly vertical, my neck straining as I look for something pretty high up amidst the canopy. I see nothing but an eyeful of magnified, far-off leaves. Then out of nowhere a sudden tiny burst of orange flame appears. I am watching an eclipse of some smaller sun without protective glasses. There is no doubt at what has lit afire the trees. It is the first Blackburnian Warbler that I have seen in far too many years. I turn involuntarily to tell my hunting partner, to share the sight of this small sun chariot come down to earth. He is nowhere to be seen. I am standing alone, shielding my eyes in the face of Apollo. The blackburnian is a black and white warbler with a bold white wing patch, black streaks beneath the wings. It has a golden crown, a kind of nimbus, atop a black head channeled with flowing, liquid gold. There is yet another sliver of gold beneath the eye; it sits within a patch of black above the molten, glowing, gold-edged orange that fills the throat and chest. I am holding my breath, trying to will this solar apparition to stay with me awhile. It is no use. We mortals are only offered glimpses. If we look too long or come too close or don't avert our eyes, we will surely burn and fall like Phaeton, or like Icarus. We are given but a moment. Such revelations must last our lifetime and beyond.

A Veery by the Equitation Field

Sounds and motion begin to return to me. I begin to think, to feel. I am in a public park, on a lawn, beneath the trees in spring and that is all. I want to share this sight, this sighting. I wander down toward what is called "the equitation field." Where the ridge levels out and the road bends left, there is a large field with an old horse fence that is ringed about by trees. There must have been riding here, but now the field is untrodden; it is filled and overflowing with a sea of buttercups. As I approach I see several more Myrtle Warblers in the woods and then an awesome sight. I have been thinking mostly about warblers, but there are other winged delights. A bird not quite the size of a robin hops onto a low branch near me from off the woodland floor. I know it is a thrush of some sort, but at first I can't be sure. I have heard the fluted notes of Wood Thrushes along the C&O Canal, but this is something different. That's all I really know. When I was younger, birding all the time, I would have known right off. I have seen this one before. But there are many possibilities until I get a better look and get my brain in gear. Veery? Gray-cheeked? Hermit? Swainson's? I can't recall the main distinguishing marks for any of these. I see that this thrush is rusty colored. I know that is a clue. There are no spots to speak of, just a few dim ones in a cluster near the throat above a creamy breast. I check the tail, the eye. I try to memorize each part, each feather. There is no time to take some notes or pull out my field guide now. Again, I try to simply see the beauty in this quiet, gentle rufous bird that has joined me in the wood. I start to think it could well be a Veery. I wish I could hear it sing. The Veery's song has enchanted birders in the woods and in the forest wherever they are found. It descends rapidly down the scale in a long set of flute-like notes that stir the soul. I associate the Veery with evenings in the woods, with the smell of campfires while camping in Canada or New England where the air is crisp and stars are tossed across the sky like pixie dust.

The official bird name, Veery, is a relatively recent one. My bird in question was first called the Tawny Thrush by the great early ornithologist Alexander Wilson in his *American Ornithology*, even though the current Wood Thrush was known by that name at the time. In 1817, in his *General Zoology*, James Francis Stephens pointed out Wilson's confusing naming and called the bird the Brownish Thrush. This humdrum appellation didn't stick.

So the bird was named the Wilson's Thrush. Elliot Coues uses both Tawny Thrush and Wilson's Thrush in his editions of *Avifauna Columbiana*, the first serious compilation of Washington birds in 1862 and 1883. Only in 1909 was the Wilson's Thrush changed officially by the American Ornithological Union to the Veery, since it replaced a "bookish" name with one in more popular use. In "Spring in the Capital" in *Wake-Robin* (1871), John Burroughs calls the bird the Veery Thrush. But whatever the name, the effect on the listener is always the same, as it was for Burroughs. "I have heard the veery thrush in the trees near the White House; and one rainy April morning, about six o'clock, he came and blew his soft-mellow flute in a pear tree in my garden. The tones had all the sweetness and the wildness they have when heard in June in our deep northern forests." My thoughts of John Burroughs rambling through Rock Creek and waxing lyrical over Veeries are interrupted when I hear the old familiar *threep!* of a Great Crested Flycatcher nearby. I find it in a big, old gnarled tree near the corner of the equitation field. I spot a pair of these noisy, colorful flycatchers and am amused again at the raucous projection of their call and the silly official genus name, a tyrant flycatcher, for this wonderful, small, blue and yellow crested bird. I turn my glasses now to look at something smaller, maybe less familiar, and hence, for the moment, more interesting. A warbler? It is small and active with a rusty cap and an eye line—whoa! A little Chipping Sparrow! I watch the first and then more appear. Chippers move in little flocks. They feed in and around the bottom of big trees in open fields. Now I hear their little chipping sounds. To me they are delightful. I first saw these birds around the trees on the wooded lawns of a big old rambling hotel in Pennsylvania near where Caryn spent some summers. I have loved them since, but they are somewhat hard to find in greater Washington. They are listed as uncommon in Rock Creek Park. As I watch the chippers, I see another old friend land on a lower snag and wag its tail as me, as friendly as a Labrador. It is a phoebe, though it does not call. It simply sits and says hello.

Then high above the elfin suns of buttercups in the field, six golden streaks go dipping, flashing by. They land nearby to feed on top some flowering tree. I now can see the razor contrast of their black upon their gold. Out here with woods and sun and Burroughs on my mind, no common birds are these. This shining flight of American Goldfinches takes on new dignity, new meaning, new feelings, wild and free.

Exotic Birds

As if to confirm my feelings for this spectacular backyard bird, I see another birder following them closely as if they were macaws or toucans or some exotic bird. He is holding a hardback birding book and is dressed in stylish shorts. I strike up conversation to see what he has found. I hear his Oxbridge accent and ask where his home in England is. He answers that now he lives in "Fronce." This British expat birder, who now lives near Lyons in France, is in love with all our birds. Yes, he has been watching the smashing goldfinches and then says somewhat excitedly, "Isn't that a phoebe?" His name is Chris and he tells me with wonderful accuracy and description how he has been fortunate enough to have just seen a Barred Owl sitting by the road behind the equitation field. We watch in awe together as the goldfinches move again, undulating, unworldly golden birds that glisten in the sun.

May 17, 2013
A Revolutionary Oak

I am away for a trustees' meeting and Commencement at Mitchell College in Connecticut in New London on the water.

There is little time for nature, though there are cool and crisp fall-like sunny days. Spring has been rolled back here for me by perhaps two, three weeks or so. Trees are not quite leafed out and the pink and white dogwoods on the lawns are still in bloom. It is a lovely setting, a special little place. But I grieve when I see that an ancient oak that filled much of central campus with a bronzed Nathan Hale standing stoically beneath has disappeared, is gone. Nathan Hale and oaken benches are standing in full sun. Superstorm Sandy, a howling mix of wind and snow, was worst here in New England. It tore the old oak down. The storm is just one of many consequences of the shifting climate we have caused. This mighty tree that stood before the living Hale was teaching here in Revolutionary times is gone forever. It cannot be replaced. I stand and pay respects to the patriot and the patriarchal oak that stood together faithfully and bravely here when our nation was still young. More will be lost, I think to myself, unless we act, unless we begin a new American, a new global revolution. I look out at the Thames River, up to the bright cerulean sky, across at other old, though not yet ancient trees, at academic buildings, at old brick walls that surround what was once the Mitchell family estate. I try to breathe in beauty. I will not, cannot, give in to mere anger, or despair. It is just such settings that I need to carry on, to restore me, fill me, give me strength for all that lies ahead.

That evening, I sit at dinner at a waterside restaurant that looks out at boats, and pilings, and the river. I am talking with the new board chair, a friend and older, pioneering female physicist. As a boy growing up on Long Island, I tell her, I used to go with my parents to just such a place for seafood and the sights and smells of nature by the water. Just then, I say, "I think I see an eagle," as a huge black bird with white head and tail sails across the window. I am mixing memory with desire. I know as soon as I speak it is surely not an eagle. The large Black-backed Gull settles down and folds its wings as it sits upon a piling. It is a glorious bird, even if not the symbolic hoped-for eagle. We watch other gulls in flight; a white ferry slowly glides along the river. I hold the moment in my mind. I want the birds and beauty to stay with me awhile.

May 19, 2013
Great Falls in Fog

I get to Great Falls in early morning fog. It feels like autumn. I wear a windbreaker and cap and keep my hands inside my pockets. Although it will rain today, I wanted even a brief chance to see how Washington in spring is progressing in the week since I've been gone. As I walk toward the historic Tavern at Great Falls, a Great Blue Heron sails above and greets me. It looks as if we are in Maine in an early twentieth-century Sarah Orne Jewett story. All the normal birds look quite exotic in this foggy, drizzled light. A Blue Jay darts across, partly shrouded, its blue and white a blur. I watch a titmouse work some woodpecker holes in the trees beside the tavern wrapped in mist. Each sound seems more important in the fog, each creak, each crunch, each groan, each rustle. I see some ghostly Canada Geese by the canal with six grey and foggy goslings. Each one is half the size of their black and white, slightly smudgy parents; the only yellow is on their heads. They are about the size I have seen a fox cart off, the long neck dangling toward the ground. These growing goslings, the lucky ones, may yet make it through the spring.

The fog is slightly lifting now, though there are miniscule, fuzzy drops of rain. I think of birding in Berkeley by the bay. But the sounds I hear from above me in a sycamore are not from California. Oriole calls, all jumbled up. I try to use my eyes. I finally spot an Orchard Oriole; its brick red chest in mist looks almost brown. Then a pair of Baltimore orioles peeks from out the leaves.

Refracted in light rain, the yellow of the female seems brighter. The handsome male looks different too, as if I have found another species. The orange that he's known for is beautiful, but dimmer, slightly duller, burnished some with age.

Another silent heron glides overhead, a goblin clad in gray. I tromp across the bridge beside the tavern, above the barge that's moored there, to the river side of the canal. I want to look up closely in the sycamore to see if the screech owl is still there. With slightly nervous anticipation, I raise my binoculars to the hole where I last saw him. As I focus in, the lenses gather light and brighten up the scene, but, if there, my Rufous Eastern Screech Owl will not be in the sun. I frame the horse collar of a hole that has formed in the broken limb. It seems the owl has never moved; it is still sitting very still. It is a chestnut brown owl now; in this moist air, with shaded view, it is no longer rufous. Sienna streaks and pointed ears with glowing, large black eyes. The screech owl is awake! Perhaps he thinks it's night, or maybe evening. I wonder when he eats, and what he eats, and if he hunts in early morning fog. I look at him with magnified eyes, and he stares back with his. We are both hunters of a kind who have come within the arms of this hazy sycamore to rest.

The morning fog is now a gentle spritzing; I can see it on my windbreaker and some dark spots on my Dockers. I can't stay long. I breathe deeply and absorb the scene around me. The lock with pouring water, the high river in the background, rushing noisily over rocks. The tavern looks like a wrinkled, faded photograph left here somehow from 1889 when things were busy, thriving, when some one hundred people worked here, when mule-pulled barges took city tourists fifty miles upstream to Harper's Ferry. Herons flew over then as two more do right now. It is the herons, the mist, the fog that are eternal; at least they are for now.

At home I watch and wait to see the white-throats who have been my close companions beneath my kitchen window throughout the winter and the spring. But they have flown further north to breed and sing either "Old Sam Peabody, Peabody, Peabody!" or "Sweet Canada, Canada, Canada!" depending on the border. I feel a sense of loss and sadness, but when it's hotter, humid here, I'll migrate, too. I can follow them to Maine. There are other losses in the yard; I feel somewhat to blame. While I was in Connecticut, Caryn found the half-eaten carcasses of two robins in our backyard birdbath. She thinks that crows may be to blame. Caryn seems as horrified and angry as Rachel Carson's friend Olga Huckins who found robins in her yard all twisted up in agony and dead from DDT. We have lured these robins into the yard. We watch them bathe and cluck and dig up worms and wet mud to build their nests for blue egg-shelled babies. We have watched with pride as huge Fish Crows that are nesting down the block come bathe and drink from our birdbath where they never did before. I should understand predation; I have seen robins carried screaming out for help or mercy in the talons of a Cooper's Hawk in woods. But this seems different, artificial, awful, an ambush made by man.

The robin is really the American best-loved bird. Every nature writer has adored and then described them since 1850 when Susan Fenimore Cooper described the widespread cheering when the first spring robins came back to Cooperstown. Among Washington writers, the robin is the first bird described by Florence Merriam Bailey, the founder of birding with binoculars, who lived in Kalorama. In *Birds through an Opera Glass* (1889) she writes, "He is full of buoyant life. He may always be heard piping up above the daybreak chorus, and I have seen him sit on top of a stub in a storm when it seemed as if the harder it rained the louder and more jubilantly he sang." Is it any wonder that Rachel Carson was distraught and then took action when the songs of cheery robins were silenced by poison sprays that filled the air?

May 20, 2013
Prothonotaries by the Pond

I return to the pond near Riley's Lock on the canal like a swallow to Capistrano, or unshaven, unwashed as I am at this hour, like a buzzard back to Hinckley, Ohio. I want to see those prothonotaries that I missed in more than just a new friend's app. I tiptoe, yet with occasional crunches and sharp snaps, down the little used narrow dirt road that leads to the canal from Tschiffley Mill Road. Riley's Lock Road, just a couple of car lengths down River Road next to Tschiffley's, is paved and sports a colorful sign that designates it scenic. Nevertheless, it runs smoothly by houses and straight on to the lockhouse and a parking lot. On my side of the stream, things are tangled, wooded, all gravel road, with weeds and wildflowers on the sides. I park in a small, dirt turnout and head out on foot. As I near the pond on the right, I look down into an overgrown, swampy pool in the woods to my left. It is practically primeval. I had heard a prothonotary down in here the other day before I met up with Mardy and Sharon on the trail. I simply stand and wait and look and listen. I let my mind and imagination wander just a bit; I am in a southern swamp where I saw my first prothonotary amidst the ancient sounds of gronking Wood Ibises and Wood Storks. Here, it is fairly dark around the shallow pool that is underneath thin trees, bushes, shrubs, and hanging vines of every kind. Into this paleo picture, a brilliant, deep flash of golden yellow suddenly appears. I have traveled back in time or at least back to Georgia in the 1970s, to the Harris Neck National Wildlife Refuge that had been an air base that was closed and, long before, a plantation whose road past where the slave cabins would have been is lined with live oaks with lengthy arms and Spanish moss that drips with parula warblers.

My new prothonotary is now close up and unafraid. Its sharp black bill and eye stand out against its golden head. Its wings are a soft blue-gray. There is a shade of olive near the back. But the rest is truly golden. One man's gold is another's dross, but you can be sure it is not just ordinary yellow. When I got my first look at a prothonotary, I gasped aloud. I had seen Yellow Warblers, yellowthroats, and goldfinches, both bright and burnished, at my feeders. But the gold on this bird is deep orange-yellow gold; it cannot be mistaken for brassy, brazen, butter, sunny, or any other yellow word. One small bird, a Prothonotary Warbler, has lit up my morning, as it does this dank and swampy pool. It is such a perfect scene, such a perfect photo op, that the prothonotary throws back it's head and warbles into song. Just then another apparition drops down from out of nowhere into the shallow water. It is a female Wood Duck who has been roosting somewhere in a tree nearby. In all my years, I have never seen a Wood Duck jump down from up above me. I have seen them on the fly, or posing like a carving, or clucking to a clutch of tiny ducklings in a row. But this is a first for me to witness what all the bird books say. The Wood Duck lives in cavities in trees or man-made boxes nailed to one so it can get some privacy. I admire her giant eye ring, her small brown helmet, her understated elegance. I pause for just a while. I don't want such moments to end or fade away, before I head on to the canal.

My eyes and senses are as wide now as a Wood Duck. I notice little things. The wild raspberries are in flower, no longer nasty vines. The path has left small arrangements for me of daisy fleabane against the sight and scent of flowers that will offer raspberries this summer to all who pass this way. They will give true nourishment for birds and beasts and body, mind, and soul. A bullfrog groans agreement in the distance as I step on to the towpath. I head left toward the bridge and lock and lockhouse at the end of Riley's Road. I stop to watch some chickadees and titmice who are feeding silently in the trees right near the water. I wonder what the tree is that I am standing right in front of. It does not look familiar. It is some kind of maple with eight or nine layered, dangling pollywogs arranged in little clusters. But the leaves are not the five-pointed kind of maple leaf that we are so familiar with. These have rounded, slight triple lobes. The leaf is nearly oval. I look it up and think I've found a striped maple. Though, if so, it must be in the southern part of its range and the temperatures here by the river cooler than elsewhere in the woods. I'll come back in fall when colors help or ask the rangers when I see them.

I look out at the Potomac. Here it is vast and wide. But today there is no wind and not much sun. All is silent, still, as on a silver lake. A titmouse floats down like a falling leaf. Close to the shore I see a goose and then a white bird as if I have entered a fairy tale or fable. It is a Mute Swan that I have never seen here along the wide Potomac. It makes barely a ripple in the glassy surface it shares with just a single goose. Its graceful neck is curved just so, the Canada's is straighter. They look like furtive lovers whom protocol must keep apart until they slip off on a cool gray morning to rendezvous far from others' sight.

I simply stand and look at the quiet morning river; faint floral smells and earthen odors fill the air. A Wood Duck drake streaks across the bridge, heads upstream, and sharply banks and lands somewhere along the river's side. I assume it is the mate of the female I just saw. This stirring sight is just the start of morning glories on the river. A Pileated Woodpecker follows soon—a silent burst of black and white and red. A squadron of looping goldfinches is next to pass my small reviewing stand. They seem fast and free out here released from backyard duties. A Carolina Wren that snatched a bug nearby now wipes its bill politely on a branch, as if it were a napkin.

Though wide awake, I am moving slowly, breathing deeply, as I retrace my steps from the other day along the towpath past the pond. I have not consciously crept up, or slowly tiptoed, as did, perhaps, the Doeg or Piscataway of long ago. But I find myself standing, one foot slightly raised, beside a Great Blue Heron who seems to mimic me. We stand still together in solidarity this morning. I look into its yellow eye, the iris, black and bold, is easy enough to see. This silent, stoic heron is looking back at me. I admire its yellowed saber bill, its grey blue feathers hanging down, its blackish wings and ancient, scrawny legs. I own a carved one just like this that stands in front of leather books in my Bethesda study. Some future archeologist will have to puzzle out why such wooden household totems were kept in our skeptical, modern times.

A little further on I see splashing, flapping, little sprays out in the water on a rock. I zero in to look and spy a mother Wood Duck with two or three good-sized ducklings playing or washing I can't be sure. Has she brought them here for me to see from the nest behind the pond? Or is this another group, the neighbors from across the wooded way? I marvel at the work and love it must have taken to get these few ducklings out of perhaps a dozen to survive and play and thrive. I promise not to take such sights for granted, to recall the connection that I feel. I may even add another totem to the small bookshelf altar in my home.

I move gently now a bit more up the path. Another heron greets me; it is standing on a mossy log. Then, in the path, pops up some friendly little critter. It moves toward me. Its cheeks are full. It stops and stands up on its hind legs with its paws in prayer position. It is a local chipmunk pretending to be a comic prairie dog. I look at its white eye line on its small and pointed tawny head. I am back in Colorado when I was eight and saw my first chipmunk close up in the wild. In the Rockies then I saw snow and hail in summertime and began to wonder how such things could come to be. Now, two generations later, I am worried about the end of glaciers and of prairie dogs, and maybe even chipmunks, if we continue on our way.

A flattish, small-sized turtle now proceeds to underscore my thoughts. It is just sitting in the path apparently without a care. I move slowly toward it to take a peek; it simply pulls back into its shell. It is then that my first fellow human of the morning walks up to me. We start a quiet conversation. I tell him I am looking for prothonotaries, but so far just a turtle. My new companion's name is Richard and he is a frequent birder. He also knows his turtles and calls them into MARA. MARA, he explains, is the Maryland Reptile and Amphibian Watch that uses volunteers to identify and call in turtles and snakes and other sightings with photos as the proof. He snaps a picture of my turtle and calls it in through his phone. I have fallen seriously behind in modern nature study out here in the trackless woods. What we are holding, Richard shows, is a musk turtle, not a mud turtle, since the shell has no hinge to bend a little underneath. The creamy pattern that looks like some sort of leaf is another way to tell. We talk of turtles and how we played with them as kids and found box turtles near our houses.

Just then, I hear a Prothonotary Warbler; I don't wish to miss it. Richard tells me that they are all around here, though he cannot tell by song. He is tone deaf and birds by sight alone. I explain the sweet, sweet, sweet, sweet song that I learned anew the other day. But it soon is not a problem since a deep golden-headed warbler soon flies into view. Before long I have seen several prothonotaries and enjoyed their melodious song. Richard points out that they are here and easily seen because a local birder has put up nesting boxes! I had seen one or two but thought that they were for bluebirds or some other dwindling species. Four or five of these small yellow pine rectangles with little holes mark the path from Riley's Lock to just beyond the pond. They are fresh and new like the empty wren box in my yard. I thank Richard for all sorts of new naturalist information and, inwardly, thank the guy that built these boxes that brought back the sweetly singing golden-headed marvels for mornings such as these.

I have marveled at the prothonotaries so much that after Richard leaves I nearly miss a glimpse of what seems to be some sort of puffed-up little chickadee. But I know my backyard friends too well to be fooled by this imposter. This is a young Blackpoll Warbler that is black and white and has a cap just like a chickadee. But it lacks the black bib to match its cap and makes no familiar "chick-a-dee-dee-dee" noises. I have not seen a blackpoll like this for many years, perhaps since Philadelphia. One fall at home when my elder daughter Rebecca was a baby bouncing gently in some springy seat beside me, I watched fall warblers every day from our small back deck. Migrants came from Fairmont Park and settled in our yard. I was very proud that I could tell each fall warbler from the others. In autumn their flashy, distinctive colors are all faded, turned into blurry shades of brown. The Blackpoll and the Bay-breasted Warblers look maddeningly the same. The bay-breasted, which is gloriously colorful in spring, can only be told from a blackpoll by the fact that its legs are buffy, not black, and it is very slightly buffier on its belly. Learning such details is rather odd to say the least. So I am very happy now to see a blackpoll in the springtime, even if in a chickadee disguise.

Now that I have paused along the trail and am attuned to tiny movements, another favorite bird of mine appears; perhaps it is the name that made me fall in love. The Nashville Warbler could be the nickname for some sashaying country singer. It is part of the colorful music scene that we fans have come to see. It is bright yellow underneath, including its chest and throat, with a blue-gray head that sets it off from other yellow warblers. But for me, it is its pure white eye ring, like a Wood Duck head done in miniature, that gives the Nashville its innocent, wide-eyed, country song appeal.

Still enchanted by my warblers, I move on by car to each choice birding spot along the canal this morning. I drive slowly out on Tschiffley Road and hear more prothonotaries serenading me goodbye. Then an odd bird with an insect in its mouth catches my eye. I stop to get a better look. It is a young bluebird that looks like some oddball thrush, or unmarked robin, or some other puzzling thing. But after many looks from every angle and a peek at the book that's in my car, I take some pleasure that this gentle little native bird is still around here, too. As if to show me what blue is really all about and to be sure I can tell the difference, a male Indigo Bunting appears and struts his stuff, the bird from the *Golden Guide*.

I pull into the Pennyfield Lock bumpy parking area near where Grover Cleveland used to stay. There are new tadpoles in the puddle and two deer watching me up ahead. And either the Indigo Bunting has followed me or another one wants me to be dazzled by its blue. He is sitting out on a snag by the lot singing in the morning sun. It is a kind of five note combination of tweet, tweet, tweet— sweet, sweet! There is minor mumbling at the end. But no need for sounds or apps to see this fellow greet the day. He seems unconcerned as a Red-shouldered Hawk flies by from the side of the canal. Perhaps blue-colored birds taste lousy or the song scares hawks away. I only know that I am glad to see both big and little birds sweep in the spring with me. I watch in close up a Turkey Vulture sitting just above me in a sycamore. Some more indigos are here. A swallowtail floats by and a cardinal, looking wild and wonderful, flies across my path.

But soon I see some flitting, rapid movement in a tree that's to my right. I scan catch a glimpse of some tiny bird in motion. It is a Blue-gray Gnatcatcher starting on its morning rounds. Like a redstart or a hyperactive child, it won't, or can't, sit still. I follow it, my binoculars bobbing all around. I few more looks and I'll be seasick. I look down at the ground. And there to test me once again is a turtle in the path. I have no app, no I-phone, no Richard to help me now. I just know it's not a childhood box turtle from Long Island. I pick it up and turn it over as if I know what I am doing. I look at a different oak leaf tawny pattern and think I see a hinge. But I'm sort of nervous to pull on it to see if it really moves. I place it on the ground in the grass that's by the path. I'll put it down as a mud turtle for now and check out books and the MARA website when I get home.

Snappers in Love

This must be turtle day today for there are many, many more along the canal. There are sliders and painted turtles on logs and at the shallow, muddy edge of the lagoon where I've seen solitary sandpipers, swallows, Eastern Bluebirds on other days. But now there are big muddy rocks that were not here before. Snapping turtles! They are huge. They have their heads in the water and are feeding. Am I related to these omnivores? Each seems at least a foot long and there are at least seven of them. Then I see two muddy boulders leaning one on top of the other. It is snappers mating, the one mounted on the other. This does not look like fun to me, no matter who's on top out there. So this is why we call it mating, not making love. There soon will be little snapping turtles all around to grab a toe, or crush a duckling, or cause some other kind of woe. This scene is straining all my talk of biodiversity, endangered species, and the rest. Do we really need such beasts? I try to think of the Canada Goose droppings that litter everywhere. OK, OK, a gosling or two, but then you get no more. No Wood Ducks, please. That really goes too far. I look back at sliders slim and sleek, but then my eyes return to this canal-side peep show primeval. Where did they come from? How did they evolve? These lumbering, ancient creatures who live on and on upon so very little. I know I will recall this spring by this May ritual laid out before me. I finally smile a bit and nod and cheer their mating on.

A little further on, I see the grandfather, the patriarch of this Paleolithic pageant. A huge old snapping turtle is propped up at an angle, just basking in the sun. Tawny underneath with jagged armor everywhere. The snout and claws are fearsome in their size. But this giant shaman snapper looks also very wise. It rests, it worships, it soaks up sun; it surveys with pride its rock-like tribe. The ancient Native Americans and Captain Smith have watched a scene like this. These wise and fearsome turtles are still here, still sitting, still serene.

The snappers are not far from a bluebird box where I often see a metallic, flashing blue Tree Swallow come and go. But I laugh out loud as I peer across at a Prothonotary Warbler now perched atop this little human-made motel. I long for one of those huge, long-lensed birder's cameras to capture my gargantuan, grizzled reptiles and a prize-winning warbler in one bright frame together.

Mud

I think I may have not appreciated mud enough, the primordial ooze we always hear about from whence we humans emerged in Genesis. Just beyond the lagoon, to my right in the canal, a small muddy peninsula has formed where bubbling, running water enters in. Gathered in the middle of this newly-formed spread of mud is a startling, showy, yellow, flapping pile of Eastern Tiger Swallowtails. They are hopping, circling, eating, like buzzards on a carcass somewhere in South Africa. All this for mud! If I am amazed at snapping turtles procreating, feeding, lounging, in a muddy small lagoon, I am simply now incredulous at this pile of beauty writhing on the sodden ground. I watch with fascination at the motion, color, abandon with which these butterflies can feed. I try to count them, maybe eight or nine, and see how well they act together, if there is bullying, or somebody in charge. But it is simply chaos theory on the ground; I can see no patterns. Just yellow wings and tiger stripes and rapture all around.

A Murder of Crows

Finally the call of a Great Crested Flycatcher distracts me from the butterfly feeding frenzy on the ground. I watch this little show-off friend and see a Black Swallowtail butterfly (it has lovely blue as well) sailing by. I pass the rocky cliffs and stop to watch two Blue Jays chase a crow. They scream and dive against this bird that's more than twice their size. An aerial battle worthy of the *History Channel* plays out before my eyes. I think it's ended, over, quiet now. When to my horror, a crow flies out from behind the cliff with something small and brown and live that's clutched within its mouth, a lone Blue Jay in pursuit. I think about the Fish Crows in my yard and start to feel like Caryn. No wonder a bunch of these cawing monsters is called a murder of crows. I start to sympathize with farmers, shotguns, poison. I need to settle down. My reaction comes from too much Disney as a child, or Emerson or Wordsworth when I was still in college. Nature is not just pastoral and sylvan scenes or tuneful little warblers. I stand and ponder for a while and wonder where I fit. Shoot at crows and declare all raptors vermin, as did naturalists of old? Stand and watch through good binoculars and let nature take its course? I remember that none of this would be here except for Justice Douglas who stopped one more modern highway in 1954. I briefly offer condolences to the Blue Jays, thank Justice Douglas, Rachel Carson, Roger Tory Peterson, and the rest. If I feel so deeply for one snatched jay; I must do something more when all of nature, our whole planet, is increasingly at risk.

A Warbler in Disguise

I go a little farther to unwind again. I watch a phoebe and then a Red-eyed Vireo each snatch and eat a bug. It doesn't bother me at all. I listen to the sounds of the river rushing. I turn around and start back home. Near where I was told last year that they nest, and, this year, are in action by the lagoon, I finally see a Louisiana Waterthrush, a warbler in disguise. It walks along with mostly horizontal posture, an eye stripe, brown back, and streaks along its sides. It looks like some sort of smaller thrush, so I suppose the name. I watch it walk along the mud in the canal side across from the dry lagoon. And then I spot another.

I am now in birder's heaven. I have wanted to see these birds that I barely can recall from years ago in Pennsylvania. But, as is the rule, each time I hunted for them, they would stubbornly refuse to show. Now I am content to watch, though I secretly pat myself on the back as a naturalist in the know whose passport has been renewed. As if to acknowledge my now recovered status, two Great Egrets fly by and relieve themselves in air. These majestic white plumed birds, with a simple splat, have put my prowess in perspective.

I am nearly done. The sun is high. A Solitary Sandpiper bobs and weaves like a boxer on the shore. We are nodding in agreement about a springtime day. Above my head a heron escort dips its wing and leads me to my car.

May 22, 2013
Spring in Shade

At home a rabbit greets me and there are tulip poplar flowers on the ground strewn everywhere, on the lawn, the patio, the driveway. They are beautiful up close; these seeds of the Northeast's most majestic shade tree attract birds and butterflies when high up in the branches. They form cups of chartreuse and lime and limpid yellow, with fingerprints of slightly rosy-tinted orange that slowly fade to browning parchment down here in the yard. My poplars aren't yet thirty years old, but they are almost three feet wide. The one in back beside the fence has some Virginia creeper growing up its side. It is another native plant that is crimson in the fall and will succor birds and bugs and keep my song birds coming. Out in the front I look again, as I do each year, at my native rhododendron. The red ones are the hybrids; this native one is white until you look more closely. A neighbor once admired it; I have loved it ever since. Each blossom is a pentagon of petals as white as is the snow. But each petal is delicately painted with tiny streaks of gold. It is incredibly tiny brushwork that defies all explanation. In the middle of this doll house English china cup is some craftsman's final touch. Set into place are little T-shaped stamens made out of old-time rose. These cups are then attached against a set of long and oval, dark green leaves. The full effect is first in show and sitting by my curb. I want to put out signs or ribbons or shout so that everyone will see.

We are nearing June. Soon heat will rise, but for now things are still in late spring bloom. There are rhododendrons, pink and red, out on many lawns. There are irises standing tall in gardens in blue and mauve and purple. Their fragrance is intoxicating, as are the linden trees in blossom. I breathe and sigh and head inside and hope that springtime lingers. I find an e-mail from my birding friend Sharon who has gone to Rock Creek Park for one last look at warblers. They are mostly gone she says. I share my Nashville Warbler and my blackpoll from out on the canal. Spring is moving northward, soon summer will arrive.

May 23-24, 2013
Tropical Spring

My fears of summer are premature, unfounded. It is cold and wet for two full days. A perfect time for work. Then off to Martinique to do some babysitting. My daughter's research is in the departmental archives in the Caribbean part of France. Caryn and I will watch Nora, see some sights, explore the tropics with our son-in-law while Emily does her work. The rain that was in Maryland is on the beaches, too. But it comes and goes throughout the day, with clouds or sunshine in between. We can watch the squalls form quickly as the wind picks up, the skies turn grey, then black, and then unleash their water. The first time that this happened, Emily simply told us, "Run!" No time for ponchos or umbrellas or slow arriving rain. If you don't move within two or so full minutes, you'll simply be soaked through. I look online and see that Bethesda has now gone up to ninety. It's slightly hotter, wetter here on a tropic island. But not by much. My fears of someday living in the tropics may yet have some real basis.

June 4, 2013
Cycling Toward Georgetown

It has been rainy since we came back to Bethesda. At least we beat the heat. Today is perfect springtime, perhaps the last I'll see. The early morning is sunny and cool, a stirring sixty degrees. It heads to seventy as I set off on my bike and stays right there all day. I am finally dressed in riding gear, black shorts and tee shirt, no long sleeves, sweatshirts, jackets. I head down Little Falls Parkway and enter in the woods at Massachusetts. There is a winding bike path here that joins up with the main Bethesda Crescent Trail. I ride as slowly as I can to savor all this green and springtime temperatures that have been hard to find this year. The path rolls by a rocky stream that will end up in the Potomac. It is beneath a leafy neighborhood with folks who walk their dogs. Along the way are saplings that have been planted, protected from the deer and dogs by rolls of chicken wire. This is a local project to clear out invasive species, then plant native trees for shade, to soak up water, hold the soil, and keep this patch of woods from being ruined. I thank again whoever makes this environmental investment. I am the beneficiary. I wonder a while why it is that we comfortable Americans like to live so close to nature. Almost all our wild spots, even little ones like this, must somehow be maintained and then protected. I think of zip codes, incomes, of mansions high up on the cliffs of the Potomac. But enough of this, I already did a sermon at my church on the Sunday nearest Earth Day. That was the time and place to wonder aloud why pollution, waste, and factories are almost always closer to the poor.

As I turn onto the Crescent Trail, I am near a small dam and reservoir that provides DC with water. Across the back is an older, low brick, peak-roofed building that gives this municipal water works the slight feel of an historic village. And sure enough I soon see colorful, fork-tailed Barn Swallows swooping, diving, eating bugs with great abandon. Like me, they must imagine that they are near a barn. I ride on some more across a bridge beneath a water tank that is labeled Washington Aqueduct - 1853 with the crenulated castle logo of the Army Engineers. I am riding through what would look to be a small and tidy college campus, but for barbed wire fences and old, fading sheet metal shield-shaped signs in red and white and blue that variously say "US Government Property" and "No Trespassing." But the land is undeveloped, open, and unspoiled, with some specimen trees on lawns that turn to woods as my Trek travels through the campus.

I pass through fields with Rough-winged Swallows now feeding overhead. They are quick, in constant motion, with white rumps and brown backs and an endless thirst for gnats and other pesky prey. I am heartened to see a hummingbird high up in the branches of an old ash tree by the trail; they have scorned my yard and feeders this time around. There are daisy fleabane stretched up and growing tall among some weedy tangles and oxeye daisy by a fence. Before too long, I come to Fletcher's Boathouse where the Crescent Trail and the C&O towpath join together. I look up before I park my bike and see a Yellow Warbler. These little beauties with red streaks on their sides prefer brushy, semi-open spots near water. This is only the second I have seen in quite a while, so I simply stand, straddling my bike, and take a good long look. Then I park my bike and walk behind the boathouse concession stand where I have heard some oriole sounds. I soon pick out an Orchard Oriole, with its brick red breast, as if sent from central casting. These orioles like a mix of lawn and trees and open woods. It need not be an orchard. As I look, a little busy Blue-gray Gnatcatcher zips around the tree, earning its name with every bite. I cheer on all the birds near the boathouse who are trying to create a gnat-free zone.

I wander down a bit to a stream and small pond beyond the boathouse where you can see the river and a boat launch. Two Great Blue Herons glide low across the water. Back in the trees, the war against the bugs goes on with reinforcements from chickadees and titmice and a flight of flashing goldfinches. I see another Orchard Oriole and somebody's orphan cowbird. Right here is where a mill once stood that was built in 1801 by Abner Cloud. Then I walk through the picnic area by the water to see what I can see. There are logs piled up all along the shore from floodwaters that have passed. They are stripped clean like driftwood on a beach. Then overhead I hear another oriole and look around to find a striking male Baltimore Oriole posed on a snag in sunshine. The ornithologists insist we now call it Northern. But tell that to us older folks and to millions of baseball fans. I sometimes think that ornithologists, though good people they must be, really should get out more and talk to you and me. My snarky thoughts are soon elevated by the thin, high screams of an Osprey that come from the river. I think of how I learned this sound when we were camped in Maine on an inlet near Mt. Desert when the kids were really little. We stared and stared as Ospreys circled, dove, and feasted on a swarm of tasty eels. Each time I see an Osprey or an eagle now I still think of DDT and how we nearly lost these splendid seafood hunters before some Washingtonians stepped in.

I head off now on the dirt towpath that runs beside the Crescent Trail that's paved. I pass a pair of geese with goslings that now are nearly grown. There are four of them about three-quarter size; there is black upon their heads and on their tails. Then I turn off the towpath and back onto the trail where steps go down at the Incline Plane, a testament to engineering and to fleeting fame. The Incline Plane was a gigantic slide of massive blocks of granite and iron bars and pulleys and all sorts of gear that pulled barges and boats down from the C&O Canal from here into the Potomac River. This prevented pileups and delays of the five hundred boats that plied the C&O and gave a gateway to unload materials at the Navy Yard and Alexandria and other parts downriver. The Incline Plane was completed in 1876 and won a prize at the 1878 Paris Exposition. But before too long, in 1889, a record flood destroyed the slide, miles of the canal, and bankrupted the company that ran the C&O Canal. Now all that's left is a few big granite blocks and some iron bars that you can see right by the towpath about three miles from its start.

Further on, the bike path runs where the Potomac now is wide and visible. An Eastern Kingbird sings from a crag an oddly sweet "eety tweet, eety tweetyou!" I have rarely heard them sing. Usually kingbirds just sit on wires or perches, or are busy chasing and eating bugs. Nearby, another tree sports what at first seems to be a daytime owl, but, it is much too slender. Then I think it is a headless bird, perhaps from Irving's *Sleepy Hollow*. But when it stretches out its long neck which has been entirely invisible, my owl becomes a cormorant. There are others perched in this bare old tree, looking eerie and too much like vultures high above the water.

But soon a single sculler and a crew of eight stroke upriver into view with muffled, amplified instructions from a coach and others trailing in a motorboat. With the boaters and a stone bridge in the background, the scene becomes an Eakins on the Schuylkill. I eye the eights in my binoculars; they seem slightly shaggy college men. Then a quickly moving kayak pulls up on them propelled by a young woman, with a white tennis visor and yellow top, paddling strongly on each side. She is worthy of a Caillebotte and seems single-handedly to overcome a century of sexism with her style, her strength, her oars. I am in awe of all these rowers, scullers, kayakers that are stroking mightily below me. Still straddling my bike, I slowly turn and vow to ride much harder. But a little group of flying birds soon undermines my good intentions. They are moving quickly in and out of a tree across the path. I shield my eyes and follow them till they are clear to me. I have found a little group of Cedar Waxwings who are also eating bugs. I usually see them eating berries, but these nomads seem, like me, to have the omnivore's dilemma. They are tawny and burnished gold and look a bit like comic crooks with their masks and backswept crests. I watch the river a little longer to regain some athletic motivation. But again I am deterred by the sight of huge fish jumping. There are big splashes and widening circles in the water and large brown backs exposed that look like little sea monsters. I have no idea if they are shad or bass or sturgeon or some other monster fish. But they call me back to Captain Smith who rowed right here in 1608. Had they held Henley or the Olympics back then, John Smith and his men surely would have won.

Not too far ahead at the end of the trail is where some modern Olympians come from. Along the right hand side before the bridge is a lengthy, green-shingled antique building with a cupola near the front. There are canoes all stacked around it and a simple, single sign. It says "We are the historic Washington Canoe Club, Established 1904. Home of Olympic Champions, 9700 K. Street, Washington, DC 20007." I think of Teddy Roosevelt and the days before the auto when walking, bicycles, rowing, and streetcars were the norm. Perhaps we should go back in time a bit, but bring along computers, modern medicine, and lots of wind and solar power.

June 8, 2013
Last Chance for Spring

There has been steady rain for two full days and more is on the way. But for now it is sunny, cloudless, and somewhere right near seventy. Hydrangeas are almost in full bloom, turning from white toward litmus blue. My sundrops, yarrow, tickseed, and other sun-seeking flowers are almost back erect. They are next to tall, colonial-style rose campions, gray-green, mossy plants topped with scarlet flowers that I hope will make my Bethesda house look something like an old-time salt box in New England. They have struggled, reseeded, moved about within our yard until we made this sunny bed out front. Now they thrive in front of an even larger rosemary bush whose fragrance is truly heaven scent. The other day I showed it to my granddaughter who broke off a piece and ran around and made everybody smell it. I do not know how or when or where we get our early taste for nature. But I do know that I will look back and smile a little bit each time I think of her delight in simply sniffing and showing off some herbs. Across the yard, small yellow, trumpet-shaped day lilies are recovering as are more old-fashioned orange day lilies that are bent a little lower. Our magnolia blossoms have moved from large white globes to open china bowls.

I must stay indoors at a downtown hotel for all-day board meetings. I'll emerge in time for thundershowers. I am ambivalent about these choices, too. I am happy to work with groups that care about the environment, population, global warming, war. But I also worry that we may be losing out, that my grandchildren may face a wasted world of wicked weather and of want. What can keep me going? How can I hope that others care? These questions are unsettled, like the springtime sunshine that I savor, but with clouds on the horizon. Somewhere between simply tending to my garden and watching passing birds, or dashing about with impatient activism and ideas, there must be some sort of balance. Tomorrow is unencumbered; it may be my last chance for Washington in spring. I think I'll get back on my bike, ride out into nature, breathe deeply, and then, perhaps, come home to write.

Bibliography

Ackerman, Jennifer. *Notes from the Shore*. With illustrations by Karen Grosz. New York: Viking Penguin, 1995.

Audubon, John James. *The Birds of America*. Popular ed. With an introduction by Ludlow Griscom. New York: The Macmillan Company, 1950.

Beston, Henry. *The Outermost House: A Year of Life on the Great Beach of Cape Cod*. With an introduction by Robert Finch. New York: St. Martin's Griffin, 1992.

Branch, Michael P., and Daniel J. Philippon, eds. *The Height of Our Mountains: Nature Writing from Virginia's Blue Ridge Mountains and Shenandoah Valley*. With a foreword by John Elder. Baltimore, MD: The Johns Hopkins University Press, 1998.

Brinkley, Douglas. *The Wilderness Warrior: Theodore Roosevelt and the Crusade for America*. New York: Harper Perennial, 2009.

Burroughs, John. *The Writings of John Burroughs, with Portraits and Many Illustrations, Volume I, [Wake-Robin]*. Boston: Houghton Mifflin Company, Riverside Edition, 1904

Carrier, Thomas J. *Historic Georgetown: A Walking Tour*. Charleston, SC: Arcadia Publishing, 1999.

Chevy Chase Historical Society. *The Place Names of Chevy Chase, Maryland: Being an Anecdotal Stroll Through the Centuries and Neighborhoods of Chevy Chase*. Portsmouth, NH: Back Channel Press, 2011.

Choukas-Bradley, Melanie. *City of Trees: The Complete Guide to the Trees of Washington, D.C.*, 3rd ed. With illustrations by Polly Alexander. Charlottesville, VA: University of Virginia Press, 2008.

Choukas-Bradley, Melanie. *An Illustrated Guide to Eastern Woodland Wildflowers and Trees: 350 Plants Observed at Sugarloaf Mountain, Maryland*. With illustrations by Tina Thieme Brown. Charlottesville, VA: University of Virginia Press, 2004.

Choukas-Bradley, Melanie. *A Year in Rock Creek Park: The Wild, Wooded Heart of Washington, D.C.* With photographs by Susan Austin Roth. Staunton, VA: George F. Thompson Publishing, 2014.

Cool Springs Press. *Field Guide to Backyard Birds of the Mid-Atlantic*. Minneapolis, MN: Cool Springs Press, 2008.

Coues, Elliott, and D. Webster Prentiss. *Avifauna Columbiana*, 2nd ed. Washington, DC: The Smithsonian Institution, 1883.

Cutright, Paul Russell, and Michael J. Brodhead. *Elliott Coues: Naturalist and Frontier Historian*. Urbana, IL: University of Illinois Press, 1981.

Dryden, Steve. *Peirce Mill: Two Hundred Years in the Nation's Capital*. Washington, DC: Bergamot, 2009.

Dunlap, Thomas R. *In the Field, Among the Feathered: A History of Birders & Their Guides*. Oxford: Oxford University Press, 2011.

Einberger, Scott. *A History of Rock Creek Park: Wilderness and Washington, D.C.* Charleston: History Press, 2014.

Ellison, Walter G. *Second Atlas of the Breeding Birds of Maryland and the District of Columbia.* With a foreword by Chandler S. Robbins. Baltimore: The Johns Hopkins University Press, 2010.

Evans, Arthur V. *National Wildlife Federation Field Guide to Insects and Spiders of North America.* With a foreword by Craig Tufts. New York: Sterling Publishing, 2008.

Fisher, Alan. *Country Walks Near Washington*, revised and expanded 3rd ed. Baltimore: Rambler Books, 2011.

Garland, Mark S. and John Anderton. *Watching Nature: A Mid-Atlantic Natural History.* Washington, DC: Smithsonian Institution, 1997.

Glassberg, Jeffrey. *Butterflies through Binoculars: The East: A Field Guide to the Butterflies of Eastern North America.* New York: The Oxford University Press, 1999.

Glickman, Barbara. *Capital Splendor: Gardens and Parks of Washington, D.C.* With photography by Valerie Brown. Woodstock, VT: The Countryman Press, 2012.

Gracie, Carol. *Spring Wildflowers of the Northeast: A Natural History.* Princeton, NJ: Princeton University Press, 2012.

Halle, Louis, Jr. *Spring in Washington.* New York: William Sloane Associates, Inc., 1947.

High, Mike. *The C&O Companion: A Complete Guide to the History of the C&O Canal National Park*, updated ed. Baltimore: The Johns Hopkins University Press, 2000.

Horton, Tom. *Bay Country.* Baltimore: The Johns Hopkins University Press, 1987.

Hugo, Nancy R. *Seeing Trees: Discover the Extraordinary Secrets of Everyday Trees.* With photography by Robert Llewellyn. Portland, OR: Timber Press, 2011.

Kaczmarek, Frank. *New England Wildflowers: A Guide to Common Plants*, A Falcon Guide. Guilford, CT: Globe Pequot Press, 2009.

Kligerman, Jack, ed. *The Birds of John Burroughs: Keeping a Sharp Lookout.* With a foreword by Dean Amadon, drawings by Louis Agassiz Fuertes. New York: Hawthorn Books, Inc., 1976.

Leupp, Francis E. *Walks about Washington.* With drawings by Lester G. Hornsby. Boston: Little, Brown, and Company, 1915.

MacKay, Brian. *A Year Across Maryland: A Week-by-Week Guide to Discovering Nature in the Chesapeake Region.* Baltimore: The Johns Hopkins University Press, 2013.

Marinelli, Janet. *The Wildlife Gardener's Guide.* Brooklyn: The Brooklyn Botanic Garden, Inc., 2008.

Maynard, Lucy W. *Birds of Washington and Vicinity, Including Adjacent Parts of Virginia and Maryland: Where to Find and How to Know Them.* With an introduction by Florence A. Merriam. Baltimore: The Lord Baltimore Press, 1898.

Minichiello, J. Kent, and Anthony W. White, eds. *From Blue Ridge to Barrier Islands: An Audubon Naturalist Reader.* Baltimore: The Johns Hopkins University Press, 1997.

Mitchell, Alexander D., IV. *Washington, D.C.: Then and Now.* San Diego, CA: Thunder Bay Press, 2007.

Montgomery Bird Club of the Maryland Ornithological Society. *A Birder's Guide to Montgomery County, Maryland,* 2nd ed. Montgomery Bird Club of the Maryland Ornithological Society, 2008.

Rice, James D. *Nature and History in the Potomac Country: From Hunter Gatherers to the Age of Jefferson.* Baltimore: The Johns Hopkins University Press, 2009.

Rountree, Helen C., Wayne E. Clark, and Kent Mountford. *John Smith's Chesapeake Voyages, 1607-1609.* Charlottesville, VA: University of Virginia Press, 2008.

Russell, Sharman Apt. *Diary of a Citizen Scientist: Chasing Tiger Beetles and Other New Ways of Engaging the World.* Corvallis, OR: Oregon State University Press, 2014.

Sabatke, Mark D. *Discovering the C&O Canal and Adjacent Potomac River.* Rockville, MD: Schreiber Publishing, 2003.

Schmidt, Susan. *Landfall along the Chesapeake: In the Wake of Captain John Smith.* Baltimore: The Johns Hopkins University Press, 2006.

Shaffer, Earl V. *Walking With Spring.* Harper's Ferry, WV: Appalachian Trail Conservancy, 2004.

Shelton, Napier. *Potomac Pathway: A Nature Guide to the C&O Canal.* Arglen, PA: Schiffer Publishing, Ltd., 2011.

Shosteck, Robert. *Potomac Trail Book,* revised and expanded, 9th printing. With a foreword by Justice William O. Douglas. Oakton, VA: Appalachian Books, 1976.

Spilsbury, Gail Dickersin. *A Washington Sketchbook: Drawings by Robert L. Dickinson, 1917-1918.* Baltimore: Chesapeake Book Company, 2011.

Spilsbury, Gail. *Rock Creek Park.* Baltimore: The Johns Hopkins University Press, 2003.

Tallamy, Douglas W. *Bringing Nature Home: How You Can Sustain Wildlife with Native Plants,* updated and expanded. With a foreword by Rick Darke. Portland, OR: Timber Press, 2012.

Teale, Edwin Way. *North With the Spring: A Naturalist's Record of a 17,000 Mile Journey with the North American Spring.* New York: Dodd & Company, 1951.

Tillman, Ned. *The Chesapeake Watershed: A Sense of Place and A Call to Action.* Baltimore: Chesapeake Book Company, 2009.

Trott, John, Jr. *The Virginia Naturalist.* With illustrations by Nicky Staunton. Middleburg, VA: Virginia Native Plant Society and Middleburg Garden Club; Kearney, NE: Morris Publishing, 2007.

Welles, Judith. *Cabin John: Legends and Life of an Uncommon Place.* Cabin John, MD: Cabin John Citizens Association, 2008.

Wilds, Claudia. *Finding Birds in the Capital Area*, 2nd ed. Washington, DC: The Smithsonian Institution, 1992.

Williams, John Page. *Chesapeake: Exploring the Water Trail of Captain John Smith*. With a forward by Gilbert M. Grosvenor. Washington, DC: The National Geographic Society, 2006.

Worthy, Kenneth. *Invisible Nature: Healing the Destructive Divide between People and the Environment*. Amherst, NY: Prometheus Books, 2013.

Wulf, Andrea. *Founding Gardeners: The Revolutionary Generation, Nature, and the Shaping of the American Nation*. New York: Alfred A. Knopf, 2011.

Youth, Howard. *Field Guide to the Natural World of Washington, D.C.* With illustrations by Mark A. Kingler and photographs by Robert E. Mumford, Jr. Baltimore: The Johns Hopkins University Press, 2014.

About the Author

Environmental leader and avid birder Robert K. Musil is the President and CEO of the Rachel Carson Council, the legacy organization envisioned by Rachel Carson and founded in 1965 after her death from breast cancer. Musil is the author of *Hope for a Heated Planet: How Americans Are Fighting Global Warming and Building a Better Future* (Rutgers, 2009) and *Rachel Carson and Her Sisters: Extraordinary Women Who Have Shaped America's Environment* (Rutgers, 2014). He teaches environmental politics and history at American University in Washington, DC where he is a Senior Fellow at the Center for Congressional and Presidential Studies. Trained in environmental health, literature and the humanities, Musil holds degrees from Yale, Northwestern, and the Johns Hopkins School of Public Health and honorary degrees in science and humane letters.

Musil was the longest-serving CEO of the Nobel Peace Prize-winning Physicians for Social Responsibility and is a Woodrow Wilson Visiting Fellow and popular lecturer on college campuses. A former award-winning, nationally-syndicated broadcaster, his most recent voicing is as narrator of the prize-winning documentary film, *Scarred Lands and Wounded Lives: The Environmental Footprint of War.*

(continued from back cover)

Praise for *Washington in Spring*

Washington in Spring is about some of my favorite subjects: sense of place, seasons, appreciation, the beauty of nature, and the fact that wild nature remains all around us, ready to grant its gifts. I hope this book encourages everyone to appreciate the wild things and seasons of their own home towns, and to scan the skies overhead for signals from a better world.

—Carl Safina, author of *Beyond Words: What Animals Think and Feel*

"With the soul of a poet and the precision of a phenologist, Robert K. Musil witnesses the coming of spring in the nation's capital. As he pedals his bike along the towpath, moseys on foot along Rock Creek, and explores his suburban neighborhood, Musil revels in the glories of butterfly flight, the songs of birds, and the unfurling of flowers from the delicate wild spring beauty to the Japanese cherry blossom. Bob Musil's traveling companions are the extraordinary naturalists who have preceded him along his springtime routes: Theodore Roosevelt, Rachel Carson, Roger Tory Peterson, and the intrepid bureaucrat who made it his mission to record the spring of 1945-Louis J. Halle, author of the local classic *Spring in Washington*. While joy and wonder reign in Musil's book, the specter of climate change is the author's near-constant shadow, as he records the too-warm winter of 2012 and ponders evidence from around the world that things are changing in unsettling ways. A must-read for everyone who loves nature and cares about our future."

—Melanie Choukas-Bradley, author of *A Year in Rock Creek Park* and *City of Trees*

In the grand tradition of classic nature writing, Bob Musil invites readers along on outdoor adventures that brim with wonder and insight. Discoveries made in DC's woods, wetlands, city parks, and suburban backyards are shared through vivid prose and stunning photographs. Leavened with wit, history, and metaphors drawn from the arts, these careful observations of skunk cabbage, warblers, and other signs of the season sometimes turn dark, as when the author reflects on how global warming threatens birds his grandchildren cherish. But an ebullient joy in nature prevails. *Washington in Spring* celebrates hope and gratitude, despite troubling changes, for all that still remains, and what we must do to protect it.

—Julie Dunlap, editor of *Companions in Wonder: Children and Adults Exploring Nature Together*

A wonderful and urbane walk and talk in the suburban and city woods, with an informative historical context that reveals Washington, DC to have been home and inspiration for many noted naturalists. Musil finds the wildness still alive—and perhaps even reviving—in the midst of manicured lawns and non-native landscaping.

—Steve Dryden, author of *Peirce Mill: Two Hundred Years in the Nation's Capital*

Praise for *Rachel Carson and Her Sisters*

"This is a long overdue book, giving great credit to the long line of women who have done so much to shape our culture's view of the world around us and of our prospects in it. We desperately need that culture to heed their words!"

—Bill McKibben, author *Oil and Honey: The Education of an Unlikely Activist*

"Rachel Carson is only the best-known example amidst an inspiring cast of pioneering and modern women environmental leaders that Musil brings to life. Readable, reliable, and rousing—a book for anyone who cares about America's past and future."

—Gene Karpinski, President and CEO of the League of Conservation Voters

"A treasure! A welcome discovery of the linkages among profoundly caring, ecologically-aware women across time, and the truths of our ecological crisis. Musil shows clear-eyed science and heartfelt story telling are not mutually exclusive."

—Rebecca Wodder, former President and CEO of American Rivers

"Bob Musil provides an important contribution to the history of the environmental movement. He paints a compelling portrait of Rachel Carson and the remarkable women who preceded her and who continue her legacy. He reminds us of the struggles and achievements of Ms. Carson and, just as significantly, the pivotal and courageous role that women have played in fighting for a safer and healthier world."

—Tom Udall, US Senator, New Mexico

"With deep grounding in women's history, environmentalism, and public health—and, just as importantly, with great reverence—Musil introduces us to a pantheon of remarkable women, true heroines everyone. This book offers a new perspective, countless wonderful stories, and inspiration. A great read!"

—Howard Frumkin, Dean, University of Washington School of Public Health

"An absolutely wonderful book! Bob Musil shows Rachel Carson not as a lone voice, but an eloquent one who drew inspiration from female predecessors and those around her. He argues persuasively that we can understand Carson better if we see her in relation to other women, to the broader environmental movement, and to working in community. Should be required reading for anyone interested in where we have been, and where we need to go."

—Geoffrey Chase, author of *Sustainability in Higher Education*

"An eloquent and moving tribute to the women at the heart and soul of the environmental movement. It is a story of brilliant science, courage, stamina, and a passion for life. We are in debt beyond counting to them and to Robert Musil for telling their stories so well."

—David W. Orr, Paul Sears Distinguished Professor of Environmental Studies and Politics, Oberlin College

"A richly detailed, documented, and eloquent history—a ground-breaking account of undaunted American women, determined to prevent environmental catastrophe."

—Lawrence Wittner, *Huffington Post*

"A great read for anybody who is interested in learning about Rachel Carson's role in a delicate web of connections that makes up the environmental movement. Also, if anybody is interested in the human aspect, the personal lives, and the trials of each of these women, this book certainly will deliver. Musil has stitched together a wonderful collection of true stories about the amazing women who have changed, and are continuing to change, the way we see the world."

—*The Prairie Naturalist*

"Bob Musil brilliantly documents the rich trajectory of women's intellectual and political influence, not just on environmentalism but on public policy and activism. Musil offers fascinating details of Rachel Carson's struggles to be taken seriously as a scientist and unearths the stories of the women—unsung heroes all—who influenced her. A must read for anyone interested in American history, science and environmental politics."

—Heather White, executive director, the Environmental
   Working Group

"A vibrant, engaging account of the women who preceded and followed Rachel Carson's efforts to promote environmental and human health. In exquisite detail, Musil narrates the brilliant career and efforts of pioneering women from the 1850s onward to preserve nature and maintain a healthy environment. Anyone interested in women naturalists, activists, and feminist environmental history will welcome this compelling, beautifully-written book."

—Carolyn Merchant, author of *The Death of Nature*, and professor
   of environmental history, philosophy, and ethics, University of
   California, Berkeley

"Musil contextualizes *Silent Spring* as the culmination of decades of work by other women in science, who were consistently overlooked, underappreciated, and dismissed by their male peers and institutions. These ladies ranged from Victorian garden observers to die-hard chemists and marine biologists. They are tied together by a fierce sense of activism and beautiful writing. Their writing is what drew Musil in. He too wants 'people to connect with science in an approachable way.'"

—Sierra Club Greenlife

"In *Rachel Carson and Her Sisters*, Musil fills the gap by placing Carson's achievements in a wider context, weaving connections from the past through the present. Readers will find new insight into Carson and contemporary figures she influenced... who have historically received less attention. Musil's respect and enthusiasm for these women is evident throughout the book, making it a deeply engaging and enjoyable read. A valuable addition to scholarship on Rachel Carson, female environmentalists, and the American environmental movement in general. Highly recommended. All academic and general readers."

—*Choice*

"Musil uses the life and writings of Rachel Carson as an exemplar of women's participation in the American environmental movement. He places Carson's achievements in contexts by illuminating the lives of trailblazing female scientists who inspired her and for whom she, in turn, paved the way. Extremely well-researched."

—*Foreword*

"*Rachel Carson and Her Sisters* makes a number of important contributions to both environmental history and women's history. Musil's genius is weaving his intriguing, thoroughly researched mini-biographies of individual women into a cohesive larger story of overlapping and mutually reinforcing actions and ideas."

—*Environmental History*

"In celebrating Rachel Carson's work, Musil takes on the important task of contextualizing this environmental luminary within a tradition of women's research, activism, and authorship."

—*Women's Review of Books*

"This book is one-of-a-kind. Musil provides a remarkable new perspective on the role of individual women in the US environmental movement."

—Cathy Middlecamp, Professor, Nelson Institute of Environmental Studies, University of Wisconsin-Madison

Praise for *Hope for a Heated Planet*

"*Hope for A Heated Planet* is an important and timely book. Musil not only makes a strong case that a real climate movement is underway, he shows how a public health perspective can help to accelerate this hopeful new movement."

—Jonathan Isham, editor of *Ignition: What You Can Do to Fight Global Warming and Spark a Movement*

"Bob Musil has had a bird's-eye view of the climate debate almost from its inception, and he paid careful attention to both the problem and the solutions. This is a masterfully comprehensive account of both where we are and where we sure better go."

—Bill McKibben, author of *Deep Economy: The Wealth of Communities and the Durable Future*

"*Hope for A Heated Planet* offers a clear-eyed assessment of the unprecedented challenge that climate change presents for today's Americans. Musil is a hard-headed yet hopeful Washington insider who is well-positioned to make the case that with a new generation of clean energy—and the energy of citizens across America—there is hope, indeed, for our heated planet."

—Chris Flavin, president, Worldwatch Institute

"Bob Musil's *Hope for A Heated Planet* is an act of faith, both secular and spiritual. This generous and thoughtful guide to understanding climate change will make all readers want to join the growing climate movement."

—Reverend Richard Cizik, vice president for governmental affairs of the National Association of Evangelicals

"*Hope for A Heated Planet* is an excellent synthesis of everything you need to know about global warming, from science to solutions. It is authoritative and accessible, often witty and wise. Musil, a long-time environment and health leader, calls on Americans to get involved—from light bulbs to legislation, from the secular to the spiritual, from the backyard to the ballot box."

—Gene Karpinski, president, League of Conservation Voters